STUDIES IN COGNITIVE SYSTEMS

VOLUME 15

The titles published in this series are listed at the end of this volume.

CONSCIOUSNESS, COGNITIVE SCHEMATA, AND RELATIVISM

Multidisciplinary Explorations in Cognitive Science

edited by

MATTI KAMPPINEN

Department of Cultural Studies, University of Turku, Finland

KLUWER ACADEMIC PUBLISHERS

DORDRECHT / BOSTON / LONDON

Library of Congress Cataloging-in-Publication Data

Consciousness, cognitive schemata, and relativism : multidisciplinary
    explorations in cognitive science / edited by Matti Kamppinen.
        p.   cm. -- (Studies in cognitive systems ; v. 15)
    Includes indexes.
    ISBN 0-7923-2275-4 (alk. paper)
    1. Philosophy of mind. 2. Cognitive science. 3. Consciousness.
4. Schemas (Psychology) 5. Explanation. 6. Relativism.
I. Kamppinen, Matti, 1961-   . II. Series.
BD418.3.C655   1993
128'.2--dc20   93-15269

ISBN 0-7923-2275-4

Published by Kluwer Academic Publishers,
P.O. Box 17, 3300 AA Dordrecht, The Netherlands.

Kluwer Academic Publishers incorporates
the publishing programmes of
D. Reidel, Martinus Nijhoff, Dr W. Junk and MTP Press.

Sold and distributed in the U.S.A. and Canada
by Kluwer Academic Publishers,
101 Philip Drive, Norwell, MA 02061, U.S.A.

In all other countries, sold and distributed
by Kluwer Academic Publishers Group,
P.O. Box 322, 3300 AH Dordrecht, The Netherlands.

Printed on acid-free paper

Printed in the Netherlands

TABLE OF CONTENTS

SERIES PREFACE

This series includes monographs and collections of studies devoted to the investigation and exploration of knowledge, information, and data-processing systems of all kinds, no matter whether human, (other) animal, or machine. Its scope spans the full range of interests from classical problems in the philosophy of mind and philosophical psychology through issues in cognitive psychology and sociobiology (concerning the mental powers of other species) to ideas related to artificial intelligence and computer science. While primary emphasis is placed upon theoretical, conceptual, and epistemological aspects of these problems and domains, empirical, experimental, and methodological studies will also appear from time to time.

This multi-authored volume provides investigations that fall into three broad areas of inquiry. In Part I, Antti Revonsuo reviews and evaluates contemporary discussions of the nature of consciousness. In Part II, Matti Kamppinen explores methodological issues, distinguishing between "intentional" and "structural" explanations. In Part III, Seppo Sajama and Simo Vihjanen consider whether humans ever have direct access to reality (in Section A), while Matti Kamppinen and Antti Revonsuo explore the consequences of the claim that our knowledge of reality is conceptually mediated (in Section B). These studies combine to provide a stimulating exploration of cognitive science that should appeal to students and to scholars alike.

J.H.F.

PREFACE BY THE EDITOR

The purpose of the book is to illustrate how empirical and conceptual problems interact in modern cognitive science. We argue that several topics discussed in contemporary research have long historical roots in philosophy. This information is especially relevant for students and scholars working in cognitive neuroscience, cognitive anthropology, and other fields of cognitive science.

The book is divided into three parts. Part I, *Cognitive models of consciousness*, reviews and evaluates the contemporary discussion concerning consciousness. Both philosophical and empirical arguments are assessed. The fundamental philosophical issue seems to be the ontological status of consciousness: some philosophers claim that consciousness is nothing but a pseudoproblem, a mirage created by naive everyday thinking which should hardly worry philosophers or scientists. Others, by contrast, respect their intuitions and take consciousness as a real phenomenon, which cries out for an explanation. On the empirical side, a number of models of consciousness have been presented recently, but as yet, no unified emerging paradigm of consciousness research has emerged. The reason for this is, we argue, that present theories of consciousness do not share a common base but stem from diverging philosophical and empirical roots. We will try to foresee what kinds of philosophical commitments and theoretical starting-points could serve as the core and bedrock of the future science of consciousness. We consummate Part I by suggesting that the first-person, phenomenological point of view must, in some way, be preserved in theories of consciousness and we investigate, how such future theories could be built from the presently existing, preliminary models.

Part II, *Cognitive schemata*, deals with methodological issues, especially with cognitive explanations in anthropmlogy. We distinguish between intentional and structural explanations. The intentional explanation is deeply rooted in our commonsense psychology, and its scientific use assumes that the "anthropological other" is sharing our basic beliefs and inferential rules, that is, our rationality. Structural explanation, on the contrary, can cope with differences in beliefs by means of abstracting the meaning structures from the belief systems. The vehicle of structural explanation is the cognitive schema, or a cluster of representations. The notion of schema is widely used in psychology, anthropology and artificial intelligence. The various theories of schemata are systematized by means of posing two questions, those concerning their nodes and links.

In Part III, *Relativism and cognitivism*, the classical problem of relativism inherent in the study of doxastic diversity is studied in the novel context provided by cognitivism. Cognitivism appears to provide a solution to the problem of relativism, but, by the same token, it invites a more profound version of relativism. Part III is composed of two sections. Section A discusses the question of whether we could have a direct access to reality, even in principle. We show how this question has ancient roots in philosophy. The conclusion argued for is that all our cognition is conceptually mediated. Section B investigates the consequences of this claim.

This book is relevant for students and scholars in cognitive science, especially those working in cognitive anthropology and neuroscience. The book does not require previous education in philosophy. The philosophical themes and their relevance in modern empirical research are presented in accessible form. The book can be well used as a university textbook for the courses that serve to introduce the students of in cognitive anthropology and neuroscience into philosophical background of cognitive science.

M.K.

ACKNOWLEDGEMENTS

This book was prepared during the research project "Cognitive Systems and the Representation of Environmental Risks", funded by the Cognitive Science Research Programme of the Academy of Finland (contract # 1071132). I did most of the editorial work while enjoying a grant from the Kordelin Foundation, which enabled me to stay at Cornell University, Ithaca, for the spring terms 1991 and 1992. The Department of Anthropology and Religious Studies Program at Cornell University provided hospitality during those visits. Section B of Part III is based on an article "Relativism and Cognitivism" which appeared in *Science Studies* 2/1991, 35-43.

I wish to thank my colleagues at the University of Turku for their comments, questions, and support.

Matti Kamppinen

INTRODUCTION

Students and scholars in cognitive neuroscience and cognitive anthropology encounter concepts like semantic network, information, meaning, representation, cognitive model, subjective viewpoint, and consciousness. Indeed, those are the very objects, as well as the tools of research in these fields. Many times they come out of blue, as if they were the innovation of modern cognitive science. But they have been around for a long time, much longer than the apparent few decade history of cognitive science proper suggests. Especially philosophers have contributed to the study of human mind throughout history.

Issues in cognitive science require a multidisciplinary approach, interplay of empirical research and philosophy for two reasons. On one hand, it shows that many contemporary problems in psychology and anthropology are deeply rooted in traditional philosophical problematics. On the other hand, it encourages us to redraw the boundaries between conceptual and empirical research; some conceptual problems may turn out to be empirical, and vice versa. Moreover, empirical research in neuroscience, psychology and anthropology benefits, not only from the analytical philosophy of science, but also from phenomenology and speculative armchair psychology.

In this introduction we will first look at the historical roots of modern cognitive science, then introduce one of its thorniest philosophical problems, namely the problem of representation. This problem has been extensively studied in phenomenology and philosophy of mind. The obstacles appear to remain the same in traditional and modern research.

1. ORIGINS OF COGNITIVE SCIENCE

Cognitive science is standardly characterized as a new branch of research uniting psychology, artificial intelligence, neuroscience, philosophy and linguistics in the study of systems which receive, store, represent and process "information" or even possess "knowledge" and, thus, can be called "intelligent". The computer and the brain are considered to be the paradigmatic examples of such intelligent systems and the main task is to explain how cognitive processes like perceiving, remembering, learning, and intelligent

1

behavior are possible in such systems.

We will first take a look at the roots of cognitive science: how between the 1940's and 60's the basic ideas of cognitive science were born in the separate special sciences and how they were connected. The important question is how cognitive science depicted human beings and what were the reasons for such a view. Then we will take a critical stance towards the original ideas of cognition. It seems that cognitive science has not found a stable philosophical footing yet and that substantial challenges must be met before we have a stable research paradigm of cognition.

Perhaps the most powerful element of the emergence of cognitive science has been the development of computers and the research program called Artificial Intelligence, or AI. Alan Turing, the renowned British mathematician, was among the first to suggest that computing machines might actually be able to think, at least in principle. In 1936 he had defined "computation" as "the formal manipulation of symbols", and he had introduced the idea of a *Turing machine*: an imaginary computer which could compute any strictly definable computational process, or algorithm. Turing and many other researchers who contributed to the birth of AI believed that also complex mental operations could be decomposed to and described in mathematical theorems and algorithms.

These pioneers saw a fundamental similarity in the working principles of the brain and the computer: both were capable of functioning by using binary codes. The computer has its on/off switches which either let an electric current through or not. These two states form the basic "vocabulary" of the machine language, often designated as "1" and "0". The brain has its neurons which were seen to embody a natural binary code: the all-or-nothing firing mechanism of neural impulses in neurons. Thus, the hypothesis underlying AI was that human intelligence was explicable as algorithms – computer programs – computed by the brain. The quest that AI was facing was to unravel such algorithms and, consequently, program them into digital computers which would, eventually, result in thinking machines.

In summer 1956, a momentous seminar was held at Darthmouth College, New Hampshire. It gathered together the most important figures in the field which they there decided to christen Artifical Intelligence: John McCarthy, Claude Shannon, Nathaniel Rochester, Marvin Minsky, Herbert Simon and Alan Newell. Their goal was the formal modelling of thought and, ultimately, the building and programming of intelligent, thinking machines. This goal, of course, no longer was an innocent mathematical or programming endeavor but, obviously, had deep implications to the psychological study of intelligence and to the philosophy of mind.

Philosophers in the 1960's caught the idea of a Turing machine and started to consider it as a model of an intelligent organism. These considerations inspired philosophers to conceptualize mental states as *functional* states of the organism. Such a novel approach was extremely stimulating, since it offered forceful arguments against the so-called "brain-state theories" in the philosophy of mind, according to which mental states are to be identified with physical-chemical states of the brain. The founders of this functionalist philosophy of mind, like Hilary Putnam and Jerry Fodor, argued that it is extremely unlikely that a certain mental state could always and everywhere have an identical neurophysiological characterization. By contrast, a mental state should be identified with its *abstract causal-functional role* in the system, the characterization of which was in principle completely independent of specific neurophysiological instances of the phenomenon; the same abstract function could be implemented in different physical systems. This view was directly connectable to AI: states of a computer and computer programs in general could also be described in a physically abstract and neutral language. Thus, it seemed that there was a safe philosophical background to the assumption that the human mind is the computer program of the brain; and perhaps some of the programs running in the digital machines could one day become the minds of the computer.

In psychology and lingustics, the cognitive views arose from the growing inadequacy of the behavioristic paradigm in the 1950's and 60's. The famous linguist Noam Chomsky presented persuasive knockdown arguments against B. Skinner's "stimulus-response" behaviorism showing that human verbal behavior could not be explained with behavioristic theories or even fit in with a behavioristic view of human beings. Behaviorism was interested only in the effects of external, physical stimuli on the external behavior – on the reactions of the physical body of the organism. It was not allowed to postulate *inner* states or mechanisms intervening these objectively observable phenomena. Inner biological states were of interest only to the neurophysiologist, not the behaviorist, and talking about inner mental phenomena would only lead back to Cartesian dualism. Chomsky, however, argued that the acquisition of language could be understood only by referring to internal linguistic, grammatical rules, which were innate and common to all humans.

In psychology, the counteraction to behaviorism resulted in a new and contrasting view of human behavior and its explanation. According to the cognitive view, behavior and psychological processes in general should be explained by referring to inner functional mechanisms. These mechanisms by no means imply Cartesian dualism, but are to be understood as completely physical. Cognitive psychology sees intelligent organisms as *information processing systems*, which receive, store, and process information, using the results in the control of their behavior. Thus, the organism was no longer regarded as a black box, as in behaviorism, but as a system consisting of *many* boxes (named, e.g., "object perception", "short-term memory", "speech output system", etc.), each of which receives, processes or stores information in a characteristic way. The postulation of inner processes and functions such as these became second nature to psychology.

The general idea was that cognition consists of *mental representations* and *computational processes* which transform such representations to others and, in that sense, "process information". This view is very close to the way mental processes are conceptualized in artificial intelligence and in the simulation of psychological processes. Both have as their philosophical ground the functionalist theory of mind and both seem to explore psychological processes at an abstract level which does not call for analyses of brain neurophysiology or computer hardware.

Here, then, is the core of cognitive science, as it appears in the 1990's, after a short existence and history of about 40 years. Many recent characterizations or definitions of cognitive science emphasize the view of human thought as the manipulation of symbols, that is, as computation:

Cognitive scientists are committed to the fruitfulness of a certain approach to understanding intelligent behaviors and capacities. That approach involves at least taking seriously ... the notion that intelligent behavior is, or at least is made possible by, the manipulation of symbolic representations. It involves taking seriously the notion that the operations on those representations can be described ... as computations. (Garfield 1990, xxii)

... we define cognitive science as the study of intelligence and its computational processes in humans (and animals), in computers, and in the abstract. (Simon and Kaplan 1989, 2)

... the view – which I defend – that cognition is literally a species of computing, carried out in a specific type of biological mechanism. (Pylyshyn 1989, 52)

Thus, the key concepts of cognitive science are "computation", "physical symbol system", and "functionalism".

2. NEUROSCIENCE AND CONNECTIONISM

Neuroscience was mentioned as one of the "mother sciences" of cognitive science, but as yet, no account of its role has been given. Indeed, its role is somewhat controversial. The founders of Artifical Intelligence did not think that neuroscience has any contributions to make to the field. Consequently, John McCarthy on purpose did not invite any neurophysiologists to participate in the foundational meeting of AI in 1956. He explains: "It was our intention to leave that nervous stuff out and to study artificial intelligence. ... I thought artificial intelligence had more of a relationship with psychology" (quoted in Ladd 1985, 37). The whole philosophy of AI and cognitive science was anti-biological, emphasizing the independence of the abstract program level with its computational algorithms from the hardware level of the brain's neurobiology or the computer's vacuum tubes or silicon chips. By definition, knowing about the neurobiological details could not help one to understand the level of cognition, and vice versa.

Nevertheless, not all shared this view of the role of neurobiology. Actually, a neurally inspired research paradigm of computation existed as early as in the 1940's. Warren McCulloch and Walter Pitts showed in 1943 that nets consisting of neuron-like units – with "all-or-none" firing-thresholds – could in principle compute the same functions as a serial Turing Machine. However, the initial success of traditional AI which ignores neurophysiology drove the neural network approach to an almost complete oblivion for decades.

The bold dreams to build thinking machines has gradually met realism: today's digital computers could not match the intelligence of a cat, much less that of a human. Consequently, the neurally inspired approach to computing, nowadays often called "Parallel Distributed Processing" or "Connectionism" is striking back. The traditional AI, or "Good Old-Fashioned AI", GOFAI (Haugeland 1985) implies that cognition is the matter of symbolic representations and logical rules for manipulating these representations in a serial manner. A connectionist network, by contrast, is devoid of explicit rules or symbols. It consists of simple *units* or *nodes*, each of which has a numerical *activation value*. These units can affect each other through their *connections*: Every connection between two units has a numerical strength value, sometimes called *weight*. Activation values and weights can be positive or negative, and positive weights can be thought of as excitatory, and negative weights as inhibitory, thus borrowing even neurophysiological terminology.

A complete network usually has input units, hidden units, and output units. The network does not have to embody any previously given "program"; it can "learn" to represent various patterns by itself if it is given feedback revealing how much the actual output differed from the desired one. We may imagine that we give as input written English words and the network is supposed to give as output the phonemes telling the pronunciation of the word. After a "training" period, during which the stimuli are run through the net a number of times, the net's activation values finally reach a rather stable state and the outputs correspond to the desired ones. We may say that the network represents a letter-to-sound conversion and each different stimulus word generates a different activation pattern across the network's hidden units. For any given letter, some units are highly activated, some mildly, and most not at all. Nowhere in the system can there be found a rulebook of pronounciation nor a symbolical representation for a given letter. The system functions *as if* it were following the rules (and idiosyncrasies) of pronounciation, but the rules are rather attributed to the network by its users than really there. And the representation of any given letter or phoneme is distributed through the whole network, and is not an explicit conglomeration of symbols.

At first glance, connectionism seems to take us a great step forward in modelling real information processing in the nervous system. First of all, its basic elements are neuron-like – at least like highly abstracted neurons – and secondly, the performance of connectionist networks – learning, perceptual categorization – gives the impression of psychological reality. For example, network models of semantic memory (e.g., Collins and Loftus 1975), according to which concepts are represented in memory by nodes and their interconnections, facilitate a connectionist interpretation. Certain empirical observations in experimental psychology have been thought to reflect the spreading of activation in such lexical-semantic networks from one externally activated concept to others internally highly associated with it (Neely 1977).

Nevertheless, even connectionism might not be the royal road to the mind-brain. In the following, we attempt to show what the principal problems of the foundations of cognitive science – both symbolic and connectionist – are.

3. PROBLEMS WITH REPRESENTATION

As defined above, cognitive science's view of the human mind has deep philosophical implications. It implies the claim that cognition or thinking quite literally is a species of computing. This position has been called "the strong equivalence thesis" (Pylyshyn 1989) which also entails the commitment to "strong AI" (Searle 1980). According to strong AI, the appropriately programmed computer literally is a mind and thus it can be said to have exactly similar mental states as humans when engaged in a similar cognitive task. Consequently, the simulation of cognitive processes in AI programs is sometimes seen as the principal methodology of cognitive science and AI is sometimes characterized as "the intellectual core of cognitive science" (Boden 1990).

Starting from these basic assumptions, some AI gurus have sketched grand visions of the future. For example, the robot scientist Hans Moravec believes that cognitive science will eventually lead us to a post-biological world of technological wonders. It will become possible to program the human mind into a computer, and even to make several copies of one mind – thus the valuable thoughts of each individual will never vanish. When we have turned to computer programs, a person will be immortal, he or she or it can be sent as a laser wave to another planet, or several programs can be united, creating a superprogram from the best available personalities.

All this seems to be manageable, in principle, if we believe that the mind is a physical symbol system which computes and for which the abstract functional organization is all that matters. But do we have reasons to question these central tenets of cognitive science? We do indeed, since the understanding of what *computation, information processing*, or *symbols* are, in the first place, appears to be deeply problematic. The notion of representation is especially relevant here, since it is involved in all the above concepts.

Let us begin with the cognitive psychologist's favourite cliché: human beings and especially brains "process information". In perception, for example, this information comes from *external* objects and events and, consequently, *represents* those external things in order to guide the organism's responses adaptively. Now, "information processing" and "representation" are notions which are used by every even remotely cognitivist researcher. But they are unclear and philosophically burdened notions. How should we understand them?

3.1. What is information?

Information is often understood as the measure of organization or complexity of a physical system, given that the universe in general is marching towards bigger entropy and disorganization, as the Second Law of Thermodynamics indicates. The amount of information or complexity a certain physical system contains has been described with probabilistic concepts: one *bit* of information corresponds to a choice between two equally probable alternatives. However, information understood in this way implies that almost all possible events in the physical world involve "information processing". The stone you throw into the air is processing information about the energy of the throw, following a path in the air which could be described as highly informational – we would need many bits to describe that path. The atmosphere is processing information about the energy of the sun, thus directing warm and cold air currents, high- and low pressures and other weather-phenomena. The DNA-molecule and the synthesis of proteins in the cell become, in this reading, immense information stores and processors.

So, understood as physical information in this sense, the brain certainly is "processing information", but so is practically everything else. Thus, this cannot be what the cognitive scientists are talking about. Perhaps we could restrict "information processing" to mean something that allegedly does happen in us when we perceive the external world. Information could then mean something like a change in the system caused by external energy. The receptors at the interface of my physical body and the external world are constantly bombarded by physical energy which causes changes in the receptors which in turn cause corresponding changes in the nerve impulses and, ultimately, in the brain. The information represents its source, for example, a red strawberry, in virtue of the causal chain that begins with the light reflecting from the real, external object and ends in the brain, where the perception is reconstructed in consciousness and categorized as a strawberry.

This characterization still seems to be too wide: does not our digestive tract, for example, change its state in consequence of getting in touch with digestible food, and creating a causal chain of processes which "represent" the food eaten. Digestion seems to be a purely biochemical and physiological process, not a case of the kind of information processing that computers and brains are engaged in. To create an appropriate sense of information processing, we must seek help from the computer metaphor. Information processing is, as we saw in the previous section, manipulation of physical symbols; representation is a matter of structured symbol systems. So we end up with a notion of information closely resembling *linguistic* information, not physical information.

But what, ultimately, *are* symbols and representations and how on earth can brains contain such things? This is an interesting and, perhaps, critical question. Let us examine some uncontroversial cases of representations and symbols. John Haugeland (1991) characterizes representations saying that a living organism must adjust its behavior to the environment and in order to do so, relevant features must be either directly present to the organism (i.e., directly guiding its behavior, like sunlight guides a plant) or indirectly represented for the organism. The evolutionary reason for the existence of representations is clear – but what are representations?

3.2. Mental acts: content and object

The paradigmatic case of representation is people having ideas, commonsense beliefs and perceptions. The standard phenomenological distinction between *mental act* (a psychological state or other event of representing), its *content*, and *object* is perhaps the most fruitful way to analyse ideas (see Sajama and Kamppinen 1987). The distinction points out that whenever we have a mental phenomenon, i.e., a case of symbol manipulation, representation, information or what have you, we should distinguish between the particular state or event, the content it has, and the object that is prescribed by the content. The content is not identical with the particular state or event of representing, since it is a universal property that can be exemplified by other states as well. Thanks to this, we can share a thought, for example. Our acts of thinking about Europe are different in many respects, but they share a universal property, the content "Europe". It is equally important to keep contents and objects apart. All mental acts (and other representing particulars) have contents, but only some of them have objects. When I am imagining a Gorgon (a species of sea-monster), the act does not pick out any object. It still has a content which prescribes the object but does not guarantee that there exists such an object. The following thought-experiment illuminates the case.

> Suppose that you are in a big, alien supermarket the shelves of which are full of opaque tincans. Your task is to find one with mushrooms inside. However, since the contents of the cans are not directly observable, you must think of a way in which something observable could stand for or represent mushrooms. Perhaps the aliens have put a picture of a mushroom to represent the insides – this would be a case of iconic representation. Or perhaps they have made patterns of ink, like the letters M-U-S-H-R-O-O-M, corresponding to the English language written symbol for mushrooms, or, who knows, when you touch the right can, it

might emit a sound pattern roughly corresponding to the phonemes of the spoken word "mushroom". Then again, the can might have a characteristic smell of mushrooms, or it might be mushroom-shaped, or mushroom-colored or it might taste of mushroom when licked. Or, if you are unlucky, the can might be coded in some symbol-system unfamiliar for you: for example, the word "SIENI" printed on it would not be of much help to you, although it means in Finnish language "mushroom". The aliens might also have a strangely arranged perceptual or association system, and subsequently they might mark the mushroom cans with pictures of strawberries, bicycles, or penguins. After all, in a Finnish supermarket you will find ice-cream, not small penguins, in a package depicting a penguin and liquorice, not small black men, in a package with a drawing of a black man.

It appears, then, that an uncontroversial way in which things can stand for or represent other things is the way in which various *experienced* and *associated* properties of a thing can stand for the whole thing, or the way arbitrary but conventional symbols, like words in a spoken or written language, might stand for the object itself. And in some way there have to be systems in the brain which connect the separate brain zones processing such properties of objects like their shape, color, smell, taste, and linguistic symbol. These brain connections form the neural basis of coherent perceptual experiences and the grasping of concepts, permitting us to understand the meanings of words (Damasio 1989).

Unfortunately, this cannot be the sense of representing that cognitive scientists have in mind. The examples above were told from the viewpoint of the subject who interprets the contents of the representations in virtue of his or her past and current conscious experiences. However, most of the processing and the symbols in cognitive science are meant to be manipulated and represented totally *outside* consciousness – in fact, they have no necessary connection to the subject's conscious mental life.

How can such symbols then exist in the nervous system? First, a symbol, we may say, always has a physical instantiation, that is, it must be embodied as something physical, like ink-marks, electric currents, or sound waves, although it does not matter which physical stuff the symbol consists of in its different instantiations. Second, a symbol has semantic content, which is to say that it *refers* to something. And finally, at first sight, the symbol must have a user or interpreter, *to whom* it means what it means. As we saw in the example of the search for a mushroom can in an alien supermarket, nothing *in itself* stands for something else: symbols and representations must always symbolize or represent *to somebody*.

3.3. Causal theories

What, then, gives meaning to the symbols and representations when we process information if not the subject himself? Some philosophers have made a bold move, claiming that the representation acquires its content from the *causal path* through which the stimulus has arrived. Thus, for example, a state in my brain might represent a strawberry because light was reflected from a real strawberry out there. The light entered my visual receptors and its effects ended up in my brain. However, it seems that the existence of any causal patterns whatsoever cannot in itself guarantee any meaning for a representation. By contrast, what matters here is whether I become conscious of the perception and whether my brain can connect it with the semantic content of previous strawberries: taste, smell, memories of previous encounters of strawberries, the linguistic symbols of the object, like the phonological or the graphemic patterns etc. There are neuropsychological patients who suffer from object agnosia: they can see perfectly clearly, but they cannot interpret what the objects are that they are looking at. Consequently, for such a patient it is of little comfort to be told that his brain is still capable of having visual representations with the content "strawberry" (because certain states in his brain are caused by external strawberries), since for him, no visual perceptions have the content "strawberry". And why would that causal chain which ends in my brain represent the strawberry but those reflections of light from the strawberry which did not end up causing anything in any organism's brain would not?

Not all causal chains represent, for sure, or everything there is would be nothing more than a huge representation of the Big Bang. Then why does a chain ending in the brain represent but others do not? Because some of the chains cause mental happenings in the brain which can be meaningful for the brain itself, activating semantic interpretations of the stimuli. The agnosia patient's brain states represent strawberries only from an external point of view, looking at the causal chain. But from an external point of view, any later node in the causal chain could then represent any previous node, also in completely non-mental systems. Thus, this notion of representation is suspect. Furthermore, if the fixation of the content of a representation is made from the point of view of an external observer, the explanation itself already presupposes the semantic interpretation made by the observer. That is, if there is somebody looking at the causal chain from the world to a subject's brain and then declaring some brain state as representing some state external to the subject's brain, our explanation entails reference to a conscious observer who is able to associate causes with effects. But do any causal chains represent in themselves, independently of possible observers? And if any states in the world really represent something other than themselves, they ought to do so without reference to observers.

The causal theory seems pretty inadequate also in such cases in which there does not exist any causal path from the external world to a meaningful mental state. Think about Little Green Men from Mars, or hobbits. They do not exist, so no causal paths can lead from them to our brain-states. Or, to take an extreme example, one can have a dream about a violet, seven-legged, furry creature, and call it in the dream a "makkara". Now, from where does this word get its meaning and the visual representation its content? Certainly not from the external world, since, during sleep, the brain is effectively isolated from processing the visual sensory information, even if the eyelids were open.

Despite the above criticism, the basic idea in the causal theory is well motivated. If we want to avoid postulating a mind's eye and the imminent infinite regress, the only solution is to assume that some causal systems involve representations even though there is no one to look at them. It happens to be the case that some causal mechanisms instantiate representations. The price we have to pay if we stick to the assumption that there are representations only where there are observers is high. Moreover, the causal theory can be relaxed in order to meet some of the above criticism. First of all, if we allow causal mechanisms to determine mental content, it does not follow that just any causal link will do. Thus we get rid of the Big Bang problem. Secondly, we can allow multiple types of entities to enter causal roles, for example, cultural facts or other entities of higher order. This way we can avoid the problem that stems from the fact that there are less "things" than thoughts.

3.4. Getting rid of representations

One possibility of explicating the idea that some causal mechanisms instantiate representations is to distinguish between intrinsic representations and "as-if" representations (or intentionality). The former is a representation without an observer. Conscious mental states have been the most popular candidate for this task; they are reflexive, representations-in-themselves. The latter involves those cases where outside observers or users of the system find it useful to attribute representations to the system. This option avoids mind's eyes and infinite regresses by getting rid of nonconscious representations altogether. John R. Searle (1990, 635–637) has recently questioned the talk of "symbol manipulation" and "computation" on the grounds that such an account implies a reference to an interpreter of the system and, thus, commits a serious explanatory mistake. Without us as the interpreters, the brain could not be said to "manipulate symbols". He asks, "Who is computing with the brain?":

> I think that the hypothesis of computationalism as a causal explanatory model of cognition has some real difficulties. ... Any physical object can be used as a symbol, but for the same reason, no object is a symbol just by virtue of its physics. Syntax and symbols are matters of the interpretations that we assign to physics; we do not discover 0's and 1's in nature the way we might discover circles and lines, because syntax is not intrinsic to physics. Some physical systems facilitate a syntactical interpretation better than others, just as some physical substances are easier to write on than others and some are easier to sit on than others; but this does not make syntax, writing, symbols, chairs, or computation into natural physical kinds. ... all those facts make implicit reference to a homunculus. ... In short, syntax and symbol manipulation are in the eye of the beholder. They are observer relative ... The application of such concepts as chair or computer to physical systems differs from such concepts as shape or voltage level, because the former but not the latter make implicit reference to an actual or possible user or interpreter. ... Because the syntax is always in the eye of the beholder, you can't discover that computations are going on in nature, though you could decide to treat certain natural processes computationally.
>
> Because computation does not name a process of physics, like photosynthesis or pumping, there cannot be any *causal explanation* provided by the specification of the program level ... if you take away our intentionality, if you remove the homunculus from the system, then there is no way you could discover that the brain intrinsically has a syntax. The most you could find would be a pattern of events that you might decide to treat symbolically. This is not to say that brains are not digital computers but rather to say that the question is empty. Because you can assign a syntax to anything, you can certainly assign a syntax to the brain. But for the same reason that anything can be described as a digital computer, nothing can be intrinsically a digital computer.
>
> In these respects, the program level is quite different from the mental level in human beings. Mental causation is indeed in some sense "emergent" from the underlying physical features of the system, but it is a separate causal level, intrinsic to the system. ... Computational models are useful in studying the brain, but nobody really believes that the computational model is a substitute for a

scientific account of how the system actually works, and they should stop pretending otherwise.

So we should be cautious in using terms such as "information processing", "symbol manipulation" and "representation" as long as there are deep philosophical doubts about their adequacy. It is all too easy to go with the stream of fashion and pretend that one understands what one is talking about. It is much more difficult to be critical towards the basic notions of cognitive science and to really examine the implications of one's terminology. We are not saying that cognitive science is necessarily on the wrong track, but at least it is based on some assumptions which are worth questioning, since they might, just might, entail as distorted a picture of the human mind as did behaviorism. And of course nobody would like to be *that* wrong again.

3.5. Simulation and the real thing

What about the "strong AI" hypothesis that an appropriately programmed computer has genuine mental processes? Here we need to make clear the distinction between *simulations* and *real instances* of something. Now, the natural sciences are advanced enough to be able to give mathematical descriptions or models of the behavior of a great many phenomena in, e.g., physics, chemistry, physiology and astronomy. When we have such a mathematical model of an X, it is in principle possible – and nowadays a standard procedure – to make a computer program, that is, a *simulation*, of X.

> Perhaps one of the most practical applications of computer simulations are models of weather phenomena. Such a model has a mathematical description of winds and their speeds, the distributions of air pressure, humidity, temperature, the topography of mountain ranges, plains and valleys, and so on. When such a program models the development of future weather, certain numerical values and equations are given from which the program starts to calculate the course of things to come. The output of the model might be visual (like a picture taken from a weather satellite) or numerical or verbal, which is then interpreted by the meteorologists to stand for certain weather conditions. Let us imagine that the computer is calculating in real time and that it is closed in a windowless room in which it is impossible to see what the real weather outside is like. After a 24-hour run of the program the computer announces that there is a violent snow-

storm going on, the wind is 24 m/s from the north-west, the air-pressure is 710 Hgmm, and the temperature –8.4 degrees Celsius. The computer obviously has no idea that the equations and the data it has been processing have something to do with weather – it has only calculated mechanically from certain initial states some later states, following programmed algorithms. Inside the computer, as well as inside the room where the computer is, there is no blizzard and the temperature is well above zero. The point of this discussion is to show that *the simulation of weather does not involve any real weather phenomena* – the digitized winds and rains represent winds and rains only from the point of view of the *users* of the program. The same goes with the simulation of chemical, physiological or astronomical phenomena: the program itself is completely ignorant of the subject matter the program is about – it couldn't care less; for the machine, the programs are about nothing at all.

Imagine now that we have a computer program simulating some cognitive task, say face recognition. On seeing the face of a person "known" to it (a description of it is stored in its memory), it prints out the name of the person. Is this case in any relevant sense different from the case of modelling other physical phenomena? Some think it is. Those who believe that mental processes are, at bottom, computations, claim that a computer simulation of a mental process *is* a mental process, because both the actual mental process in the brain and the simulated one in the computer are cases of physical symbol manipulation. Thus, according to strong AI, after scanning a picture the program prints "George Bush": the machine is having the same mental state as you or me when looking at the same picture and recognizing the person it depicts.

As we saw above, however, the assumption that there are nonconscious symbols somewhere in the brain is suspect, because it seems to involve a reference to the observer of the system. Thus, the traditional AI simulations of mental processes create real mentality to no greater extent than the simulations of atmospheric processes create real weather. Although the input-output relations might be similar in simulations and reality, it by no means guarantees that what happened between the input and the output was the same as what happened in the atmosphere or the person.

3.6. Connectionism and representation

Since the "symbol-manipulation" paradigm is largely inheritage from traditional AI, "GOFAI", and from the exaggeration of the digital-computer metaphor, we must ask, does connectionism escape this criticism. And if it does, does it imply some other problems. In connectionist systems there are no explicit symbols or rules, and the processing architecture is often claimed to be "brain-style". However, it is as yet unclear, to which level of nature connectionist networks correspond. They are not faithful imitators of real neural networks: real neurons are horrendously more complicated systems than the abstract "units" of connectionism. And at the network-level, connectionists are not trying to find out how real neurons are connected to form networks – they are not doing neuroanatomy. On the other hand, connectionist models are also not thought to correspond to the conceptual level of thought, but they have been said to be "subconceptual" and "subsymbolic", higher-level than neurons but lower than conceptual thought (Smolensky 1988). Thus, it is at least unclear whether there is any natural level of organization in the brain (or in the mind) to which the connectionist modeling corresponds and, subsequently, is a model of. Furthermore, the notion of "subsymbolic" does not solve the problem of representation, since subsymbolic items *are* representations.

Could a connectionist model of a cognitive process be the same as the real thing, after all? Unfortunately, as far as pure computations are concerned, no relevant difference exists between connectionist and traditional AI: any function that can be computed with a connectionist machine can also be computed with a traditional machine. So we cannot say that mental processes are functions which could only be computed in parallel machines: if mental processes are essentially computational, then they can be programmed as well to serial as to connectionist machines. In fact, most of the connectionist programs that exist today are simulations of real networks. That is, the serial computer has a mathematical description of a network and it changes the activation values one by one according to the input, thus ending up with the same result a real network would have – the digital computer is mimicking network behavior.

Let us assume then that we build a real connectionist network, and not just a simulation. Is it still only a model or could it have real mental processes? The answer, of course, depends on what we believe "real mental processes" to be. We suggest that systems with real mental processes have to have at least some kind of consciousness, whereas completely nonmental entities do not have any conscious processes occurring in them at all. We must remember that many processes in the human brain can proceed automatically and nonconsciously. Consequently, if connectionist machines are able to reproduce only such processes, totally devoid of consciousness, it is dubious to think of them as embodying *mental* processes at all. Exactly this seems to be the case: consider the neuropsychologist Daniel Schacter's analysis of connectionist models or, as he calls them, Parallel Distributed Processing (PDP):

> Would a system that operated purely according to PDP principles consciously remember a prior experience or, like the amnesic patient, would such a system merely show implicit effects of a prior experience in performance, without any conscious or explicit recollection? My own guess is that systems depicted by PDP models are largely implicit memory machines: When a new pattern of activation partially matches an existing pattern of activation, the existing pattern is automatically strenghtened and affects the response tendencies of the system, without any recollective experience or conscious awareness of a past event. An important future task for PDP models will be to come to grips with the problem of conscious recollection and more generally with the role of consciousness in learning and cognition. (Schacter 1989, 709)

To sum up, cognitive science is still plagued with the computer metaphor and the questionable dogmas of mental processes as physical symbol manipulation and computation. These notions are philosophically loaded and entail a commitment to functionalism and strong AI. Researchers in cognitive neuroscience and psychology use the standard "information processing" jargon perhaps without realizing that the concepts are not quite as innocent as their widespread use would suggest. Even the new approach offered by connectionism has not yet been shown to reach beyond blind imitation or simulation of mental phenomena. This is probably because we do not have so clear ideas of how the authentic mental phenomena are realized in the brain: is neurochemistry, -physiology or -anatomy important? Or is it just a matter of imitating a few abstract properties of neurons, as the units of connectionist networks do?

4. ONTOLOGY AND PHENOMENOLOGY

Cognitive science construes human beings as intelligent systems whose "behaviour can only be explained by appeal to internal cognitive processes, that is, rational thought in a very broad sense" (Haugeland 1981, 243). Cognitive science is inherently interested in how things appear to human beings, their first-person or "phenomenological" view. Yet research into cognitive mechanisms is bound to utilize the outside perspective, so-called third-person or "ontological" view, which is interested in how things really are. The crucial question is, how to balance these views.

Ontology deals with the problem of what really exists, whereas phenomenology is concerned with what appears to us. Of course these two studies are closely related: we cannot put forward any theories about what exists if we do not have some sort of an implicit theory of what it is like for an existing thing to appear in our stream of consciousness. It is important to keep these two studies and their typical points of view apart. If we can learn something from Descartes, Kant and Husserl, it is precisely this: don't mix up ontological and phenomenological talk. Descartes expressed this idea by saying that what we really know is within our consciousness. Everything else is uncertain. We know, for instance, only that there appears to be a horse in the field, but we can never be one hundred per cent sure that there really is a horse (or even a field) out there. Kant put this point by saying that what we know are phenomena or appearances. We can never grasp the things-in-themselves, the supposed causes of our appearances. Husserl insisted that one has to adopt a totally new attitude when one starts to examine what is really given, that is, phenomena, in order to avoid the mistake of smuggling ontological elements into the phenomenological description of experience (or phenomena). We will not deal with the elaborate proofs and systems that these three philosophers built upon this sound insight. Instead, we will try to show that it must be revived in modern philosophy. We believe that many difficult problems in modern cognitivism can be solved – or at least seen in a new light – if one keeps in mind this elementary lesson: don't confuse phenomenology with ontology.

Many contemporary problems can be seen as attempts to articulate the proper places of ontology and phenomenology. The distinction is reformulated in several disguises. The problem of consciousness, for example, is currently approached from two, radically different camps. One claims that there is no way to explicate the subjective phenomenology in terms of objective ontology, or to replace the first-person account with the third-person view. The other camp feels that phenomenology should not be taken as the starting point to begin with, but rather, it should be discarded from our scientific worldview. We think that some issues can be settled only by empirical research, mainly cognitive neuroscience. There has been progress since Descartes, Kant and Husserl.

In cognitive and cultural anthropology, explanatory models are balanced between the emic and etic viewpoints, that is, between how things appear to the informant and "how things really are" (from the viewpoint of the researcher). Thus, the distinction between the first-person view and the third-person view appears in another disguise. Cognitive schemata are one major explanatory vehicle in cultural anthropology. They are supposed to match the structures of experience. One prominent question is whether there are universal, cross-cultural schemata which are specific enough to have explanatory power. Another is whether there is a direct, nonconceptual access to reality.

5. INTENTIONALITY AND RATIONALITY

We have to get back to the problem of representation discussed above, since it borders with the distinction phenomenology - ontology. There are two pertinent philosophical themes: (1) theories of intentionality, (2) functional identification of mental representations, or the question of rationality and the ascription of mental content.

Intentionality means "aboutness" of mental phenomena. Most mental phenomena are directed towards their objects. That is their distinctive feature, the one that tells them apart from other types of states. The distinction between the Content Theory and the Object Theory of intentionality borders with the distinction between phenomenology and ontology. Content Theory is a thesis that mental states are intentional if and only if they have contents, whereas the Object Theory claims that intentionality is due to extramental objects. Accordingly, a Content Theorist proposes to individuate mental phenomena in terms of their contents, and the Object Theorist is hoping to accomplish the same task with objects. The starting point in contemporary cognitivism is the Content Theory. We have proposed earlier that the Object Theory is infested with problems (see Sajama and Kamppinen 1987). Both theories start from phenomenology, but the Object Theory smuggles in pieces of ontology when it refers to extramental objects in explaining mental phenomena. (Similar instances of smuggling can be found in some theories of acquaintance, *de re* acts and indexicality which will be examined in Part III, Section A.)

Functionalism is a major answer to the problem of intentionality. It claims that mental contents are identified by means of their functional roles. The versions of functionalism have differed from each other in that they have emphasized different sets of functional roles; intramental, social or ecological. Methodological solipsism and other intramental versions of functionalism could be classified as Content Theories of intentionality, and sociofunctionalism and other naturalistic psychologies could be termed Object

Theories. Recently the question of intentionality has been transfused with the question of consciousness. Intentionality appears to require consciousness, not vice versa. The notion of intrinsic intentionality plays a crucial role here. It seems that those who accept the first-person view, also postulate intrinsic intentionality and consciousness, whereas those who favour the third-person view, are willing to postulate derived intentionality only.

Rationality is intricately tied with problems of intentionality and functionalism for the following reason: the identification of mental content, that is, the identification of intentionality, involves a reference to a network of functionally characterized links, the functional roles of the item. This network makes up the semantic or epistemic context of the item in question. In case of human beings and other intelligent systems, the network has to make rational sense. That is, not just any network will do. Therefore the identification of mental representations assumes an answer to both functionalism and rationality.

The interconnections between intentionality, functionalism and rationality has been nicely captured by Daniel Dennett (1978, 163), who has characterized the notions of "function" and "content" as follows:

$$\text{function} =_{df} \text{function of structure}$$
$$\text{content} =_{df} \text{function of function}$$

The first proposition says that by function we should understand what some structure does. Notoriously, it is impossible to identify the one and only function of any structure, because structures perform various functions simultaneously. A system of neurons, for example, emits electronic signals, vibrations, chemical compounds, even information. The functions are identified by means of theories, which specify the level of interaction we are interested in. Transmitting electronic signals, for example, is a function that is specified with respect to a pertinent theory. The second proposition says, roughly, that contents are higher-order functions, or functions of functions. Thus, a pattern of electronic signals may serve a function in the information-processing system of the brain with respect to which the content of the electronic pattern is identified. This larger network includes such components as visual input, speech-processing, etc. Contents, in Dennett's view, are not any exotic entities, radically different from other functions performed by the system, but generically of the same kind. To put it shortly, contents are identified by means of functional networks, just like other functions.

If functionalism as a general approach is *not* found satisfactory, cognitive science needs to take even more critical stance towards its use of intentional concepts. When attributing "representations" and "symbol manipulations" to the brain, we must always be careful to think, to whom or in virtue of what fact do those things represent or symbolize. Neurophysiological brain events in themselves do not *represent*; they are not *about* anything at all any more than hemoglobin refers to oxygen: physiological processes are engaged in multiple causal chains, but to say that some state represents something else *might* always implant the external observer into the observed system. By contrast, if conscious thought can represent without presupposing observers external to the system itself, then the major – but this far largely neglected – challenge to cognitive science is how the blind neurobiology can give rise to the conscious mind.

6. SYNOPSIS

This study is composed of three parts. Part I, *Cognitive models of consciousness*, reviews and evaluates the contemporary discussion concerning consciousness. Both philosophical and empirical arguments are assessed. The fundamental philosophical issue seems to be the ontological status of consciousness: some philosophers claim that consciousness is nothing but a pseudoproblem, a mirage created by naive everyday thinking which should hardly worry philosophers or scientists. Others, by contrast, respect their intuitions and take consciousness as a real phenomenon, which cries out for an explanation. On the empirical side, a number of models of consciousness have been presented recently, but as yet, no unified emerging paradigm of consciousness research has emerged. The reason for this is, we argue, that present theories of consciousness do not share a common base but stem from diverging philosophical and empirical roots. We will try to foresee what kinds of philosophical commitments and theoretical starting-points could serve as the core and bedrock of the future science of consciousness. We consummate Part I by suggesting that the first-person, phenomenological point of view must, in some way, be preserved in theories of consciousness and we investigate, how such future theories could be built from the presently existing, preliminary models.

Part II, *Cognitive schemata*, deals with methodological issues, especially with cognitive explanations in anthropology. We distinguish between intentional and structural explanations. The intentional explanation is deeply rooted in our commonsense psychology, and its scientific use assumes that the "anthropological other" is sharing our basic beliefs and inferential rules, that is, our rationality. Structural explanation, on the contrary, can cope with differences in beliefs by means of absracting the meaning structures from the belief systems. The vehicle of structural explanation is the cognitive schema, or a cluster of representations. The notion of schema is widely used in psychology, anthropology and artificial intelligence. The various theories of schemata are systematized by means of posing two questions, those concerning their nodes and links. Even though the notion of schema provides a powerful explanatory tool, it leaves some fundamental issues unanswered; for example, the question of emic/subjective versus etic/objective viewpoint in the study of cultural cognition.

In Part III, *Relativism and cognitivism*, the classical problem of relativism inherent in the study of doxastic diversity is studied in the novel context provided by cognitivism. Cognitivism appears to provide a solution to the problem of relativism, but, by the same token, it invites a more profound version of relativism. Part III is composed of two sections. Section A discusses the question of whether we could have a direct access to reality, even in principle. We show how this question has ancient roots in philosophy. The thesis argued for is that all our cognition is conceptually mediated. Section B investigates the consequences of this claim. The issue of relativism is perhaps the paragon case of balancing the first-person view and the third-person view. In cultural anthropology, the fact of cognitive diversity states the pertinent problem clearly: Are those apparently incompatible beliefs comparable; Is there a common measure? Behind this question lies a profound philosophical issue: Do some of our cognitive states provide a direct access to reality?

BIBLIOGRAPHY

Boden, M.A. (ed.): 1990, *The Philosophy of Artificial Intelligence*, Oxford: Oxford University Press.
Collins, A.M. and Loftus, E.F.: 1975, 'A Spreading-Activation Theory of Semantic Processing', *Psychological Review* **8 2**, 407–28.
Damasio, A.R.: 1989, 'Concepts in the Brain', *Mind and Language* **4**, 24–28.
Dennett, D.C.: 1978, *Brainstorms*, Montgomery: Bradford Books.
Garfield, J.L.: 1990, 'Introduction', in Garfield, J.L. (ed.), *Foundations of Cognitive Science*, New York: Paragon House.
Haugeland, J.: 1981, 'Semantic Engines: Introduction to Mind Design', in Haugeland, J. (ed.), *Mind Design*, Montgomery: Bradford Books.
Haugeland, J.: 1985, *Artificial Intelligence: The Very Idea*, Cambridge MA: MIT Press.
Haugeland, J.: 1991, 'Representational Genera', in Ramsey, W., Stich, S.P. and Rumelhart, D.E. (eds.), *Philosophy and Connectionist Theory*, London: Lawrence Erlbaum Associates.

Ladd, S.: 1985, *The Computer and the Brain*, New York: Bantam.
Neely, J.H.: 1977, 'Semantic Priming and Retrieval from Lexical Memory: Roles of Inhibitionless Spreading Activation and Limited-Capacity Attention', *Journal of Experimental Psychology: General*, 1 0 6, 226–54.
Pylyshyn, Z.W.: 1989, 'Computing in Cognitive Science', in Posner, M.I. (ed.), *Foundations of Cognitive Science*, Cambribge, MA: MIT press.
Sajama, S. and Kamppinen, M.: 1987, *A Historical Introduction to Phenomenology*, London: Croom Helm.
Schacter, D.L.; 1989, 'Memory', in Posner, M.I. (ed.), *Foundations of Cognitive Science*, Cambribge, MA: MIT press.
Searle, J.R.: 1980, 'Minds, Brains, and Programs', *The Behavioral and Brain Sciences* 3, 417–457.
Searle, J.R.: 1990, 'Who Is Computing with the Brain?' Author's Response, *Behavioral and Brain Sciences* 1 3 (4), 632–640.
Simon, H.A. and Kaplan, C.A.: 1989, 'Foundations of Cognitive Science', in Posner, M.I. (ed.), *Foundations of Cognitive Science*, Cambribge, MA: MIT Press.
Smolensky, P.: 1988, 'On the Proper Treatment of Connectionism', *Behavioral and Brain Sciences* 1 1, 1–74.

PART I

COGNITIVE MODELS OF CONSCIOUSNESS

COGNITIVE MODELS OF CONSCIOUSNESS

In the following chapters, I will first take a look at the philosophical problems surrounding consciousness (Chapter 1). After that, I will review different mind-body theories, functionalism, its predecessors as well as its current competitors, and their answers to questions of consciousness (Chapter 2). I will also probe the arguments that have been given for and against the importance of consciousness as a respectable scientific concept and phenomenon. Finally, I will focus on the most fundamental ontological question: Does consciousness exist at all?

The contemporary cognitive models of consciousness arise from these philosophical roots. I will make a critical review of the most important cognitive models of consciousness (Chapter 3). These models by no means agree on the status of consciousness and, eventually, I will try to find out, on which basic assumptions the science of consciousness could be built. Thus, I will be making some predictions about the future course of consciousness research and theory, and I will also create my own view which coherently combines certain philosophical foundations with certain models and empirical findings about consciousness (Chapter 4). But, to start from the beginning, Why is consciousness a philosophical problem?

1. CONSCIOUSNESS AS A CONTEMPORARY PHILOSOPHICAL PROBLEM

Intuitively, consciousness seems to form the center of our minds – it is the stuff that mental phenomena really are made of. What would be left of my mind, were all my conscious thoughts, beliefs, sensations, emotions and dreams eradicated? Without consciousness I would be a mere puppet, robot, or a mindless zombie – a vacant body wandering around and going through human motions. Behind my eyes and the voice-patterns I utter there would be but darkness; there would be no subject there, which could in some way feel that it exists.

If consciousness truly is such an essential feature of our minds, what in the world *is* it? Unfortunately, we have no universally accepted answers to this question. We are still at the point of research, in which philosophers are

27

just charting the different possibilities and seeking for the right questions to ask. Some philosophers even think that there is no such phenomenon, about which questions could be formulated. Therefore, not even the most fundamental ontological question – whether or not consciousness exists – is settled so far.

1.1. Consciousness-related problems in the philosophy of mind

Consciousness is the real enigma of the mind-brain relationship. Presumably a philosophical mind-body problem could hardly even exist, were all mental events as non-conscious as the rest of the physical processes. The whole mystery crystallizes in the following question: How is it possible that blind neurobiological processes going on inside the darkness of the brain can cause all the subjective, qualitative, and contentful conscious states? Precisely those three properties of conscious states have puzzled philosophers. The *subjectivity* of consciousness is known as the problem of the subjective point of view. The different *qualities* of conscious experience have been discussed under many names: the problem of *qualia* or *raw feels*. And the *contentfulness* of conscious states is in philosophy the problem of *intentionality*. The debate on the nature of these problems is the never-ending story of modern philosophy of mind.

1.1.1. Subjectivity

Consciousness seems to involve something essentially subjective. In every instance of a conscious mind, there is a subjective point of view, which is accessible only to the conscious entity itself. Consciousness is not a phenomenon to be measured, observed or experienced in public: it seems to be a private matter, concealed from outsiders. It can only be known from a first-person perspective, never from the third-person, objective, scientific perspective. For Thomas Nagel, subjectivity is the fundamental cornerstone of consciousness. His illustrious formulation of what it means to be conscious captures this idea well:

But fundamentally an organism has conscious mental states if and only if there is something it is like to *be* that organism – something it is like *for* the organism. We may call this the subjective character of experience. (Nagel 1974, 436)

The real puzzle with subjectivity is that it is irreconcilable with a scientific approach to phenomena in general. Undoubtedly, a wide variety of thoroughly *alien* minds exist in the universe – from bat and dolphin minds to inconceivable extraterrestrial beings. Their subjective, experiential worlds are presumably totally out of our reach. Now, can science ever tell us what kind of a subjective consciousness an alien mind enjoys? Or, vice versa, can an alien mind ever find out what it is like to be a human being? Scientific explanation of ordinary physical phenomena leads to a more general, objective and precise account of the real nature of things. Thus, lightning or rainbows can be characterized by referring to concepts and properties which are not dependent on a specifically human standpoint: they are accessible also to other than human minds. The point is, then, that we move from how objects *appear* to us to what those objects *really are* behind appearances. But how could this scheme be applied in the case of subjective consciousness? How could we move from the way conscious mental states appear to us to something else that supposedly is the real nature of those states? Such a fatal move would not in the least take us closer to those states – make us understand what it is like to have them – but, on the contrary, it would totally destroy them. The essence of conscious states is precisely their appearance, and science is unable to take this fact into account.

Among those philosophers who consider subjectivity as a crucial problem are Thomas Nagel (1974, 1979 and 1986), John Searle (1984b, 1987, 1989 and 1990) and Colin McGinn (1983, 1989 and 1991). However, an opposing camp also exists. For example, Richard Rorty (1982a and 1982b) insists that the real problem in consciousness is not how to take into account its special, intrinsic nature, but how to convince people that persons have to no greater an extent any "inside" than do particles. Daniel Dennett's (1982) comments about the ontological status of subjectively experienced mental entities are also revealing:

This is what I meant: the heterophenomenologist describes a world, the subject's heterophenomenological world, in which there are various *objects*, in which *things happen*, but if we ask, "what *are these* objects and what are they *made of?*" the answer is "Nothing"! (Dennett 1982, 175)

... the purple flank of the cow you imagine, does not exist. (Dennett 1982, 179)

Dennett thinks that we should get rid of our confused everyday intuitions, according to which subjective points of view exist.

In sum, we seem to have two alternatives from which to choose. Either we can take the intuition that *there is something it is like to be a conscious being* at face value and admit that at the moment no solution is in sight. Or we can leave intuitions behind as aberrations originated in common sense folklore and go on with "real" science without such irrelevant pseudoproblems. The gap between the subjective and objective points of view is wide open.

1.1.2. Intentionality

Intentionality means *aboutness*: that one thing can stand for or be about another thing. Thus, ink-marks – words or pictures – on paper, sounds uttered, or thoughts might all be about, say, strawberries. How is it possible for a thing to represent something that it is not in itself? According to some philosophers, a sharp distinction between intentionality outside and inside the mind must be made. Things that stand outside the mental realm, like books, pictures, computers, and stones, can only have *derived* or *metaphorical* intentionality (Searle 1979, 1984a and 1988). These kinds of intentionality are dependent on how people happen to use and interpret these non-mental entities. However, mental states themselves – e.g., thoughts, beliefs, or mental images about strawberries – have *original* or *intrinsic* intentionality.

The main proponent of intrinsic intentionality, John Searle, thinks that only beings capable of conscious states can have intrinsically intentional states. He has argued that intentionality cannot be totally separated from consciousness, but that they have a necessary connection. He also criticizes modern cognitive science just because it is trying to describe and explain intentional mental states without referring to consciousness at all (Searle 1989 and 1990).

As in the case of subjectivity, also here we have contrary views, most clearly expressed by Dennett. He strictly denies that mental representation would be somehow different from all other representation and he explicitly rejects the idea of intrinsic intentionality:

... – the "right program" on a suitably fast machine – *is* sufficient for *derived* intentionality, and that is the only kind of semantics there is. ... There is no such thing as intrinsic intentionality, especially if this is viewed, as Searle can now be seen to require, as a property to which the subject has conscious, privileged access. (Dennett 1987, 336–37)

A shopping list in the head has no more intrinsic intentionality than a shopping list on a piece of paper. (Dennett 1990, 62)

Moreover, Dennett (1987) sees the belief in intrinsic intentionality as a "Great Divide" in contemporary philosophy of mind, which keeps the opposing philosophers worlds apart. So, again we have a philosophical problem which either boils down to consciousness or is abandoned as falsely posed.

1.1.3. The qualitative character of experience

Conscious experiences contain qualitative properties, or qualia, which define what these experiences feel like for the subject. The taste of wild strawberry, the sound of a church organ, the blueness of the sky, and the fragrance of jasmine are all experiential qualities. It seems to us that we subjectively discriminate our experiences from each other just because we can *feel* the differences of, e.g., pain and pleasure, sweetness and sourness, or redness and blueness. Subjectively, what it is for something to be a pain is its experienced painfulness: the outward stimuli or behavioral responses or neurophysiological spiking frequencies in the brain seem to be only indirectly connected with the pain itself.

Qualia seem to be, then, something essential, private, and directly accessible to the consciousness of the experiencing subject, whereas the outwardly observable sensory inputs and behavioral outputs seem to be only accidentally connected with certain qualia. That is, we can perfectly well imagine cases, in which the private and public criteria for certain experiences are disconnected. Let us assume that there is a sort of "parallel Earth" somewhere in the universe. At first glance, the people there all seem to be exactly like we are down here, including their linguistic and other behavior. Imagine yourself visiting this parallel world and discussing how beautiful their planet is: how deep blue is the sky, how emerald green the forests, and how bright red is their sun. However, suddenly a disturbing thought arises in your mind. What if these people, although they call green "green" and red "red", nevertheless do not *experience* these colours as you do. Perhaps when *they* talk about green, they experience the same that you experience when you talk about red. How could you ever know? Their behaviour would never betray them. But, to come to think about it, how could you ever know about *anybody*, parallel-earthling or not, if his or her experiences are the same deep inside?

This thought-experiment is known as the problem of *inverted qualia* (or inverted spectrum, Shoemaker 1982). In similar vein, the problem of *absent qualia* invites us to imagine a robot or an extraterrestrial, which seems to behave like us, but which is constructed in such a way that it makes it very hard to believe that it has any qualia at all: it is merely an unconscious automaton. These examples have been extensively used as arguments against functionalist theories of mind. As we shall later see in more detail, functionalists claim that mental states are to be identified according to their causal roles. The purpose of these qualia-based arguments is to show that the functional characterization of mental states is not exhaustive, but it leaves something out. The argument from the possibility of an inverted spectrum to the falsity of functionalism is, simply, that if two different mental states can play exactly the same functional role, then there is an aspect of mentality that a functionalistic characterization cannot capture (Block 1990). Nothing in the functional organization of behaving systems can reveal which systems are enjoying which kinds of qualia or, indeed, whether or not they are enjoying any qualia at all. Especially Ned Block (1978, 1980 and 1990) has explored different kinds of qualia arguments, and he recommends that we give up functionalism as a theory of experience or at least as a theory of the qualitative aspect of experience, but that functionalism can be preserved as a theory of the cognitive aspect of the mind.

Not surprisingly, many functionalist philosophers have been prepared to deny the importance or reality of qualia. P. M. Churchland and P. S. Churchland (1981) try to save functionalism from qualia by claiming that all that is common to different kinds of pain – burning headaches, electric shocks, ear-breaking noises, pains of snakes, fish and dogs – is their functional role, not any underlying physical nature. And the qualitative sensations that we do have are in fact to be identified with an underlying physical nature, e.g., with certain spiking frequencies in specific parts of the brain. Qualia are under attack also in Dennett's article 'Quining Qualia' (1988). He tries to demonstrate that our concepts of the qualities of conscious experience are not coherent, and that we do not even know what we are talking about. In Dennett's view, it is a thoroughly misguided way to think that there can be such things as "*the way a strawberry tastes to person P1 at time t1*" or "*the way a harpsichord sounds to person P2 at time t2.*" Subjective qualities of conscious experience simply cannot be isolated or extracted from everything else – especially not from dispositions to believe or behave.

In conclusion, the fate of subjectivity, intrinsic intentionality, and qualia seem to go hand in hand. Some philosophers claim that they are fundamental unresolved questions for the philosophy of mind, whereas others insist that all this trouble stems from our confused everyday intuitions which create artificial pseudoproblems. All we need to do is to have a reformation of everyday beliefs and open our eyes to see that current theories of mind are quite sufficient for explaining the mind exhaustively.

Our suggestion is that these problems have a common undercurrent, namely consciousness, which is the real and so far neglected core of all mental phenomena. As long as no satisfying account of conscious phenomena in general is available, the only alternatives are just to admit or to deny the problem. In the course of this article, I will try to shed some light on which approaches to consciousness are fruitful and which are not. The problem of consciousness, if depicted correctly, is not a hopeless cul-de-sac – at least so I will argue. But, the correct depiction requires a comprehensive re-evaluation of both the philosophical commitments we are ready to make and the empirical evidence currently at hand.

2. PHILOSOPHICAL THEORIES OF CONSCIOUSNESS

By a philosophical theory of consciousness I mean the different kinds of answers that have been given to the question "What on earth *could* consciousness be?" Of course, there are almost as many answers as there are philosophers of mind, and our purpose here is to concentrate on those answers that are currently relevant. I shall begin by briefly summarizing the basic ideas of so-called "central-state identity theories" and behaviorism, which are the main predecessors of present theories. Our emphasis will be on functionalism and its relations to Cognitive Science. The main opponent of functionalism, in our view, is eliminative materialism, which argues for the non-existence of consciousness. I will show that none of the currently available mind-body theories can offer conclusive or even convincing solutions to the problem of consciousness. Therefore, I introduce alternative approaches, which could serve as a philosophical foundation for empirical theories of consciousness.

2.1. Past and current theories: A review

2.1.1. The predecessors of functionalism: Identity theory and behaviorism

According to central-state identity theories or type-identity theories, mental states should be individuated by referring to their common, materialistic or neurophysiological basis. Certain types of mental states, e.g., feeling pain, seeing red, or hearing a sound, are *identical* with certain, as-yet-unknown states or processes of the central nervous system. In this view, pain *is* the firing of C-neuron fibers, and seeing red could be the firing of some other type, say Z-neurons.

Psychology and psychological concepts will one day be reduced to neurophysiology and thus the unification of science will take one great step. As water is really H_2O or light is really electromagnetic radiation, so smelling a rose is really the firing of X-neurons. Identity theory presupposes, then, that behind the folk psychological typology of mental states there is a more fundamental, materialistic world order, and both of them "carve nature at the same joints" – only the level and language of description is different.

Identity theories have been heavily criticized, but here I will mention only two points of criticism. First of all, identification of folk psychological mental states to neurophysiology has to be strict. That is, if water is identified with H_2O, then anything that is not H_2O – no matter how much it looks, tastes or feels like water – is *not* water, but something entirely different. In psychology, consequently, if consciousness (or any other psychological category) is identified, for example, with firing of ABC-neurons, then *no creature without exactly those kinds of neurons can be said to be conscious*, no matter how much it seems to be so. Identity theories are highly "species chauvinist": if the identification of consciousness with human neurophysiology one day takes place, then any other creature with a different neurophysiology will forever be denied to have consciousness. This kind of result seems to be remarkably counterintuitive: we probably would like to claim that chimpanzees, dolphins and intelligent extraterrestrials can have the same kinds of mental states, although they might have a different neurophysiology than humans. Thus, mental states are likely to be *multiply realizable* and not strictly identified with any specific neurophysiology. This is a point which especially functionalists like to make against type-identity theories.

A different line of objection criticizes type-identity theories for taking folk psychology seriously. We have no reason to believe that those categorizations of mental phenomena that folk theories make are anywhere even near the true nature of things. Many examples from the history of science indicate that common sense theories of physics, chemistry, or biology have not been in any way *reduced* to modern natural sciences, but, on the contrary, they have been completely overthrown as fundamentally wrong. It is naive to believe that our folk theory of mind should fare any better than other folk theories. Thus, mental states and processes as understood today will probably never be reduced to anything at all; instead, psychology and neuroscience must make progress to reveal the real entities relevant to science. This argument is advocated by eliminative materialists, as we shall later see.

Behavioristic doctrines were strongly opposed to identity theories, and historically preceded them. For behaviorists, psychology was first and foremost the science for predicting and controlling the behavior of organisms. The observational data of behaviorist psychologists was strictly confined to physical input stimuli and behavioral outputs. Behaviorists did not worry themselves with any internal events, be they mental or neurophysiological. Such events, if they exist, are not a proper object of investigation for psychology. Consequently, no talk about "mental states" was permitted for the behaviorist: the organism was simply a "black box", the behavior of which was to be predicted on the basis of physical stimuli. Behavior is not an indirect way to study something behind it – like mind, consciousness, or brain. Behavior is studied for its own sake: it is what psychology is all about.

Needless to say, the main line of objection against behaviorism pointed out that the theory leaves something very important out. It was intuitively highly implausible that no internal states of an organism would be relevant for psychology. Again, the functionalist could take pride in his theory, which allows internal states to be postulated for the organism.

2.1.2. Functionalism

Damaging knockout arguments were pushing behaviorism and identity theories to ideological bankruptcy. Then a new doctrine appeared on the stage, which seemed to dodge all the worst curses of its predecessors. Functionalism takes the philosopher of mind into the promised land where physicalism, autonomy of psychology, and internal explanatory mechanisms are resurrected and all live together in peace. How does functionalism manage this brilliant feat?

In functionalism, mental states are individuated by referring to their causal, that is, functional role. For example mental state M is defined as follows: M is that mental state which is typically caused by sensory stimuli S (the functional relation to the input) together with mental state N, and which typically causes mental states O,P, ... (the functional relations to other mental states) together with behaviour B (the functional relations to the output). Thus, pain would be the mental state which typically is caused by *tissue damage*, causes *a want* to remove the cause of damage and *behavior* that fulfills this want if possible. Infatuation would be roughly the mental state typically caused by the presence of a beautiful or interesting person of the opposite sex; it normally causes a strong want or need to be close to the chosen one and perhaps even dreams related to this person, and it also causes all kinds of ingenuous behaviour, the purpose of which is to satisfy the burning desires.

Functionalist explanation takes place at different levels. At the highest level, which D. Marr (1982) calls *computational*, although a better term would be the *functional* level, the different functions of the subsystems are identified. The second level Marr calls *algorithmic*, and at this level the inner workings of the functional boxes are mathematically defined. At the bottom there is the *hardware* level, which in the case of humans means neurophysiology.

The first level of functionalist explanation is the common sense level of beliefs, desires, fears, pains, and thoughts. Common sense psychological explanation aims to show how mental states cause other mental states and behaviour. A more scientific version of this functional level can be called sub-personal cognitive psychology (Dennett 1987). The general strategy here is some sort of "reiterated behaviorism" (Wilkes 1989): the black box that stands for the organism is opened, but only to put more smaller black boxes inside (Fig.1). Every smaller box has its own causal relations from the external world or from other boxes to other boxes or behaviour. This functional decomposition can go on inside every box, always identifying more simple and "stupid" functions, which are together in charge of the complex total behaviour of the system. At the basic level the functions are so simple that there is hope of finding the neurophysiological implementations for these functions: an example are the neurons in the visual cortex, which are selectively reactive to very simple properties of the visual world (Hubel and Wiesel 1962; Zeki 1990). To explain the mind of a person, functionalism postulates many smaller, simpler and more stupid men, homunculi, inside the mind: thus is the mind divided and conquered.

Input (sensory stimulus)

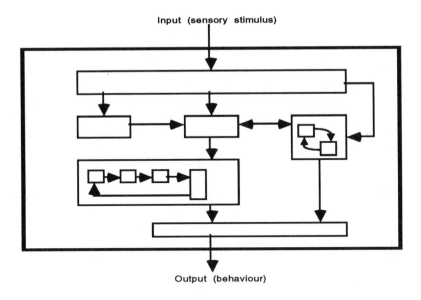

Output (behaviour)

Fig. 1. A Functionalist Box Model. The behaviour and input-output connections of a system are explained by referring to separate functions and their causal relations inside the system.

Functionalism does not allow the reduction of psychology to neurophysiology. Functionally individuated entities are multiply realizable, that is, they are not tied to any specific material composition. Every instantiation of a clock, chair, or money is material, but there is nothing in common in the materials themselves that would unite all instances under the same category. The unifying factor is the causal role of those things, not their physical nature. According to the functionalist, the same goes for mental states. What counts is the causal role, not the neurophysiology, and thus every being realizing the right sorts of causal roles in its mental life has exactly the same kinds of mental states as we do – no matter whether they are instantiated in neurons, silicon, or ectoplasm. Every instance of a mental state is *some* kind of a physical state, but they need not be the same kinds of physical states in all creatures, or even in the same creature at different times. This particular version of physicalism is often called token-identity theory.

Many functionalists believe that, at bottom, the functioning of the whole sub-personal box model of cognition can be described and also actually *is* composed of abstract mathematical algorithms, which are computed by the brain. So, there is a sort of "computer program of the mind", and if we just could unravel it, we could program any general-purpose computer to have a mind. This kind of functionalism is often called "computationalism" or "Strong Artificial Intelligence". These ideas were born with the launching of artificial intelligence in the 1950's, when it was proposed that the ontological relation between a computer and its program is the same as the relation of brain and mind. Computer programs are entirely defined at an abstract level which is totally independent of the physical features of the machine on which the program happens to run.

Functionalism, then, allows minds to be realized, not only in human brains, but in all kinds of animal and extraterrestrial neurophysiology and even in computers. Consciousness, for a functionalist, would be a mental process with certain kinds of causal relations to the inputs, to other mental states or processes, and to certain behaviours. For a computationalist, some of the computations in the brain are conscious and others are not. To perform or instantiate exactly those computations in any arbitrary system which can function as a Turing machine would, on this account, produce consciousness. Unfortunately, no computationalist has been able to tell which kinds of computations are conscious and why.

However, functionalism has been accused of ignoring, for example, the problems arising from qualia. Many critics have pointed out that systems which apparently have no conscious states at all can anyway realize the same functional organization as a human being does. A box model of cognition tells us no more about what it feels to have certain mental states than the behaviorist models did. So, is this regression of functional black boxes only a trick – like the epicycles in Ptolemaic astronomy, which can hide the symptoms for a moment, but do not cure the disease? I will argue later that functionalism is not an exhaustive theory of mental phenomena and that a computationalist theory of consciousness is outright impossible.

2.1.3. Eliminative materialism

The main idea behind eliminative materialism is that our common sense psychology and the entities it postulates form a fundamentally erroneous conceptual framework. Functionalism and identity theory have gone wrong in assuming that such mental states as "belief", "desire", "fear" or "love" are well-defined phenomena, which somehow have to be incorporated into science. They have been desperately seeking for something real – at the neurophysiological or causal-role level – behind those notions. The eliminative materialist points out that if such identities are sought for, then folk psychology must be considered as a theory. However, it seems to be a remarkably poor scientific theory. It is vaguely formulated, its concepts and categories are contradictory and its "laws" are overgeneralizations and it has not shown any signs of progress for centuries (Churchland 1979 and 1981; Churchland and Churchland 1981; Stich 1983).

A much more believable solution is that folk psychology will never reduce to neuroscience, because it is an obscure, incoherent and unscientific doctrine, which should have nothing to do with "real" science at all. The entire folk theory as well as all concepts and explanations derived from it should be eliminated from science. P. S. Churchland (1988) complains that a general assumption about reduction seems to be that mental phenomena – as understood in current folk-based psychology – should be reduced to neurobiological phenomena – as understood in current neuroscience. It is, however, extremely unlikely that the present-day categories would prove to be the explanatory relevant ones. For one thing, it is rather unclear what the psychological macro-level phenomena are that neuroscience is supposed to explain. Furthermore, neurobiology lacks theories which would describe neural organization and function at higher and more complicated levels. The co-evolution of neuroscience and psychology will probably show that the present psychological concepts are untenable and must be replaced by a coherent conceptual framework, which coincides with a macro-level description of neural processing. Consequently, if our familiar folk concepts will be radically revised, it is false to say that they were in any way "reduced" to neuroscience. On the contrary, they are thrown out of science, because their ontology proves to be based on unscientific folklore (Churchland 1983 and 1986).

It is easy to see the fate of consciousness according to the eliminativist. Consciousness is a fine specimen of our obscure folk notions. Numerous critics have argued that the term consciousness is a mixed bag. They believe that underlying all the confusion there is no unitary phenomenon, about which theories could be constructed.

Kathleen Wilkes (1984 and 1988) has tried to demonstrate how vague and heterogenous the term "conscious" is, and that there are languages, in which there is no counterpart for it. She is convinced that consciousness cannot be adopted to science, because there is no theoretical need to do so – ignoring consciousness in no way leaves anything out:

... I shall question the existence of a 'problem of consciousness', suggesting that in fact consciousness as such is not at all important, and that psychology and the neurosciences would lose nothing, and gain much, by refusing to chase this will-o'-the-wisp. (Wilkes 1984, 224)

We are then, I suggest, thrown back on the idea that 'consciousness' and 'conscious' are terms of the vernacular which not only need not but should not figure in the conceptual apparatus of psychology or the neurosciences, for the concepts required in those theories will want to group phenomena along different, more systematic principles. (Wilkes 1984, 236–237)

Aaron Sloman's paper 'Why Consciousness Is Not Worth Talking About' (1991) echoes Wilkes's points: consciousness is an ordinary-language term, and we should not attempt to theorize scientifically about it. Alan Allport (1988) comes to the same general conclusion: we do not have criteria for identifying instances of the phenomenon, and thus, we do not know what we are talking about. His view is that no criteria can ever be found for consciousness, for the simple reason that there is no such phenomenon.

P.S. Churchland (1988) leaves at least the door open for consciousness. Perhaps the co-evolution of psychology and neurobiology will ultimately preserve a macro-level phenomenon that can be called consciousness, which the micro-level neurobiological theory will explain. At the moment, however, psychology and neurobiology are too far from each other for a reduction to take place. And perhaps it never will, suspects Churchland, because the phenomena we call conscious form a remarkably diverse collection and our definitions of consciousness are as obscure as the term itself. In addition to this, our concept of consciousness seems to work only in unproblematic cases, but there are a host of strange neurological and other anomalies that our folk theory is utterly unable to handle. So, after all, it seems to her that consciousness is not of a "natural kind": there is no one neural configuration to unite all the diversity. The concept of consciousness, like other present-day psychological categories, will be revised before it can be incorporated into science – or it will be replaced with better concepts and thus altogether eliminated from real science.

2.2. The ontological status of consciousness: Does consciousness exist?

As we have seen, the deepest philosophical question concerning consciousness is the question of its existence. It is futile to long for a theory of something that does not even exist. We must be prepared, then, either to discard consciousness altogether or to defend it against elimination. Let us then see, how strong the case is against consciousness.

There are two main lines for rejecting consciousness: Daniel Dennett's line and the eliminativist line (for a detailed criticism of these positions, see Revonsuo, in press). In the previous chapter we have already seen, what the eliminativist arguments against consciousness are. Daniel Dennett is making a more indirect attack against consciousness, but anyway he apparently wants to maintain the concept. He stresses that he is *not* an eliminativist towards consciousness. However, I shall argue that his position differs in name only from explicit elimination. I first argue that elimination of consciousness seems not to be what is going on in the cognitive neurosciences, and then, I criticize the Dennettian way of treating consciousness.

The eliminativists claim that a science of consciousness is impossible, because no such phenomenon even exists. This is a fairly radical claim. What is true is that we do not currently have any scientific theory of consciousness, and also that we do not have exact definitions or criteria for the phenomenon. This is, however, no reason to believe that no progress could be made. Neuropsychologist Lawrence Weiskrantz emphasizes that it is unreasonable to demand exact characterizations of consciousness at the present stage of research:

Each of us will have his or her own idea of what, if anything, is meant by 'consciousness', and what its value might be as a concept, or cluster of concepts, in scientific discourse and theory. But to insist that the value must depend, as a *prerequisite*, on the availability of a precise definition would, I think, be a mistake. Indeed, if we always insisted on precise definitions we all would be speechless almost all of the time. Definitions and precise theoretical constructs are the final product, not the starting point of enquiry. (Weiskrantz 1988, 183)

It also seems to be simply not true that psychology and the neurosciences would be much better off without asking any questions about consciousness, as Wilkes (1984) has strongly suggested. On the contrary, it seems that this far those sciences have exactly been trying to avoid facing consciousness – excepting "the speculative perorations of retiring professors of neurology" (Dennett 1969, ix) – but that approach to the mind is proving to be not sufficient anymore. Consider the comments of neuropsychologists working with peculiar, brain-damaged patients, about which we hear more later:

We claim no special expertise in approaching the philosophical or psychological problems associated with the study of consciousness and awareness. The truth is that we had no more than a general acquaintance with such issues until they were forced upon us by research findings. (Young and DeHaan 1990, 30)

In fact, we have at the moment many promising lines of research which are showing not only the possibility but also the usefulness of introducing consciousness into science. If eliminativists are right, no such science can survive for long because it is making some fundamentally false ontological commitments. No sign of the elimination of consciousness is in sight on the empirical side, as we shall see.

Daniel Dennett certainly is an eliminativist towards many consciousness-related phenomena: he rejects qualia, intrinsic intentionality, and the subjective point of view. Unfortunately this is not the proper place to study his arguments in detail. Anyway, we must ask, what is the place of consciousness in Dennett's theories? Dennett's views on consciousness are, of course, deeply interconnected with his general approach to psychological explanation. Intentionalistic explanations and folk psychological concepts can be used only when we are considering the organism as a whole – as a proper object for "intentional system theory". As soon as we move *inside* the skull, the strategy of explanation must change: now we have "sub-personal cognitive psychology". The goal of this strategy is to decompose the information processing functions of the organism all the way down to the implementation level, neurophysiology, in order to explain how a multitude of stupid and simple subsystems are able to produce all the intelligent behaviour we observe at the level of the whole organism (see e.g., Dennett 1987).

Now, since "consciousness" is a folk psychological term if any, Dennett is very reluctant to let it refer to anything going on inside the organism. This attitude is most clearly manifested in his article 'Toward a Cognitive Theory of Consciousness' (1978), in which he opens the curtain by saying:

That of which I am conscious is that to which I have *access*, or (to put the emphasis where it belongs), that to which *I* have access. Let us call this sort of access the access of personal consciousness, thereby stressing that the *subject* of that access (whatever it is) which exhausts consciousness is the *person*, and not any of the person's parts. (Dennett 1978, 150)

The first step is to sketch a sub-personal flow-chart, a cognitivistic model that by being sub-personal "evades" the question of personal consciousness ... (Dennett 1978, 154)

It is clear, then, that for Dennett, consciousness is a matter of intentional system theory, about which he says the following:

The *subject* of all the intentional attributions is the whole system (the person, the animal, or even the corporation or nation) rather than any of its parts. (Dennett 1987, 58)

So, though we can rightly say of a *person* that she is conscious, it would nevertheless be a big mistake to ask, which of her *parts* are conscious. Consciousness is something at the personal level that must be explained by non-conscious mechanisms working at the subpersonal level – it should not itself be pushed into the subpersonal level. In a recent talk, Dennett made this point rather clear by telling that his favorite *wrong* question about the modularity of mind is " *Where does it all come together?*" He is very carefully trying to avoid the postulation of any cognitive subsystems with suspicious properties like "understanding" or "consciousness".

The ever-present-worry is that as we devise components – lesser homunculi – to execute various relatively menial tasks near the periphery, we shall be "making progress" only by driving into the center of our system an all-powerful executive homunculus whose duties require an almost Godlike omniscience. (Dennett 1978, 164)

Dennett's strategy is clever, since he does not at any point deny the existence of consciousness. Instead, he first externalizes it by using it to refer to only whole intentional systems and not to their parts. After this manoeuvre, it is time to divide and conquer consciousness in the same way as has been done with other entities of intentional systems theory: by postulating a multitude of unintelligent, unconscious sub-personal components that operate beneath the surface to produce outward behaviour.

We have, then, Dennett's convictions that consciousness cannot be a property of some subsystem or processing mode of the brain and that mind is essentially centerless, and, furthermore, the eliminativist's claims that consciousness is not and cannot be a scientifically respectable phenomenon. What can be said about these affirmations?

Dennett takes consciousness to be essentially included in accounts of the external behaviour of whole intentional systems and their interactions with the environment. This attitude is reflected, in addition to what has been reviewed above, also in his denials of intrinsic intentionality and the possibility of zombies. When writing against intrinsic intentionality, Dennett (1990) emphasizes that having a mind is a matter of "the right sorts of environment-organism interactions." Dennett (1982) mentions the possibility of zombies, but he ends up denying that such a creature – or even such a concept – is possible:

I have been playing along with this zombie idea – for tactical reasons that should now be obvious – but in fact I think (in case you have not already guessed) that the concept is just incoherent. The idea of a being that could pass all heterophenomenological tests but still be a merely unconscious automaton strikes me simply as bizarre. (Dennett 1982, 178)

It seems to us that Dennett is here making a mistake concerning the proper level of explanation for consciousness. A much more plausible assumption is that consciousness is a property of some subsystems or processing modes of the brain. On this account, for "having a mind" it is necessary to have this subsystem or something sufficiently like it, and not merely a facade of outward behavior and the pretense of conscious states. Certainly the concept of the zombie is not as confused as Dennett seems to think: zombies are not round circles and it is rather simple to characterize them in understandable terms. Just consider the bulk of science-fiction literature dedicated to describing the adventures of those loathsome, unfeeling aliens as they threaten to infiltrate humanity and replace us with outwardly indistinguishable impostors (see e.g., J. Finney's novel *Invasion of the Body Snatchers*, 1978).

If the necessary and sufficient conditions for consciousness are to be defined at the level of the neurophysiology of the brain, it follows that a zombie is a creature which does not have this kind of neurophysiological system, but which nevertheless replicates the outputs of this system at the behavioral level of the whole organism. It also follows that the mere existence of this brain-system (with appropriate stimulation) is sufficient for there to exist any kind of subjective, conscious phenomena, although they would in no way be expressed at the behavioral level. For example, when we are dreaming, our brains are informationally insulated from the outside world: neurobiological dream research has found out that the brain is then blocked both from the input and the output sides (Hobson 1988). However, especially the visual cortex is being activated internally, and the brain processes this activation as if there would be sensory information coming from the outside world. Furthermore, the motor cortex sends movement commands to the muscles, but they are all barricaded at the spinal level – and thus no real, external behaviour occurs. Dream researcher J. Allan Hobson (1988, 171) phrases the neurobiology of dream aptly: "As far as the neurons are concerned, the brain is both seeing and moving in REM sleep." This picture is nicely in accordance with the phenomenology of dreaming: we have all kinds of colourful subjective *conscious* experiences in dreams, which are created somewhere entirely inside the brain. Also John Searle has emphasized in his "principle of neurophysiological sufficiency" that no external relations are necessary for experiences to occur inside the brain:

Whenever a mental phenomenon is present in the mind of an agent – for example he is feeling pain, thinking about philosophy or wishing he had a cold beer –

causally sufficient conditions for that phenomenon are entirely in the brain. (Searle 1987, 229)

It seems that processes in the brain can be divided into conscious and unconscious ones: preperceptual, automatic, modular processes and, e.g., syntactic rules and unretrieved long-term memories seem to be totally unconscious, yet instantiated inside the brain. So-called controlled, central or effortful processing, by contrast, is conscious as well as e.g., our currently attended percepts and retrieved memories. We definitely have good reasons to believe that the proper level of explanation and, accordingly, the level in which consciousness is in fact instantiated, is the level of some processing mode of the brain, in virtue of which the whole organism can be said to be conscious.

What about the centerlessness of mind? It is not a very convincing general argument to say that even if the mind *seems* to be centered around consciousness, it *really* cannot be so. Both the claim that there is some kind of central processing system and that there is not, are just hypotheses to be falsified or strengthened through empirical research. The functional decomposition of mind is not an a priori enterprise, and the possibility of a consciousness-centered theory of mind should not be overthrown prematurely. It is quite possible to find such a neurophysiological system or processing mode in the brain which integrates the separately processed features from different sense-modalities into a coherent model of the world. At the moment we have reasons to believe that such theories are successful and that they will survive (see Chapter 4). And finally, even though the consciousness-centered view of mind would be discarded, some kind of explanation must be required for the seeming unification, coherence, and centralization of our mental life. We must have a theory to explain how a distributed reality can produce a phenomenological unity. Current Dennettian and eliminativist theories offer no such comfort.

2.3. The ontological status of consciousness: The realist alternative

To be a Realist towards consciousness is to believe that conscious mental phenomena really exist in the world: our intuitions about our minds as consciousness-centered are not illusions, but reflect the true nature of things. Consciousness is as important an object of scientific inquiry as any other real things. However, the Realist must be ready to give some kind of explanation for consciousness, since he cannot hide the problem under the stairs like the eliminativists do.

John Searle (1987 and 1984b) explicitly confesses to being a Realist in the case of consciousness. Searle himself calls his view "naive mentalism": there really are internal mental states, some of which are conscious, others unconscious, some intentional and others not. For him, it is a simple fact concerning the world that there are such things as conscious mental states. It is the duty of neurobiology, not of cognitive science, to explain this fact. Conscious processes are real biological processes like digestion or photosynthesis.

2.3.1. Searle, supervenience, and intrinsic intentionality

John R. Searle (1987) has tried to show how it is possible to incorporate consciousness as a neurobiological phenomenon into science. All mental states are caused by biological processes inside the brain. For example, someone can be in horrible pain without any pain stimulus in the peripheral nerves, and without manifesting any pain-behaviour. The experienced pain sensation seems to be caused by stimulation in the basal parts of the brain. All that matters for our internal, subjective mental life is dependent only on processes deep inside the brain. They are quite sufficient for causing any kinds of mental states. Even though the external events would exist, but they would not cause anything inside the brain, no mental states would exist, but if only the internal happenings of the brain existed, all mental events would also exist.

What, then, is the explanatory strategy we should use for consciousness? Searle suggests that mentality does not differ in principle from other natural phenomena. We must remember that in nature there are many different levels of organization, e.g., subatomic particles, atoms, molecules, cells, organs, organisms, ecosystems, planets and galaxies. For the purposes of science, there are convenient levels of explanation, like particle physics, biochemistry, and ethology. It seems that entities at different levels of organization have different kinds of properties, which cannot be exhaustively characterized in terms of lower-level entities and properties. So, for example, subatomic particles do not have properties like liquidity, gaseousness, temperature, replication, metabolism or spiking frequency. However, all the entities that instantiate these properties are composed of nothing but subatomic particles. The crucial point is the *organization* of the particles: higher levels can exist only if the lower levels are organized in a certain way.

At this point we must introduce a new philosophical concept, *supervenience*, with which to characterize the psychophysical relation. To say that the mental supervenes on the physical is to say that no two things could differ with respect to some mental property unless they differed also in some physical property (Kim 1984). In other words, there can be no mental differences without corresponding physical differences – if a system is in two different mental states at two different times, then it must have a corresponding difference at the level of physical properties also. According to J. Kim (1990), the central ideas or components of supervenience as a philosophical concept are: (1) Covariance – supervenient properties covary with their base properties; (2) Dependence – supervenient properties are dependent on or determined by their base properties; (3) Non-reducibility – supervenience is consistent with the irreducibility of the supervenient to their base properties.

There are many different kinds and strengths of the supervenience relation. The one that seems to be relevant here is a variety of supervenient dependency, not mere covariance. Part-whole-dependence or *mereological dependence* seems to be what Searle has in mind when he talks about supervenience:

Indeed, it seems to me a merit of the view advanced here that the superveniènce of the mental is simply a special case of the general principle of the supervenience of macro-properties on micro-properties. There is nothing special or arbitrary or mysterious about the supervenience of the mental on the physical; it is simply one more instance of the supervenience of higher-order physical properties on lower-order physical properties. (Searle 1987, 229)

Searle takes the supervenience of the mental on the physical to be a special case of mereological supervenience, according to which wholes and their properties supervene on parts and their properties. That is, any real higher-level organization in nature depends on the specific micro-level particles that it is composed of, but yet, at the macro-level, new kinds of properties are manifested, which would have been impossible at the lower level or in a system composed of a different kind of micro-level. For example, gaseousness is a property which can be manifested at the level of molecule systems, but not in individual molecules or subatomic particles: one cannot make gas out of photons. Similarly, mental phenomena are dependent on the neuronal networks of the brain, although we do not yet know the details.

As was mentioned above, Searle has emphasized the distinction between intrinsic and derived or original and as-if intentionality. Now we can elaborate the details of Searle's philosophy, especially bearing in mind the connection between intentionality and consciousness. Searle's quest against AI and computationalism began in 1980 with the publication of his famous Chinese Room Argument. This is not the place to redescribe that ingenuous thought-experiment: however, I will present a shortened account of the central points of this argument, according to Searle (1987). He starts from four "axioms" that he thinks are accepted by most if not all:

(1)   *Brains cause minds.* This means that the relevant causal processes in the brain are sufficient to produce any mental phenomenon.

(2)   *Syntax is not sufficient for semantics.* This is the logical truth that formal symbols do not have any meaning in themselves: the level of meaning is distinct from the level of syntax. It is possible to have a perfect description of the syntactic level of some formal system, and yet have no idea of what those symbols refer to, what they are about.

(3)   *Minds have contents; specifically, they have intentional or semantic contents.* With a mind's "semantic content" Searle means simply that our thoughts and other intentional mental states are about strawberries, planets, people, and that we really do understand what we mean when we talk or think about these things. We know what our mental states are about.

(4)   *Programs are defined purely formally, or syntactically.* Computer programs are formal and the computer executes the program by following syntactic rules: these rules tell how to combine and manipulate symbols (e.g., the "ones and zeroes" of machine language), but they do not and cannot tell anything about what the symbols are symbols of.

From these premises, Searle concludes that instantiating a program by itself is never sufficient for having a mind and that the way the brain functions to cause minds cannot be solely by instantiating a program. To put it briefly, brains can somehow cause states with semantic content, but purely formal systems, such as computer programs, certainly never can by virtue of their syntactic, formal nature alone cause any semantic contents. The notion of intentionality that Searle here denies of computers is of course *intrinsic* intentionality. Computer programs can very well have "as-if" intentionality – that is, we can treat them, for practical purposes, as if they had intentional states – but we can treat virtually anything like that. Why then can brains have not only as-if, but genuine intentionality?

The real difference between intrinsic and as-if intentionality is that intrinsically intentional states have an essential connection to consciousness.

The nature of this connection and why computations lack it, is discussed recently by Searle (1989 and 1990). He claims that intrinsic intentional states have always *aspectual shapes*, which are essential to them. It means, roughly, that intentional states always matter to the subject and they are enjoyed from a certain point of view and with certain features. Thus, we can separate thoughts about water from thoughts about H_2O – the aspectual shape constitutes the way the subject thinks about or experiences a subject matter. These aspectual shapes can never be exhaustively characterized solely in terms of third person, behavioral, or neurophysiological predicates; they are irreducibly subjective. And, what makes them subjective is that they are always either actual or possible contents of consciousness.

But what in my brain is my 'mental life'? It is just two things; conscious states and those neurophysiological states and processes that – given the right circumstances – are capable of generating conscious states. (Searle 1990, 588)

All intentional states are thus dependent on consciousness. From this conclusion Searle proceeds to refute cognitivist and computationalist explanations of mind. They postulate intentional states which are in principle not accessible to consciousness and in doing this, they commit themselves to the same crime as pre-Darwinian biology: they anthropomorphize the brain's non-conscious phenomena, as e.g., the behaviour of plants was anthropomorphized: the plant turns its leaves to the sun because it wants to survive. However, as there are no wants and goals in plants, so there is no non-conscious rule following, mental information processing, languages of thought or mental models in the brain.

But just as the plant knows nothing of survival, so the non-conscious operations of the brain know nothing of inference, rule following, or size and distance judgements. We attribute these functions to the hardware relative to our interests ... (Searle 1990, 590)

As in the case of biology, so in cognitive science the anthropocentric style of explanation must be overthrown. The level of non-conscious intentionality must be eliminated, and this radically alters the ontology of cognitive explanations. Like the behaviour of plants, so the mechanisms of non-conscious brain processes must be made in hardware, biological terms.

2.3.2. Arguments against computationalism

Searle's most important point is that there is not in itself any specifically cognitive or computational level of organization in nature and, accordingly, there should not be any cognitive or computational level of explanation, either. He (1990) gives one more argument against the view of the brain as a biological computer. He argues that it is impossible to scientifically discover that brain processes are, in fact, computational processes. Computation, after all, is defined in terms of syntax and symbol manipulation. Now how could we *find* syntax or symbols in Nature? What physical or material properties differentiate symbols from non-symbols? The problem is exactly that symbols are not waiting out there to be discovered by us, because nothing in nature is a symbol in itself:

> Any physical object can be used as a symbol, but for the same reason, no object is a symbol just by virtue of its physics. Syntax and symbols are matters of the *interpretations* that we assign to the physics. ... In the case of computation, the most you could discover in nature would be a set of patterns to which you could *assign*, not *discover*, a computational interpretation. (Searle 1990, 636)

The only causal level is the physical level – the program level cannot offer any causal explanations over and above the implementation level. The program level of the computer is thus completely different from the mental level of the brain. Since it is possible to assign or interpret a program level to anything, a program level can be assigned also to the brain. But that has nothing to do with those properties that the brain has without any interpreted symbol-manipulation level. The mental level somehow naturally, in itself, supervenes on the brain; it exists without reference to an outward interpreting homunculus, whereas the computational level is entirely dependent on our ways of treating the brain. Mentality is a genuine phenomenon of certain physical systems, namely (at least) animal and human brains, and it is dependent on the physical properties of those systems; by contrast, symbols are not.

There is also another line of argument open from the starting points of Searle to the refutation of a computational account of consciousness, which I develop here. The purpose of this argument is to show that if one accepts that consciousness is supervenient on brain function like other high-level phenomena are supervenient on their micro-levels, then one cannot consistently accept that consciousness is a computational property. I present five claims, which demonstrate the inconsistency.

(1)   Mereological supervenience (part-whole-dependence) explains the different properties that physical, chemical, and biological systems have at different levels of organization (physics-chemistry-biology). Examples: properties of an atom depend on

its subatomic constituents; properties like temperature or liquidity are dependent on the collective behaviour of molecules; neural impulses or electric signals in a neuron are dependent on ionic currents into and out of the cell, which depend on proteins functioning as ionic channels and ionic pumps on the cell membrane. We may, therefore, make the reasonable assumption that there is only one hierarchically arranged world, and that consciousness is at some level in this hierarchy.

(2)   Supervenient properties have alternative supervenience bases (or realizing bases, see Rowlands 1990 and 1991) – base properties that are each sufficient for the supervening property. The minimal supervenience base for a certain property p is the property that is minimally sufficient for the supervenient property p – any property weaker than the minimal base is not a supervenience base for p (Kim 1984). The minimal basis for something to be an instantiation of a hydrogen atom is that, at the subvenient level, it has one proton and one electron, but the number of neutrons might vary from none to two.

(3)   A computational theory of consciousness is true. That is, consciousness is a property of some (unspecified set of) computations: there is a finite set of computations, say, $C_1, C_2, C_3, \ldots C_n$, which are identical with, or which cause consciousness, all other computations are totally non-conscious.

(4)   A universal Turing machine can execute any computations. Specifically, it can execute those computations that are identical to, or that can cause consciousness.

(5)   The computations of a universal Turing machine can in principle be executed in any material substance, and in any time scale whatsoever without thus affecting the identity of those computations. Specifically, the computations that underlie consciousness can be executed in any given material system acting as a universal Turing machine. From this it follows that consciousness – as computations in general – can be realized in principle in any kind of matter.

Now we can start to see where the difficulty lies. If consciousness is taken to be like other higher-level natural properties, it cannot at the same time be taken as a computational property. Mereological supervenience of macro-level properties constrains the possible properties of the micro-level phenomena.

Liquidity can be had only in systems composed of molecules or of other particles enough like them (that is, satisfying the minimal supervenience base, whatever it might be). Liquidity, certainly, cannot be instantiated in a system composed of, say, gluons, photons, grains of sand, or banana peels.

Now, the functionalist might point out that, after all, it is not at all important, what precisely is realizing, e.g., the *role* of an ionic pump on the neuronal cell-membrane, but the *function* that the pump has. And then we are, again, back where we started from, that is, functionalism. This will not do, however. We can perfectly well admit that anything that can function as an ionic pump would well suffice for there to occur real neural firings, but we must stress that this is far from the "multiple realizability" that functionalism or computationalism offers us. Supervenient physical properties are multiply realizable *only within the boundaries of possible minimal supervenience bases*. That is, they are not at all so multiply realizable as you would think at first glance. For example, it would be highly difficult to replace a membrane protein with something composed differently and still maintain the normal function of the neuron. Of course, perhaps in different possible worlds proteins themselves are composed of different microparticles than here, but that level is not relevant when we are confined to those properties where the protein is at the micro-level and the neuron at the macro-level.

So, we might say that physical properties in general are multiply realizable within narrow boundaries. They certainly are not realizable in arbitrary pieces of matter like computations are. If we take consciousness to be this kind of property, it makes no more sense to say that we could produce consciousness by executing computation C_n in any matter or time-scale than it makes to say that we could produce liquid or ionic channels by executing the right computations in any universal Turing machine.

To summarize this discussion, if consciousness is a mereologically supervenient property of neural organization, then functionalism and computationalism are in difficulties. As we remember, functionalism says that the right kinds of causal relations in any kind of matter constitute consciousness, and computationalism that the right kinds of algorithms computed in any kinds of machines are conscious. However, a mereologically supervenient property is always dependent on the specific micro-level, in which it is instantiated. There are some necessary base-properties that a micro-level must have in order for it support a certain macro-level property. Computations, by contrast, can be instantiated in any arbitrary material basis. Now, if some properties of neuronal networks are the base-properties necessary for consciousness, then abstractively defined algorithms or functions cannot be the correct way to explain consciousness. Rather, we would need a neurobiological theory which tells us the difference between unconscious and conscious brain processes.

For Searle (1989 and 1990), subjectivity is a real property of the conscious mental level of organization, and he thinks that all intentional mental states have an essential connection to consciousness. His concept of "intrinsic intentionality", then, means that only consciously representable states can really "mean" or "be about" something: all other talk about intentionality is just a convenient shorthand for describing some entirely non-conscious entities, like books or computers.

To be sure, Searle is not the only Realist about consciousness, but he is one of the few who have some kind of scheme for incorporating conscious phenomena into the general scientific picture that natural sciences are offering us. For Searle, consciousness is not an obstacle for the theoretical synthesis of biology and psychology – it is merely a reminder of the multiple levels of organization in Nature.

2.3.3. Other realist views

Next I shall briefly take a look at some other Realists who perhaps do not have readymade solutions to offer, but who nevertheless take consciousness to be something real. Robert Van Gulick (1988a, 1988b and 1989) has tried to navigate between Searle and functionalism by claiming that there is a difference of degree only between machine and human understanding. He has introduced the concept of *semantic transparency*, which is what systems understanding the semantic contents of symbols can have to a different extent; and human conscious understanding simply has a remarkably high degree of this property. Essentially, semantic transparency means an ability to combine and interrelate "symbols with symbols and symbols with the world in a sufficiently rich and flexible range of ways":

The internal component of understanding need be nothing more than an ability to interrelate a great many diverse mental representations very quickly. (Van Gulick 1988b, 95)

It seems to me that Van Gulick's attempt to separate intentionality or understanding from consciousness fails. It is misleading to use the same concept of "understanding" for all kinds of systems that have "semantic transparency", that is, are able to combine semantically related symbols. The distinction between conscious understanding and unconscious symbol combining is fundamental – not a mere matter of degree. This is most clearly manifested in neuropsychological patients. For example, patients with severe deficits in face recognition or language comprehension have been shown to display so-called *semantic priming*, which means that processing of incoming stimuli is affected if the stimuli are semantically related (this might be manifested e.g., in reaction-time tasks; see Neely 1977). Semantic priming is assumed to reflect the spreading of information in memory to semantically related items. Now some patients show intact priming effects, although they do not consciously understand the content of the stimuli. That is, the patients do not, e.g., understand a word or recognize a face, although in their unconscious processing systems the relevant connections become activated (Young and DeHaan 1990; Schacter et al. 1988). If semantic transparency is at issue, these patients should have it to the same extent as normal subjects. However, the mere activation of the relevant representations does not in itself guarantee any understanding of the contents of perception at all, if the results of this processing cannot reach the level of consciousness. Our conclusion is, thus, that genuine understanding requires consciousness and that to call something that we have without consciousness "understanding" is like calling the dead in fact living but *with a low degree of metabolic transparency*.

However, Van Gulick (1989) has made some valuable observations about the relations between consciousness and functionalism. He points out that it is a much stronger claim to say that mental states are computationally definable than to say that they are definable in terms of their causal relations to inputs, outputs, and each other. A functionalist need not accept that the relations are to be defined at the abstract level of formal or syntactic relations. He can very well be interested only in the psychological roles that mental states play in humans. And, Van Gulick proposes, in studying consciousness, the functionalist should ask: "Do phenomenal, qualitative mental processes play such psychological roles that non-conscious processes do not play?" And if, in fact, we find such psychological processes, we should ask: "What, if anything, do these psychological processes have in common?" Van Gulick himself observes that phenomenal representation of information seems to be a necessary condition for the initiation of voluntary actions. This may not be very helpful, since it is unclear whether "voluntary" can be defined independently of "conscious" – and if not, all we are saying is that consciousness is necessary for conscious acts, which is not particularly informative. Van Gulick (1989) ends up suggesting that all phenomenal representations involve "reflexive metacognition" and a "high degree of semantic transparency".

I think that the questions formulated by Van Gulick are more interesting than the answers he suggests. As we see later, a promising empirical research strategy is simply trying to articulate how the roles of conscious processes differ from those of unconscious processes. This does not mean that empirical psychology should commit itself to the view that the functional role consciousness plays somehow exhausts it. Separating the different roles of mental or brain functioning is only a methodological tool to approach consciousness – if we can catch something by casting the functionalist net, afterwards we must probe into the neurobiology of the captured system and not just announce that consciousness *is* this functional role.

Max Velmans (1990) argues that we have misleading conceptions and intuitions about what the contents of consciousness actually include and how they should be contrasted with the external, physical world. In everyday thinking, we make a sharp distinction between the perceived objects out there, and the pains, thoughts, and dreams, which seem to take place in our bodies and minds. The world seems to be divided into inner experiences like thoughts; bodily experiences like itches, and experiences of objects out there. The difference between the inner experiences and the outer objects seems to be fundamental – it seems to be the problem of the relation of physical to mental. However, this picture is a serious misconception. Velmans points out the old philosophical insight that

... the contents of consciousness include not only 'inner' experiences such as images, thoughts, and dreams but also the body as-experienced, and experiences of physical objects beyond the body-surface, which are, in a sense, *none other* than physical objects as-perceived. The physical objects we perceive, therefore, cannot be contrasted with the contents of consciousness, for they are *included amongst* the contents of consciousness. (Velmans 1990, 82–83)

Velmans puts forward a "reflexive model" of the relationship between consciousness and the physical world. According to it, the experienced world as a whole – with its sounds of distant thunder, visions of far-off galaxies, and intimate inmost emotions – is a "projection" made by the brain – the brain can produce conscious events experienced as with no clear location, or located in the body, or located in the three-dimensional world projected around the body. This experienced world is the content of consciousness and it can be regarded as a useful model of the real world, as described, e.g., by physics. The real world is radically alien to our experienced world: it has no sounds – only vibrations of air – or colours – only different wavelengths of electromagnetic radiation – no centers from which to observe it and no objective present moment. Also Van Gulick (1989) makes a point similar to

Velmans:

One might say that conscious phenomenal experience involves a construction of a model of the world that in some sense *is itself a world*, but it is so only from the subjective perspective of a self which is also built into the model. (Van Gulick 1989, 226)

We symphatize with this kind of a view because it puts the problem of consciousness into the right perspective. It is not so, one might say, that inside my head – as I perceive it – is somewhere a model of the world inhabited by a small homunculus-me, but rather, *I*, as I perceive myself and my body, *am a sort of homunculus adventuring in the virtual reality created by the physical brain in interaction with the real, physical world*. This virtual reality is a biologically useful, but not necessarily truthful, model of the real world. One consequence of this kind of view is that the specifically human experienced world is crucially dependent on the existence of humans, since presumably every species has its own model, biologically useful for its purposes, of reality.

McGinn (1989) has investigated the grim implications this has for our abilities ever to understand the experienced worlds of other, alien creatures, or of the nature of reality itself. This variety of realism towards consciousness we may call "desperationalism", since McGinn argues that his view entails that we will never be able to solve the mind-body or the brain-consciousness problem. McGinn's views are thoroughly discussed in the chapters devoted to relativism (Chapters 17–18), since our cognitive construction seems to imply a strong form of it.

Recently, it has been proposed by many that quantum physics could offer a solution, or at least a different approach, to the problem of consciousness (Penrose 1989; Lockwood 1989; Squires 1990; Zohar 1990). It has, however, remained unclear, what the precise relation of quantum phenomena is to the workings of the brain and, as Penrose (1989, 518) and Squires (1990, 204) admit, it is a rather speculative enterprise to treat the brain as a distinctively quantum mechanical object. After all, we certainly do not know in any classically based terms – physics, biochemistry, neurobiology – what kinds of mechanisms underlie the conscious processes of the brain, and perhaps it is not unjustified to presume that the answers are to be found in those branches of science. And if it is quantum phenomena and not the macro-organization of the brain that makes us conscious, why do we need a complicated brain to be conscious in the first place? Would it not suffice to have those quantum phenomena appearing in any kind of classical system? It is hard to believe that the macro-properties of the brain would be totally irrelevant to consciousness. So, even if there is some truth in it that we cannot ignore quantum physics, I think that there is *more* truth to it that we cannot ignore the neurobiology of the brain.

Quantum mechanics and consciousness are both deeply mysterious, but that does not imply that both mysteries stem from a common cause. Fascinating connections between them exist, like the role of a conscious observer in quantum systems. Furthermore, the complementarity of particle and wave descriptions has been compared by Velmans (1991) to "psychological complementarity" between first-person and third-person descriptions of the world. Despite being largely metaphoric, the analogy has some force: if the Baserock of Science contains dual descriptions, why not neurobiology and psychology?

2.3.4. Conclusions: The philosophy of consciousness

Do subjective, conscious mental states really exist? As we have seen, this question is far from settled among philosophers. The eliminativists want to ban all talk about consciousness, and Dennett tries to get rid of consciousness by turning the mind inside out and treating consciousness as an external description of the whole person. Realists, like Searle, assure us that consciousness is somehow produced inside the brain, although all the details remain unexplained.

As I have argued above, it seems to be unwise and indefensible to reject consciousness at this stage: the study of consciousness is just beginning to gain a foothold in cognitive and brain sciences. Dennett's account was equally unsatisfactory in its denial of consciousness as something intrinsic and real. I dare say that it is a much lesser mistake now to take consciousness seriously and later to find that it has been a wild-goose chase than now to ignore consciousness and later to admit that the core of mentality cannot be understood without it. The burden of proof is heavily on those who eliminate consciousness, and thus far their arguments are nowhere near convincing.

Evidently the advisable direction in the problem of consciousness is, for Realists, to show that it is possible to make progress in science with consciousness. But how could this be achieved? Well, anything that is actual is possible, and as we will see in the following chapters, there are ways for treating consciousness scientifically. A cognitive approach is to ask what kinds of functions or roles do conscious processes have that distinguish them from unconscious processes? How can conscious processes be incorporated into the flowchart of the mind? I shall review several proposed models of the cognitive role of consciousness in the next chapter, which try to answer exactly these questions.

3. CONSCIOUSNESS AND MODELS OF COGNITION

3.1. Introduction

Regardless of the ontological and philosophical problems surrounding consciousness, a handful of bold theorists have introduced consciousness into cognitive models of mind. As we remember, cognitive or "information processing" models of mind describe the different subfunctions of mental processes and their interaction. Thus, they are in vivo examples of functionalistic box models described in the chapters devoted to functionalism.

In this chapter, I shall review several models of consciousness, which arise from different sources, but nevertheless have much in common. Daniel Schacter (1990) bases his model on certain surprising findings in cognitive neuropsychology, which demand an interpretation in terms of consciousness. This model I call "the Neuropsychological Model". Bernard Baars (1988) begins with William James's suggestions and he reinterprets a large body of empirical findings from cognitive psychology in the light of a proposed cognitive theory of consciousness. This model I call "the Cognitive Model". Ray Jackendoff (1987) has computationalism as his starting point, and he tries to reconcile consciousness with the computational mind. His model I call "The Computational Model". Daniel Dennett (1991) argues for a "Multiple Drafts Model" of consciousness, which stands in grave disagreement with the aforementioned models. Antonio Damasio (1989b) builds his theory on functional neuroanatomy, which leads to certain new views on the architecture of consciousness. Damasio's ideas, together with the theories of F. Crick and C. Koch (1990) and G. Edelman (1989) I call "The Neurobiological Model".

Before we go into the details of these models, we must get acquainted with the general outlines of present cognitive models of mind. Jerry Fodor (1983) has put forward a general model of the cognitive structure of mind. In his important book *The Modularity of Mind*, Fodor explicates the concept of a *module*, which is perhaps the most important concept that the different models of consciousness share, at least in some form. Another significant point Fodor makes is that in addition to modules, the mind must also have

other kinds of systems, which he calls "central systems". I shall now take a
closer look at Fodor's theory and its most central concepts. I will also
explicate what the place of consciousness is for Fodor, although he reveals it
only indirectly. After that I will go on to review and criticize the above-
mentioned models of consciousness.

3.2. Fodor's general model of the cognitive structure of mind

3.2.1. Historical background

The historical roots of Fodor's theory are in so-called "faculty psychology"
which, like contemporary cognitivism, individuates psychological faculties
according to their typical effects, that is, functionally. There are two forms of
such theories of mind: horizontal and vertical.

In horizontal faculty psychology, mental processes are believed to result
from the interaction of different faculties, like attention, perception, and
memory. These faculties are independent of the contents they are acting upon,
that is, the same memory faculty, for example, takes care of all kinds of
memories – autobiographical, factual, musical, etc.

The father of vertical faculty psychology, F. J. Gall, denied the possibility
of horizontal faculties. According to him, psychological processes are
distinguished in terms of their subject matter, that is, in terms of what kind
of information those processes are handling. Thus, Gall's "intellectual
capacities" are domain specific, and the psychological mechanisms underlying
those capacities are correspondingly separate, too.

Fodor ingeniously uses these historical accounts as a basis for a modern
synthesis. He proposes a trichotomous functional taxonomy of psychological
processes, which preserves the main ideas from both versions of faculty
psychology.

3.2.2. Fodor's functional taxonomy of psychological processes

Fodor (1983, 41) distinguishes three kinds of psychological processes:
transducers, input systems, and central processors. We can think of them as a
processing chain that describes the flow of input information (Fig. 2).
Accordingly, transducers translate the physical, chemical or other stimuli into
a form that is understandable for the organism, that is, into neural impulses.
Transducers, then, roughly correspond to sensory organs operating at the

interface between the external world and the organism's body. After this translation, information is processed in the input systems. Their purpose is to deliver representations for the central systems. In Fodor's words, input systems function to interpret transducer information and to make it available to central processes. They "present the world to thought" (Fodor 1983, 101).

Central processes include such "higher" cognitive functions as "thinking" and "fixation of belief". They use as their raw material the representations produced by input systems plus all available background information which might be in some way relevant.

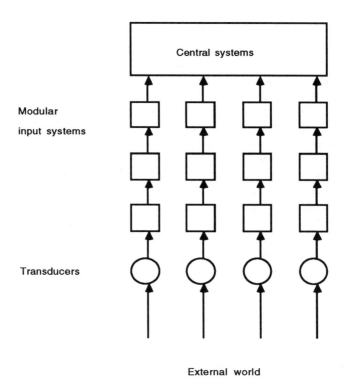

Fig. 2. Fodor's functional taxonomy of psychological processes: Transducers, Modular Input Systems, and Central Systems.

Now, we may ask, what is the proper place for conscious processes to reside? Is consciousness a property of input systems or of central processes? I shall investigate a bit closer the properties of those systems and, although Fodor never says it aloud, it is fairly obvious that conscious processes can happen in only one of them.

3.2.3. The modularity of input systems

Fodor (1983, 27) introduces the notion of a cognitive module. For a psychological process to be modular it means that it possesses most or all of certain properties which Fodor lists as the hallmarks of modularity. I will take a brief look at those nine properties.

I   *Domain Specificity:* A module is specialized in handling only one kind of information and it can accept as its input only the right kind. Evidence for domain specificity, according to Fodor, comes e.g., from many eccentric perceptual domains, like colour, face, or sentence perception, in which the stimuli demand unique computations, different from every other domain. To put it the other way around, a face processor module could do nothing with acoustic inputs, and vice versa.

II   *Mandatory Operation:* The operation of modules is mandatory in the sense that whenever appropriate input is present, the module will process it from beginning to end, whether or not the owner of the module approves of it. Modules are not under voluntary control: we cannot turn the modules off and, e.g., hear just babble instead of words and sentences, or see just colour patches and contours instead of three-dimensional objects.

III   *Limited Central Access:* The analyses in the input systems proceed through a number of intermediate levels, but the subject does not have equal access to all levels. The lowest levels are completely inaccessible, and the further we get from the transducer outputs, the more accessible the representations become to central systems. Thus, we cannot "see" the retinal pictures or the outputs of retinal processing, no matter how hard we try.

IV   *Fast Processing:* Although recognition of objects, faces, or sentences is an immensely complicated computational task, it takes place instantaneously. Input systems function like reflexes: they are totally automatic and mandatory, and hence fast. The

obvious advantage is that no time has to be wasted in deciding
how an analysis should be made, but the almost as obvious
disadvantage is that reflexlike responses are essentially
unintelligent.

V   *Informational Encapsulation:* The essence of modularity, says
Fodor (1983, 71) is the informational encapsulation of modules.
It means that an input system has only a very restricted access to
information – it usually has access only to its own domain. This
means that input analysis is insensitive to much of what one
knows. It is ignorant of the hopes and expectations of the
organism as well as of what is currently being analyzed in other
input systems. The point of perception is to inform the organism
about the world even – and in particular – when the world is not
what was expected. Evidence for informational encapsulation
comes, e.g., from the persistence of perceptual illusions: although
we know that an illusion is an illusion, we cannot help seeing the
illusory effect. The input module cannot interact with our
background knowledge, and thus our experience is untouched by
it.

VI   *Input Systems Have Shallow Outputs:* The categorizations that a
module is able to make must be totally determined by modality.
Thus, the visual input system can only use information detected
by the visual transducers, e.g., shape and colour. This means that,
at best, the outputs of visual input systems are based on visual
categorizations. The output can, then, be something like "a dog",
"a face", "a tree". By contrast, we can never *see* e.g., protons,
because to conceptualize something as a proton requires access to
a large body of other than visual background knowledge.

VII   *Input Systems Have Fixed Neural Architecture:* It seems that each
input system has its neurological counterpart in the brain. This
fits in well with informational encapsulation.

VIII   *Input Systems Have Specific Breakdown Patterns:* Many known
pathologies (like aphasias and agnosias) suggest that input
systems can be selectively damaged independently of each other,
whereas central processes cannot.

IX   *Input Systems Develop In Certain Ways:* The neural mechanisms
subserving input systems develop according to endogenous
patterns. Thus, input systems are innate and their development
genetically controlled.

3.2.4. Central systems

Central processes stand in strict contrast with input processes: they are neither modular, domain specific nor informationally encapsulated. The most important function of central processes is, according to Fodor, "perceptual belief fixation", which means, roughly, judging what the world must be like. This judgment means that the representations handed over by the input systems are corrected in the light of background knowledge:

To a first approximation, we can assume that the mechanisms that effect this process work like this: they look simultaneously at the representations delivered by the various input systems and at the information currently in memory, and they arrive at a best (i.e. best available) hypothesis about how the world must be, given these various sorts of data. (Fodor 1983, 102)

Fodor argues that central processes typically are processes of "rational non-demonstrative inference". This kind of inference is, first, quinean and, second, isotropic. The former means that the confirmation of each perceptual hypothesis is dependent on the total background web of beliefs, the latter that any arbitrary piece of background knowledge might prove to be relevant in the confirmation of a perceptual hypothesis or in fixating the organism's beliefs. Analogical reasoning is an illustrious example of isotropy at work: information is transferred between otherwise separate cognitive domains.

It seems, then, that "thinking" uses a global architecture quite different from the modular architecture. Globality is, suggests Fodor, exactly what makes central processes intelligent in a way that modular processes are not. He further proposes that the neural structures underlying central systems are, unlike modular systems, diffuse and equipotential, and that connections in them are unstable and instantaneous rather than innate and neurally hardwired.

All in all, Fodor ends up claiming that, after all, both the vertical and the horizontal version of faculty psychology are correct. Input systems, or modules, behave like vertical faculties and central systems like horizontal faculties. Fodor is extremely pessimistic about the future of cognitive science: he thinks that it is not possible to formulate good cognitive theories about the global factors relevant in central processes.

What has been reasonably successfully developed is a sort of extended psychophysics. A lot is known about the transformations of representations which serve to get information into a form appropriate for central processing; practically nothing is known about what happens after the information gets there. The ghost has been chased further back into the machine, but it has not been exorcised. (Fodor 1983, 127)

3.2.5. The place of consciousness in the modular mind

Fodor hardly even mentions consciousness or conscious processes in his book, but nevertheless it is possible to infer approximately what kind of role conscious systems in this model have. To begin with, Fodor (1983, 94 and 136) mentions that the output of the visual input processor has to be "phenomenologically accessible", that is, accessible to conscious experience:

It seems to me that we want a notion of perceptual process that makes the deliverances of perception available as the premises of *conscious* decisions and inferences. ... I want a vocabulary for the output of the visual processor which specifies stimulus properties that are phenomenologically accessible and that are, by preference, reasonably close to those stimulus properties that we pretheoretically suppose to be visible. (Fodor 1983, 136)

Phenomenological access and conscious reasoning do not take place in modules but in central systems. It seems then that input systems work totally in the dark and they have no traces of consciousness, but their outputs consist of representations that can be consciously manipulated and experienced. It seems to be fairly obvious that whatever goes on inside modules is not itself conscious: consciousness belongs to the central systems. The next question to be asked is, then: Are all central processes conscious, or only a part of them?

Central systems look at what the input systems deliver, and they look at what is in memory, and they use this information to constrain the computation of 'best hypotheses' about what the world is like. These processes are, of course, largely unconscious, and very little is known about their operation. (Fodor 1983, 104)

In sum, modular processes are not conscious but some central processes are. Thus, conscious processes form a subset of all central processes. To return back to Figure 2 about the functional taxonomy of psychological processes, we can now complete it by placing conscious processes among the central systems (Fig. 3).

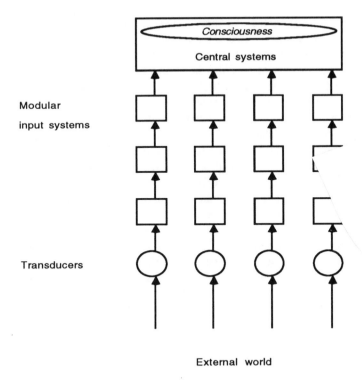

Fig. 3. The place of conscious processes in Fodor's model of mind.

3.3. Consciousness and cognitive neuropsychology

3.3.1. The principles of cognitive neuropsychology

Cognitive neuropsychology has taken the idea of modularity seriously. One of its starting points is called "The modularity hypothesis", which says, roughly, that the mind and brain are so organized that cognitive skills are mediated by large numbers of semi-independent cognitive processes or systems, each of which is capable of separate impairment. Each module handles its own form of processing independently of others, apart from those it can directly communicate with (Ellis and Young 1988).

Theoretical progress in cognitive neuropsychology takes place in two complementary ways. First, the patterns of impaired and intact cognitive performance in brain-injured patients are explained by referring to damage in certain components or modules in a model of normal cognitive function. Second, those impairment patterns are used to constrain and test theories about normal cognitive functioning. If a certain pattern of impairments occurs, we can infer that only certain kinds of normal organization could, even in principle, be damaged in that way.

The most important evidence to constrain theory formulation is based on so-called dissociations of impaired functions. A dissociation occurs whenever a patient is severely impaired in one sort of cognitive task, say object recognition, and yet performs quite normally in some other task, say, auditory word comprehension. An even stronger case for the independence of cognitive operations is achieved through double dissociations, in which one patient is impaired in task A and normal in task B, and another patient exhibits the contrary pattern. If it is possible to find a double dissociation between any two cognitive tasks, then there are good grounds for assuming that the tasks demand separate cognitive processes. Even a single case of double dissociation can be used as powerful evidence for arguing what is *possible*: to confirm an existence claim we need to have only one convincing case.

Cognitive neuropsychologists are actually conducting a functional decomposition of cognition by using data about the different manners of cognitive breakdown. The objective is to build a complete box model of the mind. That model shows what kinds of processors underlie our normal cognitive capacities, and what kinds of breakdowns can explain the behaviour of brain-injured patients. The model can also predict which kinds of impairment patterns are possible and thus should be observed and which are impossible. Hence, the model lends itself to empirical testing. In Dennett's (1987) terms, cognitive neuropsychologists are practicing sub-personal cognitive psychology.

How far can empirical evidence guide us in the problem of consciousness? It might seem that the "evidence" offered by cognitive neuropsychology is extremely weak and based on questionable single-patient analyses. And after all, which questions can even *in principle* be answered by empirical enquiry, and which are metaphysical, pre-empirical commitments? As I will try to show in Chapter 4, different models of consciousness do make differing philosophical commitments. I argue that empirical evidence can take us somewhere only in case our pre-theoretical understanding of consciousness is somehow captured by the scientific constructs that our theories are composed of. Now, neuropsychologists like Schacter (1990) seem to have a pre-theoretical account of consciousness which neatly preserves enough of the everyday intuitions we have of consciousness. The question then becomes, how appropriate are the methods and experimental techniques of neuropsychology in uncovering the mental structures of mind. Note that this question is not specific to the problem of consciousness, but a general query about the scientific value of neuropsychological research. This is not the place to make a comprehensive analysis of neuropsychology, but it is advisable to keep in mind that the methods of neuropsychological research have been severely criticized, and also successively defended. An excellent treatment of what we can learn from neuropsychology and how reliable its results are, is Tim Shallice's (1988) book *From Neuropsychology to Mental Structure* and its précis (1991) with commentary in the *Behavioral and Brain Sciences*. All taken together, it seems that neuropsychology does provide us with evidence which, combined with evidence from other branches of cognitive neuroscience, contributes to the understanding of the mind-brain. Thus, the neuropsychological results reviewed below ought to be taken seriously and not discarded on methodological grounds.

3.3.2. Implicit knowledge

Daniel Schacter et al. (1988) suggest that there is ample evidence of a different kind of dissociation of cognitive functions than the traditional ones. As we mentioned above, the paradigm cases in cognitive neuropsychology have demonstrated the independence of different cognitive functions: language, object recognition and face processing can be damaged separately and thus are considered to be independent functions. The new and somewhat surprising dissociation is not between two different tasks but, rather, between doing one task in two different ways.

The pattern of dissociation is generally something like the following: a patient is, after brain injury, found to be severely impaired in performing certain cognitive operations, say remembering recent events, recognizing faces, or comprehending words. The patient usually complains about these defects and is painfully aware of his handicaps. Also the patient's overt behavior and test performance reflect his cognitive inabilities. However, if the same cognitive function is tested indirectly or implicitly, the patient might perform significantly better, sometimes even normally (on these tests). It seems that those patients have implicit, unconscious knowledge of the stimuli although they cannot explicitly or consciously access the same information.

Implicit knowledge is knowledge that is expressed in performance without the subject's phenomenal awareness of possessing any such knowledge. The existence of implicit knowledge in a wide variety of neuropsychological syndromes is a challenge to cognitive neuropsychology: what does this dissociation reveal to us about the normal organization of cognition and consciousness? I shall first make a short review of implicit knowledge in neuropsychological syndromes and then I will present Schacter's (1990) model.

Amnesic patients can remember virtually nothing of what happened just a few minutes ago. They are fully aware of the present moment, but they usually have no idea about the chain of events that led to it. It is possible to introduce yourself to the patient, then leave the room for a moment, and when you re-enter, you can introduce yourself again, since the patient thinks he has never seen you before. It is possible to continue this game indefinitely, and every time you will be as new for the patient as you were the first time you met.

Such a loss of memory is obviously deeply incapacitating for the patient. No wonder that it came as a surprise when reports revealing a massive amount of implicit memory in amnesic patients started to accumulate. The first finding was that amnesics can learn motor skills at a normal rate despite their inability to remember that they had ever done the task before. However, their performance became faster and more accurate exactly like the normal subject's performance did.

Implicit skill learning was dramatically manifested in experiments conducted by E. L. Glisky, D. L. Schacter and E. Tulving (1986) and Glisky and Schacter (1988 and 1989). They showed that amnesic patients could learn even to use microcomputers and to make simple programs for them. However, some of those patients could not consciously remember having learned any such things. One patient insisted, after months of training, that he has never worked on a computer before; yet his performance showed implicit memory.

Recently, it has been found that amnesic patients show intact repetition priming effects after a single exposure to a target stimulus. This means that after e.g., having seen a list of words, the patient cannot consciously recall them, but nevertheless if he is asked to complete word fragments with whatever first comes to mind, he very often retrieves the previously seen words. The earlier stimuli, then, still have some effects in the processing of present stimuli, but the patient's awareness and recall of the past happenings is virtually nil.

After these experimental findings, the conceptual division of memory into implicit and explicit has become central (Graf and Schacter 1985; Bowers and Schacter 1990; Musen and Treisman 1990). Memory is implicit when previous experiences have their effect on performance, although the task itself does not demand the conscious or intentional recall of those experiences. By contrast, explicit memory does necessarily demand the conscious re-experiencing of the remembered past. The existence of implicit memory has not been noticed before presumably because most of the traditional memory tests require and measure only explicit memory (Schacter 1987).

Tulving (1987) suggests that amnesia is not really a disorder of memory but, rather, a disorder of consciousness. Abundant experimental evidence (Graf et al. 1984; Cermack et al. 1985 and 1988; McAndrews et al. 1987; Gordon 1988; Nissen et al. 1989; Gabrieli et al. 1990) shows that amnesics are able to learn many kinds of new skills as well as to store new knowledge: their main problem is that they cannot explicitly remember those skills and pieces of knowledge – they are not conscious of them.

Blindsight is perhaps the most widely known example of implicit knowledge. It may be manifested in patients whose primary visual cortex is damaged, resulting in blindness in a part of the visual field. The patients claim to be absolutely blind in those parts of vision. When a visual stimulus is projected onto the blind field, the patient reports seeing nothing. However, when these patients have peen pushed to guess various properties of those unperceived stimuli, it has been found, curiously enough, that their responses are far more accurate than pure coincidence would allow. The stimulus properties thus discriminated include the location of a bright stimulus in the blind field, simple figures and line orientations. Despite these preserved visual abilities, the patients are highly surprised when informed about the accuracy of their "guesses", and they strongly insist that they cannot *see* anything. They do not have any kind of visual experience of the stimuli, but some patients report having a "feel" (Weiskrantz 1980, 1987 and 1988; for a review, see Young and DeHaan 1990; Schacter et al. 1988).

An analogous phenomenon has been reported in the touch modality by J. Paillard et al. (1983): the patient could not consciously experience the touching of her skin, but still she could point with her hand to the location. In sum, blindsight and blindtouch are manifestations of implicit knowledge of stimuli unaccessible to conscious experience. Blindsight-like phenomena have been produced through certain experimental manipulations also in normal subjects (Graves and Jones 1991).

Unilateral neglect is a syndrome in which the patient pays no attention to one side of perceptual space. Usually the damage is in the right cerebral hemisphere, which results in neglect of the left side of space. In severe cases, the patients draw half-pictures, they read text only from the right side of the page – and complain that it does not make any sense, they use only the right side of paper when writing, they eat only half of the food on the plate. Sometimes the patient dresses himself, brushes his hair or shaves his beard only from the right side; he might even deny that the left leg and arm belong to him at all (Newcombe 1985; Bisiach et al. 1979; Young and DeHaan 1990).

When two pictures are simultaneously flashed for the patient – one to the right field, the other to the left – the neglect patient can reliably name only the picture on the right side. However, they can amazingly often judge whether or not the pictures shown were identical or different – even though they might claim that there actually was only *one* picture (Volpe et al. 1979; Karnath and Hartje 1987). In another kind of experiment, a patient was shown two pictures of a house (Marshall and Halligan 1988). One was just a plain, ordinary house, the other was identical, apart from bright red flames coming out from the left side of the house. Now the patient insists that the pictures are identical, but when asked which one she would like to live in, she consistently preferred the one without flames, although she did not know why and considered the whole question silly. We can again use the concept of implicit knowledge to describe those findings.

Prosopagnosia, or inability to recognize familiar people from their faces (Damasio et al. 1982), has become an important source of evidence for implicit knowledge. The patient cannot recognize his friends, family members, and celebrities from their faces – he might not recognize even his own face in the mirror. Usually prosopagnosic patients do discriminate faces from other objects – they know when they are looking at a face. They are even able to describe facial features or judge the age or sex of the person from the face, but nevertheless the patient is totally ignorant of the identity of the person: he does not have the slightest idea, whose face he is looking at. To recognize a person, the patient must use some other than facial information: voice, clothes or hair might trigger recognition (Young and DeHaan 1990).

In an explicit task the patient is often totally unable to classify faces according to their familiarity: for him, all faces seem equally unfamiliar. However, a wide variety of physiological and behavioral measures have revealed that the patient, after all, does recognize the familiar faces, albeit unconsciously (for a review, see Bruyer 1991). For example, the patient's skin conductance may change when a familiar face is seen (Bauer 1984; Tranel and Damasio 1985 and 1988). His eye movements might be different when scanning a familiar face as compared to scanning unfamiliar ones (Rizzo et al. 1987). Even the event-related potentials of the brain might react to the category difference between familiar and unfamiliar faces (Renault et al. 1989). At the behavioural level, there is evidence from, e.g., priming procedures, interference designs and learning tasks, which show that the patient has at some level got the information concerning the familiarity of the faces. Not all patients, however, show implicit recognition: there are cases where the whole recognition system seems to be damaged (Newcombe et al. 1989).

A. W. Young and E. H. F. DeHaan (1990) describe their prosopagnosic patient PH, who was asked to match two photographs at a time on the grounds of whether the pictures were similar or not. His performance was faster when the faces were familiar, although he did not have any idea of their familiarity. In an interference task it was found that the semantic category of the pictures affected PH's performance. He was supposed to classify printed names into two categories: as politicians or as non-politicians. His reaction times for these words became longer if the names were paired with conflicting or misleading faces from the opposite category (e.g., Margaret Thatcher's name paired with Steffi Graf's picture) compared with pairings from the same category or no picture at all. So, although PH was unable to tell whether or not a given face was the face of a politician, the information interfered with his response speed.

The most interesting results with PH came from a cross-modality priming study (Young, Hellawell and DeHaan 1988). In the priming paradigm, the first stimulus is called the prime. The idea is to observe whether or not exposure to the prime affects the processing of a subsequent stimulus, called the target. The most familiar case of priming effects is so-called semantic priming, where the subject is first shown a word (e.g. mouse) and then another related word (e.g. cat). Now if the words are semantically related, the subject should process the second word faster than in a condition where it is preceded by an unrelated prime (Neely 1977).

First PH was put in a situation in which both the primes and the targets were names of people, which he could of course read and recognize, and the targets were also names. The processing was faster when the prime and target were related, compared to unrelated conditions. The same is true of normal subjects. The surprising effect was that when the primes were pictures of faces, which PH of course could not overtly recognize, the priming effect was

still found. The information from the face must have been analyzed to
semantic and identity level and then it must have interacted with the don
of name representations. The knowledge of the familiarity must have b
distributed rather widely across domains unconsciously, which is theoretic
a most significant observation.

R. Bruyer illustriously summarizes the state of the art:

... we now have empirical data showing that some prosopagnosic subject
manifest simultaneously covert behavioral signs of recognition and overt
behavioral signs of nonrecognition. What is (un)recognized can be the face
familiarity, semantic properties of the person seen, or its name. These data
suggest that the "conscious subject" does not recognize or identify familiar faces,
while her/his "information processing system" does. (Bruyer 1991, 230)

There are still other forms of implicit knowledge found from different
kinds of neuropsychological patients, e.g., Wernicke's aphasics, which seem
to be sensitive to the semantic features of words despite their severe language
comprehension difficulties (Milberg and Blumstein 1981). Anyway, we may
conclude that a wide variety of neuropsychological patients show preserved
implicit knowledge in the absence of explicit, conscious experience of that
knowledge.

3.3.3. The neuropsychological model of consciousness

Amazed by these observations, Schacter (1990) and Schacter et al. (1988)
have sought for a reasonable interpretation for them. This dissociation cannot
be characterized like the traditional ones in cognitive neuropsychology, but
anyway it seems that we have here something that can teach us a lesson about
the normal organization of cognition and consciousness.

Schacter et al. (1988) emphasize the generality of the pattern of
dissociation and they think it is useful to seek a common explanation for this
pattern. They put forward a descriptive model that is based on the following
principles:

(1)   Conscious or explicit experiences of perceiving, knowing, and
       remembering all depend in some way on the functioning of a
       common mechanism. In other words, conscious awareness of a
       particular stimulus requires involvement of a mechanism that is
       different from those mechanisms that process the various
       attributes of the stimulus.

(2)   This conscious mechanism, or Conscious Awareness System

(CAS, Schacter 1990), must be sharply distinguished from modular systems. CAS normally accepts input from and interacts with a variety of processors or modules that handle specific types of information.

(3)   Conscious experience of various types of information depends on intact connections between the conscious awareness system and individual modules. In cases of neuropsychological impairment, specific modules can be disconnected from the conscious mechanism.

Figure 4 shows schematically the relationships between the conscious and other mechanisms. Implicit knowledge, on this account, is manifested when a module is relatively undamaged but its outputs cannot reach CAS. However, the modules have also certain other routes to response systems, through which the processed information can be manifested indirectly and without the subject's knowledge.

Schacter's model is thus in harmony with Fodor's ideas: consciousness seems to be a central process which must be separated from modular systems, which are thoroughly unconscious.

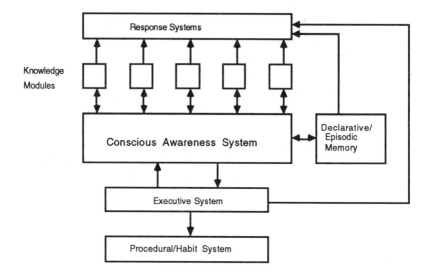

Fig. 4. Daniel Schacter's model for describing cognitive processes underlying the dissociation between explicit and implicit knowledge in neuropsychological syndromes. All processes involving phenomenal experience depend on the functioning of the Conscious Awareness System. (Modified from Schacter 1990.)

3.4. The cognitive model of consciousness

Bernard Baars (1988), in his book *A Cognitive Theory of Consciousness*, takes as his starting point a suggestion made by William James: conscious processes should be approached through "contrastive analysis". The basic idea here is to contrast two psychological processes, in which the only difference is that one of them is conscious and the other not. We can compare, for example, the memory of last Christmas, when it lies dormant in a long-term memory-store, to the same memory now, when I consciously recall it. We can contrast an unattended stream of speech to the same speech when attended and consciously understood. We can juxtapose subliminally presented stimuli with supraliminally presented ones; or the same stimulus when it is new and surprising, causing an orienting response, with when it has been repeated to the stage of habituation and it fades from consciousness.

In all these cases we can ask: why is one process or representation conscious and the other unconscious? These kinds of contrastive pairs constrain any possible theory of consciousness, and a good theory should explain them all in a simple and plausible way. Baars is trying to formulate the fundamentals of such a theory. He suggests that conscious and unconscious phenomena are realized in different kinds of processing architectures in the nervous system.

The basic architecture behind unconscious processing is that of specialist processors, which are, according to Baars, functionally unified, or modular. Thus, he broadly agrees with Fodor about the modularity of mind. However, Baars' specialist processors are more flexible than Fodor's modules. For Baars, each module may be variably composed or decomposed, depending on goals and context. In addition, Baars counts the development of automaticity with practice as evidence of skill modularity. Such skills, however, are not innate and thus do not completely fulfill Fodor's characterization of modules. The specialists, unconscious processors are very efficient and fast, they make relatively few errors, and a multitude of such processors may work in parallel, without interfering with each other. Specialists are relatively isolated and autonomous and they can handle only certain kinds of information.

The architecture behind conscious processes is quite different. In studies of attention it has been shown that there seems to be a central attention system with limited capacity. Experiments on selective attention have revealed that subjects can be conscious of only one coherent stream of events at any one time. Also, it has been shown that especially similar cognitive tasks compete with each other, probably because they require the same processing resources, and even very dissimilar tasks interfere with each other if they are both consciously executed. In general, conscious processes are, according to Baars, computationally inefficient, slow, prone to errors and interfering with each other. They can have a great range of different contents over time, but at any one moment there is only one conscious process going on, which must be internally consistent. The conscious system thus has limited capacity and it operates serially.

Conscious processes are globally distributed in the central nervous system. Any conscious event in any sense-modality seems to disturb the experiencing of any other simultaneous conscious event, although, if represented only unconsciously, these events in no way interfere with each other. Classical conditioning shows that almost any kind of stimulus can function as a signal for some totally different kind of stimulus – thus the information must have travelled widely in the brain. For humans, any stimulus can function as a signal for executing any voluntary action. By biofeedback it is possible to learn to control practically any neural system. Such connections from any arbitrary stimulus to any arbitrary output would suggest indeed that somewhere in the middle, a global distribution of information must have occurred. In addition, neurophysiological measures can show that a typical conscious event (the orienting response) activates the brain rather globally, whereas a typical unconscious stimulus representation (a habituated stimulus) has only local effects in the brain.

If it is the case that the same information must be accessible for the whole system at one moment, it follows that there can be only one truly global message at any one time. There is only one system as a whole, and if all its components are to receive the same message, only one message at a time can be sent. This is Baars's interpretation of the seriality of conscious processes.

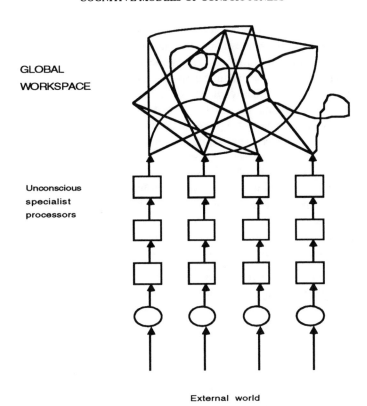

GLOBAL
WORKSPACE

Unconscious
specialist
processors

External world

Fig. 5. Differring architectures for unconscious and conscious processes (based on Baars 1988). A multitude of specialist processors work fast, automatically, and in parallel. The basis of conscious processes is the Global Workspace, which functions as a dense communication network between the specialist processors.

The system where information can become globally distributed and consciously experienced is called *Global Workspace*. It is the communication network that unites all the unconscious processors (Fig. 5). Conscious processing is a specific mode of processing realized in the Global Workspace. *Contexts* are stable coalitions of unconscious processors, which have a privileged access to the global workspace and thus they shape the messages processed in that system. The processing principles of these systems are *competition* and *cooperation*. The former lowers the activation levels of messages in the workspace, whereas the latter raises them.

The neural substrate of the Global Workspace is, suggests Baars, the so-called "extended reticular-thalamic activation system" (ERTAS). This system is known to have excellent connections to virtually every input and output channel in the brain and it is also concerned in the regulation of global states of awareness, like coma or sleep. The specialist processors, by contrast, reside in the cerebral cortex. The whole picture that emerges is that cortical specialist processors compete or cooperate with each other to get just their own message into the global workspace of ERTAS. A message that gets through must be, among other things, globally broadcast, coherent and informative. Such messages then become the contents of the stream of consciousness.

The necessary conditions which any consciously processed information must have are, according to Baars, the following (see also Fig. 6):

(1)   Conscious events involve globally broadcast information. This means that only those messages which can spread across the whole system (or at least more widely than any other messages), can become conscious.

(2)   Conscious events are internally consistent. This means that contradictory interpretations of the same information cannot be included in one message. If the message is internally inconsistent, its consistent parts will compete with each other and decrease the activation levels.

(3)   Conscious events are informative. This means that they must place a demand for adaptation on other parts of the system. Completely uninformative (i.e. totally predictable) information fades from consciousness, although it is still represented within the nervous system.

Baars is not quite clear about the next requirements, but he seems to claim that it is also necessary that

(4)   Conscious processes have access to an unconscious context. That is, they must invoke some previous pattern of activation, through which the current information is interpreted.

(5)   A message must be broadcast for at least 50–250 milliseconds before it becomes conscious.

So, a paradigm case of a conscious event, e.g., seeing an apple in front of you, requires that the unconscious specialist processors first construct the relevant features (form, colour, lightness, possible movement) and evoke an unconscious context of, e.g., fruit, then they cooperate to gain internal consistency (so that you will see it *as an apple*, although perhaps other interpretations, like a ball, a peach or a pear, would also be possible). This message is informative: it is a new fact that there is an apple in front of you and you must adapt to it. This informative, consistent and contextual message is then globally broadcast for about at least 100 ms, and you have a conscious experience of seeing an apple in front of you.

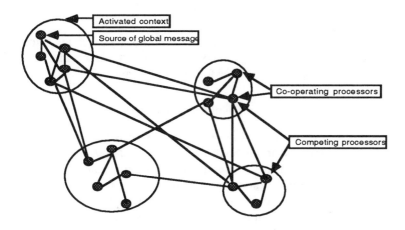

Fig. 6. The main principles of conscious processing in Baars's theory. Specialist processors compete and cooperate to send their messages to the Global Workspace. Informative, consistent, and globally distributed messages can become conscious.

Baars's theory fits in nicely with Schacter's neuropsychological model: we can think of the Conscious Awareness System as depicting that fragment of processing in the Global Workspace that fulfills all the necessary and sufficient conditions of conscious processes, whereas those processes that underlie the expression of implicit knowledge represent processing that is somehow lacking one or more of the necessary conditions, but nevertheless has its effects outside the module. The theory is also very consistent with current theories of attention, like that of R. Näätänen (1990). He has used so-called event-related potentials to reveal on-line electrophysiological processes in the brain and he proposes that a certain potential seems to control the access to consciousness:

> Thus, access to conscious perception is determined, on the present hypothesis, by the strength of the N1 generator process activated by the stimulus in relation to some threshold controlled by the direction and intensity of attention. In addition, analogous attention-triggering processes might occur in each modality, judging from the somewhat analogous N1 components in the auditory, visual, and somatosensory modalities. ... The sensory physiological events in each modality might compete for the focus of attention by the means of the respective N1 generator processes. This competition may be both inter- and intramodal. (Näätänen 1990, 229)

Baars, Schacter and Näätänen all seem to contribute converging evidence from slightly different vantage points, which leads us to suspect that the core for a theory of consciousness is to be found somewhere here.

3.5. The computational model of consciousness

The linguist and philosopher, Ray Jackendoff, presents his suggestion for a theory of consciousness in his book *Consciousness and the Computational Mind* (1987). He makes a fundamental distinction between the phenomenological mind and the computational mind. The former encompasses conscious experiences, the latter is the brain understood as a biological computer. Apart from in the problem of consciousness, Jackendoff thinks that computationalism and functionalism are sufficient explanatory strategies. The real task, for him, is therefore to explicate the relationship between the computational and the phenomenological mind.

Jackendoff takes the computational mind as primary: phenomenology supervenes on computations but not vice versa. This is most clearly expressed in his "corollaries":

> *Hypothesis of Computational Sufficiency*: Every phenomenological distinction is caused by/supported by/projected from a corresponding computational distinction.

> *Hypothesis of the Nonefficacy of Consciousness*: The awareness of an entity E cannot *in itself* have any effect on the computational mind. Only the computational states that

cause/support/project E can have any such effect (Jackendoff 1987, 24–25).

Consciousness is, in Jackendoff's view, some sort of projection or externalization of some subset of elements of the computational mind. This projection is itself causally inert, and as he admits, it means that consciousness is not good for anything. The mechanism of this projection is unknown, but instead of studying the mechanism, he proposes to examine those representations in the computational mind that are projected into consciousness.

Information enters the nervous system and the mind in different forms: the sensory receptors in different sense-organs encode quite different kinds of distinctions. However, because we are able to understand the world as integrated, there must be ways of transforming information from one form to another: otherwise we could not identify the same objects through different sense-modalities. Jackendoff distinguishes different levels of representation. The lowest levels interface rather closely with the physical world, and the most central levels are more abstract and, e.g., "thought" presumably consists of computations over a rather central level of representation (cf. Fodor's model).

Each faculty of mind has its own characteristic chain of representation levels, leading from the peripheral to the central levels. These chains might intersect at various points, and especially at the central levels at which thought occurs, independent of sense-modality. Jackendoff points out that consciousness is sharply distinguished by sense-modality. Tactile, auditory and visual experiences differ like night from day, and it is practically impossible to confuse them. Thus, he argues, consciousness must be projected from such a level of representation that is still faculty specific and not independent of sense-modality. The rest of his book is dedicated to the determination of the appropriate levels of representation in vision, language, and music.

At each representation level, there is a selection function, which selects one representation and puts it into the short-term memory. However, we are not conscious of all these levels. In vision, we have the primal sketch, the 2D sketch and the 3D model (these terms Jackendoff has adopted from Marr's (1982) theory). The level of visual structure that corresponds to the experienced visual world is the 2D sketch, since it is binocular and viewer-centered. The other levels are structured in ways that have no correspondence in visual consciousness. In the case of language, the levels of representation are phonological, syntactic, and conceptual structure. Jackendoff argues that we are aware of "linguistic images" in hearing language or thinking in inner speech. The linguistic structure that most closely corresponds to the phenomenological form of linguistic images is that of phonological structure. We are not aware of the syntactic or conceptual structures: they are not accessible to consciousness.

Jackendoff summarizes his "intermediate-level theory of awareness" as follows (see Fig. 7):

The distinctions of form present in each modality of awareness are caused by/supported by/projected from a structure of intermediate level for that modality that is part of the matched set of short-term memory representations designed by the selection function and enriched by attentional processing. Specifically, linguistic awareness is caused by/supported by/projected from phonological structure; musical awareness from the musical surface; visual awareness from the 2D sketch. (Jackendoff 1987, 298)

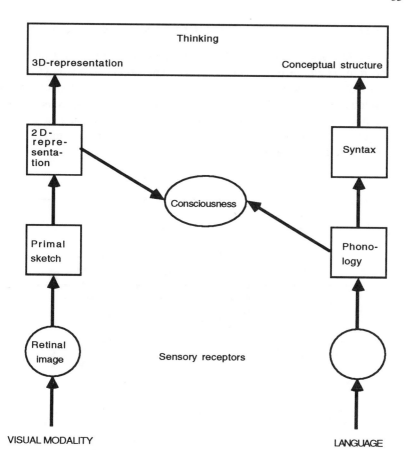

Fig. 7. The relations between the computational mind and the phenomenological mind (based on Jackendoff 1987). Conscious experiences are projected from modality-specific levels, whereas thinking occurs centrally, independently of consciousness.

3.6. The Multiple Drafts Model and Dennett's philosophy of consciousness

The philosopher, Daniel Dennett, has made a number of suggestions concerning cognitive models of cognition. In his article 'Towards a Cognitive Theory of Consciousness' (1978) he demands that "the cognitivist must take consciousness seriously" and he proposes to do this by treating consciousness as a black box from which introspective and retrospective statements issue. The relations of this box to the other boxes in the cognitive model of the mind should be explicated, suggests Dennett.

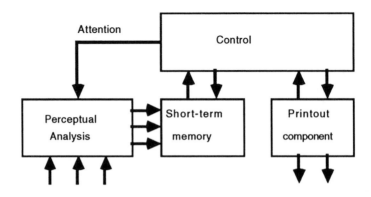

Fig. 8. A simplified depiction of Dennett's (1978) proposal for a cognitive model of consciousness.

The main components of Dennett's model are called Perceptual Analysis, Short-Term Memory Store, Control, and Print-Out component. Perceptual analysis proceeds at many different levels and the results from those levels are sent to the short-term memory. Also the control unit sends information to the short-term memory. The print-out faculty gets all its directions from control, but it has access (through control) to the pool of information in the short-term memory. The control unit allocates attention or processing resources to the most important topics in the perceptual analysis systems.

After this perhaps arises the question, what, if anything, does this obscure collection of boxes have to do with consciousness? Dennett admits that it is difficult to see this model as an explanation for consciousness, but he insists that our intuitions concerning consciousness can be persuaded to go away. It is, he asserts, just by virtue of having this kind of functional organization that we have an inner life.

What, exactly, corresponds to the black box of consciousness that Dennett was referring to in the beginning of his article? It seems that there is no unequivocal answer to be found to this question. Dennett says (p. 169) that "the content of one's experience includes whatever enters the buffer memory", that is, the short-term memory component. However, it is perfectly possible to have a communication breakdown between the short-term memory and the print-out faculty and, therefore, "what one wants to say is not an infallible or incorrigible determinant of what one has experienced or is currently experiencing."

Nonetheless, the content of consciousness cannot, it seems, be identified with the contents of the short-term memory, since Dennett says – almost in the same breath as the previous quotation – that

One's access to one's experience is accomplished via the access relations between M [short-term memory] and PR [print-out]. As Anscombe would put it, we simply *can say* what it is we are experiencing, what it is we are up to. This is accomplished without any inner eye or introspective faculty beyond the machinery invoked in the model. (Dennett 1978, 170–171)

So, after all, if in addition to *having* conscious experiences I need to have *access* to those conscious experiences before I can know anything about them – presumably even about their existence – then it becomes problematic to tell which box in this model is taking care of conscious processes and which are not. Although Dennett promised to clarify the relations of the box of consciousness with other boxes of the model, it now becomes obvious that he is not keeping his promise: in his model there is no unique box reserved for consciousness. Why, we may ask, is this the case?

The subject of conscious access, for Dennett, is the whole person and not any of the person's parts. Thus, as we have pointed out in the chapter concerning elimination of consciousness (see Chapter 'Does consciousness exist?'), Dennett does not want to postulate any special box, which has the mysterious property "consciousness". For him, such a model is only reproducing the problem of consciousness at a deeper level.

Recently, Dennett has put forward a new model of consciousness, which he calls "The Multiple Drafts Model of Consciousness" (Dennett, 1991; Dennett and Kinsbourne 1992). Dennett and Kinsbourne offer this model as an alternative to the traditional view according to which consciousness is a central "place" in the flowchart of the mind; a place where it all comes together as a multimodal, coherent representation of the world. Dennett and Kinsbourne (1992) criticize such consciousness-centered models and mock them by calling them "Cartesian Theatre Models" of mind. They claim that "nothing in the functional neuroanatomy suggests such a general meeting place" and that positing such a center means that its own activity remains unexplained or must be decomposed to subsystems which duplicate the subsystems of the whole brain – that is, leads to infinite regress.

Dennett and Kinsbourne claim that "there is no longer a role for a centralized gateway, or indeed of any functional center to the brain." They think that it is a fundamentally erroneous assumption that somewhere in the brain there occurs a multi-modal conscious representation. Different types of information are processed in isolated modules, but these separate rivers of information-flow never meet in any general meeting place. We should not ask, about the modularity of mind, "Where does it all come together?", since the answer, according to Dennett and Kinsbourne, is "Nowhere!"

The brain itself is Headquarters, the place where the ultimate observer is, but it is a mistake to believe that the brain has any deeper headquarters, any inner sanctum arrival at which is the necessary or sufficient condition for conscious experience. (Dennett and Kinsbourne 1992, 185)

What do Dennett and Kinsbourne offer in exchange for the Theatre model? They argue for the "Multiple Drafts" model of consciousness, according to which all perceptual operations are accomplished by "multi-track processes" that result in distributed and multiple content-discriminations. There is, then, a multiple stream of contents in the brain, or multiple drafts of experience, and different drafts have different effects on behaviour. The stream of consciousness is not a single, definitive narrative, but a parallel stream of conflicting and continuously revised contents. None of these streams is the actual, definitive content of consciousness: there is no unanimous and determined content of consciousness. There is no one place where these streams meet, that is, there is no place where all the differentially processed features and discriminations come together (Fig. 9). Feature detections, claim Dennett and Kinsbourne, only have to be made once – they do not have to be sent somewhere else and represented again to some central "master discriminator" or "audience".

It seems that the Multiple Drafts model is making explicit what was implicit all along in Dennett's earlier writings: there simply is no such processor, system, or module which alone would possess the property consciousness. (For a criticism of Dennett's philosophy of consciousness, see

Revonsuo, in press.)

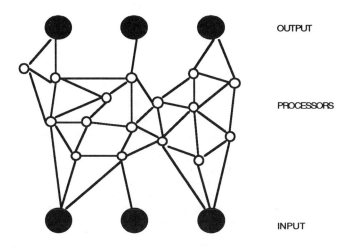

Fig. 9. The Multiple Drafts Model of consciousness. Isolated discriminations and separate streams of processing never meet in any functional center, and none of the streams forms the determinate contents of consciousness. (Based on Dennett 1991; Dennett and Kinsbourne 1992.)

3.7. The Neurobiological Model

A.R. Damasio (1989b and 1990) proposes a neurologically and cognitively motivated theoretical framework for the understanding of the neural basis of memory and consciousness. In neurology, the problem of consciousness has often appeared as "the binding problem" (see also Crick and Koch 1990). This name refers to the discrepancy that exists between what we know about experiences and about the brain. Our conscious perceptions, the experienced world, is a united, multimodal, and coherent whole. By contrast, it seems that the brain has only a multitude of detached sensory fragments to work with. How does the brain put this shattered puzzle together?

Current knowledge from neuroanatomy and neurophysiology of the primate nervous system indicates unequivocally that any entity or event that we normally perceive through multiple sensory modalities must engage geographically separate sensory modality structures of the central nervous system. ... The experience of reality, however, both in ongoing perception as well as in recall, is not parcellated at all. ... Features are bound in entities, and entities are bound in events. How the brain achieves such a remarkable integration starting with the fragments that it has to work with is a critical question. I call it the *binding problem*. (Damasio 1989b, 28–29)

The traditional solution to the binding problem has been that different sensory modalities all project to so-called multimodal cortices, in which a representation of integrated reality is achieved. Damasio criticizes this view and shows that lesions in the presumed structures of perceptual integration do not lead to disturbances in perceptual experience as should happen were the traditional view correct. He then poses this purely neuroanatomical question:

Which area, or set of areas could possibly function as a fully encompassing and single convergence region, based on what is currently known about neural connectivity? The simple answer is: none. ... The hypothesis suggested by these facts is that the integration of sensory and motor activity necessary for coherent perception and recall must occur in multiple sites and at multiple levels. A single converge site is nowhere to be found. (Damasio 1989b, 36)

Instead, neuroanatomy of the cortex suggests that first information is separated into divergent and parallel streams of processing of, e.g., colour, form and motion. There is, however, evidence of local integration at the next stage, in which there are back-projections to the feeding cortical origin. After that, there occurs convergence into functional regions, where projections from visual, auditory, and somatosensory cortices are combined. These convergence regions also feed back divergently to their feeding cortices. Thus, there seems to be a general pattern of forward convergence and backward retrodivergence.

Damasio proposes that these so-called convergence zones return the chain of processing to the earlier cortices where the chain can start again towards another converge zone and that there is no need to postulate an ultimate integration area. He denies that processing occurs only in one direction: rather, it is recursive and iterative. The converge zones do not embody refined representations of the sensory activity, but instead they store amodally the formulas for the reconstitution of fragment-based momentary representations. No representations of reality as we experience it are ever transferred in the system and no concrete contents or psychological information ever move in the system.

The neural activity and the representations that experience can access reside in fragmented fashion and in geographically separate areas located in modal sensory cortices. The integration of these multiple aspects of reality in experiences, within and across modalities, depends on the time-locked co-activation of geographically separate sites of neural activity in sensory and motor cortices. Only the feature-based components of a representation assembled in a specific pattern can become a content of consciousness.

However, there is one important reservation in this model for experiences to occur. The success of the time-locked activation is dependent on attention, which is defined as a critical level of activity in each of the activated regions, below which consciousness cannot occur. Damasio (1989b) describes attention also as "the 'spotlighting' process that generates simultaneous and multiple-site salience and thus permits the emergence of evocations" (p. 49). Consciousness, on this account, "emerges when retroactivations attain a level of activity that confers salience. Coincident salient sites of activity define a set that separates itself from background activity and emerges, in psychological terms, as a conscious content on evocation as opposed to non-salient retroactivations that remain covert" (p. 54).

In short, consciousness is a set of fragmentary but simultaneously activated representations that momentarily transcend a certain threshold level of activation (Fig. 10). A rather similar view is that of Crick and Koch (1990), who also have neurobiology as their starting point.

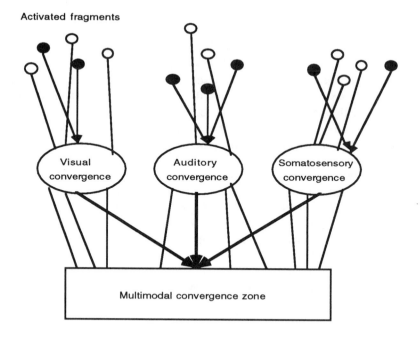

Fig. 10. The graph based on A. R. Damasio's (1989b) model of multiregional, time-locked activation. The black dots represent the fragments activated above the threshold of consciousness. The connections between the fragments and the convergence zones symbolize multidirectional processing.

3.8. Models of consciousness: A summary and a look ahead

In this chapter, I have reviewed all the most important cognitive models of consciousness that have been introduced recently. Thus, we should now be in a position to evaluate them and take a look into the future. As we saw, most cognitive theories have a more or less fodorian view of the mind lurking in the background. The models of Fodor, Schacter and Baars seem to be well in accordance with each other. They are also based more on interpretation of empirical data than Jackendoff's or Dennett's models. Dennett's and Damasio's models are in radical disagreement with the basic assumptions of Fodor, Schacter and Baars, since all those models depict consciousness as a central and multimodal system, in which the definitive contents of consciousness occur. Jackendoff's theory is also rather different from the more empirically based ones: for him, consciousness is not good for anything, and it is mysteriously projected from computations.

In the next chapter, concerned with models of consciousness, we shall try to catch a glimpse of the future science of consciousness. In other words, I will first attempt to resolve which of the presented models of consciousness are appropriate for guiding research to come. Presently, those theories do not agree on even the basic structure of a model of consciousness, and consequently, all of them simply cannot be right. But who is wrong and why? Before we know the answer to this question, it will be futile to long for a true science of consciousness. We need to make the basics clear; we must determine what the core assumptions of such a science should be. Only after an agreement about the fundamental questions can true progress emerge.

I will argue that a paradigm of consciousness research is possible and I will try to characterize its present and predict its future. Finally, I will sketch the outlines of a theory of consciousness that unifies the philosophical and empirical into a coherent whole. That is my vision of the future of consciousness and I will consider its implications for cognitive science.

4. THE FUTURE SCIENCE OF CONSCIOUSNESS

4.1. Introduction

Imagine psychology, cognitive science and neuroscience twenty, fifty, or perhaps a hundred years from now. Will they still have "a problem of consciousness" or has it been solved, abandoned, or is it just out of fashion? If the eliminativists won after all, there will perhaps not even be any independent "science of the mind" anymore: just talk about neural networks, neurotransmitters and spiking frequencies. The concept of consciousness would, at best, be deformed beyond recognition or, more likely, banned forever from true science.

We, however, are not among those who bet their money on the success of the eliminativist alternative. As I argued in Chapter 2, eliminativism is not a particularly convincing alternative at the moment. Thus, we have reason to believe that one present theory or a conglomeration of several current theories will survive to see the future science of consciousness. It would be fascinating indeed to know how the cards turn out, but unfortunately we have no time-machines available at the moment. Thus, we will have to be satisfied with arguments and speculations. I will try to uncover the weak points of each model of consciousness by argument and I hope that the fittest theory or theories will survive. Then, I will build the future predictions onto the emerging model. Before that, a number of difficult questions must be answered.

4.2. Are future models still models of consciousness?

The first question to be addressed is how do we know whether a future model of mind really talks about consciousness? After all, it is always possible to use the word "consciousness" to refer to something in one's theory, but there is no guarantee that the theory speaks at all about what we currently mean by "consciousness".

Now, the starting point is that "consciousness" and "awareness" are ordinary-language terms and as such cannot be directly adopted into any scientific theory. Instead, we must extract certain core ideas that are included in the everyday terms and then see if they fit into a scientific model of the mind. What, we may ask, are those central ideas of consciousness that we should preserve if our theory is to be a theory of consciousness and not of something else. I suggest the following:

(1)   The essence of conscious experience has been captured by philosophers who have pointed out that what it means to be conscious is that it is something like to be a conscious organism: it can in some way feel that it exists (Nagel 1974). This is the basic and perhaps most difficult problem: how can any configuration of purely physical matter have experiences of pain, pleasure, light, or colour, and in that way feel its own existence? So, the first thing that a theory of consciousness must include is that it includes a system that has or causes phenomenal experience.

(2)   The contents of normal human consciousness are manifested as an "experienced world". This world is a projection made by the brain of the real, physical world and its most prominent features are that we experience it from a spatiotemporal center and as having certain qualitative properties. This experienced world is a multimodal representation in which different kinds of experiences are integrated into a united whole. Thus, though colour, form, distance, smell, movement, feel, and sound are processed

differentially in the brain, they are united into one coherent picture of a world in consciousness (cf. Velmans 1990).

(3)   This model of the real world is a biologically useful model; that is, it enables the organism to adapt its behaviour to the real world in ways that increase the likelihood of its survival and production of offspring. It makes the control of behaviour possible so that the organism can choose an optimal alternative of the wide variety of possible behaviours.

A theoretical construct in a cognitive theory should thus, if it is to be a theory of consciousness, have these three properties: (1) its functioning is the necessary and sufficient condition of phenomenal experience; (2) it should have access to a wide variety of perceptual and somatosensory information and explain how they can be integrated in experience, and (3) it should have access to the initiation of a wide variety of behavioral responses.

This kind of characterization seems to be exactly what Dennett and Kinsbourne (1992) criticize as the "Cartesian Theatre" model of consciousness. It seems to us, however, that if we want to have a model of consciousness it must preserve this much of our ordinary intuitions or otherwise we are calling a thing consciousness although it does not deserve the name anymore.

In order to avoid a verbal disagreement concerning what can be called consciousness, let us formulate the problem in more accurate terms. The principal claim that Dennett and Kinsbourne are making is, thus, that there is not to be found in the brain/mind any system which has one or more of the three properties mentioned above. More specifically, *no subsystem of the brain has a processing mode which*

(1)   is the necessary and sufficient condition of conscious experience and determines its content;
(2)   has access to many different sensory (and perhaps other) inputs and integrates them;
(3)   has access to a wide variety of possible behavioral outputs.

However, as we have seen, empirically-based models of consciousness, advocated by e.g., Schacter (1990) and Baars (1988), postulate exactly this kind of system into the cognitive flow-chart of the mind. Dennett (1991) does not present an alternative interpretation of the data that Schacter et al. (1988) and Baars (1988) use as the basis of their theories. It seems to us that such an alternative interpretation is impossible or at least implausible and that we have several reasons to reject the Multiple Drafts model.

The Multiple Drafts model violates both intuitions and empirical results. As I have argued previously, Dennett's philosophy of mind implies that "consciousness" is an instrumentalistic term used to refer to only complete intentional systems by external interpreters. Dennett's philosophy thus makes two intuitively extremely implausible claims:

(1)   Conscious beings do not have determinate contents of consciousness. That is, there is no fact of the matter; no right answer to the question inquiring what there actually is in my consciousness at a certain moment: if some brain mechanisms are processing music, others visual, tactile, gustatory, etc. information, there is no principled way to say that some of these "multiple drafts" are in consciousness and others are not. Our phenomenological experience, by contrast, is determinate; I enjoy only certain percepts and not others, or think certain thoughts and not others, no matter what additional information is currently being unconsciously processed in the brain.

(2)   Consciousness cannot be a property of a subsystem or a processing mode of the brain, but a property of the whole organism in interaction with its environment. Thus, the Multiple Drafts model is, in fact, all the time describing the whole brain and it does not allow a distinction to be made between unconscious and conscious brain processes. However, we have numerous reasons to believe that such a distinction can and should be made at the level of the subsystems of the brain (see above).

Hence, I am afraid that the Multiple Drafts model of consciousness would lead us not towards a theory of consciousness, but away from it. The model does not so much answer our ponderings about consciousness – it seems to, rather, reconceptualize the whole matter in such a way that it becomes questionable, whether we have a *theory* of consciousness or an *elimination* of it (for a more detailed criticism of the Multiple Drafts model, see Revonsuo in press).

4.3. Theories of distributed consciousness: Multiple Drafts or multiregional activation?

We have two slightly differing accounts, according to which consciousness is not created in an integrated fashion, but is essentially fragmented. Are these views competitive or complementary?

The Multiple Drafts model of consciousness is, I fear, too deeply grounded in certain philosophical presuppositions previously expressed by Dennett in his writings. To repeat, Dennett (1978 and 1987) thinks that consciousness should not be pushed to the subpersonal level at all: only persons, not their parts, can be conscious (see discussion above). Consciousness is a matter of Intentional System Theory, and thus what a person is conscious of is a matter of interpretation. There is no determinate content of consciousness; no "intrinsic intentionality" (Dennett 1987 and 1990). If we want to study consciousness, we should study the narratives expressed by the subject, but no real objects of consciousness exist behind those interpreted narratives (Dennett 1982).

And this is what the Multiple Drafts model is all about: there can be many mutually contradictory "contentful traces" (contentful for the external interpreter) in the brain, but there is no ground to claim that one of them is the real content of subjective consciousness. It is, however, highly counterintuitive to claim that there is no fundamental difference between the "traces" or "drafts" available for outside observers, and those forming the subjective content of consciousness. Just consider "implicit knowledge" in neuropsychological syndromes (Schacter et al. 1988), where this difference is highlighted.

In conclusion, the Multiple Drafts model arises from certain philosophical presuppositions, which imply the denial of consciousness as a subsystem of the brain and the denial of determinate, real contents of consciousness. I do not share these presuppositions, and, I guess, neither do many others.

How does Damasio's model differ from the Multiple Drafts model? At first glance, they seem to share a lot. Both agree that neuroanatomy does not suggest any general integration place for experience. Furthermore, both think that the brain makes every discrimination only once:

Once a localized, specialized "observation" has been made, the information content thus fixed does not have to be sent somewhere else to be rediscriminated by some "master" discriminator. (Dennett and Kinsbourne 1992, 185)

In my proposal, the brain would not re-inscribe features downstream from where it perceives them. (Damasio 1989b, 33)

Nevertheless, Damasio apparently does not agree with Dennett that there is no principled way to distinguish conscious from unconscious processing, and that there are no determinate contents of consciousness. The level of activation in the fragmentary representations determines the contents of consciousness: those below the level at a given moment are unconscious and those simultaneously above the level together form the determinate contents of consciousness. Thus, even Damasio does not share Dennett's philosophy, although he agrees in many other ways with Dennett.

It seems that this disagreement is, after all, rather fundamental, and it tears Dennett and Damasio worlds apart. Consider Dennett's (1991) following comments:

... – and this is the fundamental implication of the Multiple Drafts model – if one wants to settle on some moment of processing in the brain as the moment of consciousness, this has to be arbitrary. (Dennett 1991, 126)

Damasio would hardly agree, since, in his view, it is just the time-locked activation properties which determine what is conscious. The same can be said about Crick and Koch (1990), whose model is closely related to Damasio's:

At any moment consciousness corresponds to a particular type of activity in a transient set of neurons that are a subset of a much larger set of potential candidates. (Crick and Koch 1990, 266)

Thus, Damasio's and Crick's and Koch's theories clearly imply that the moment of consciousness of some representation is, in principle, possible to determine. Since these theories do not share the philosophy that conscious contents are not determined, it seems that Dennett and Kinsbourne are ready to condemn also them as "Cartesian". They do admit that "the idea that content becomes conscious not by entering a subsystem, but by the brain's undergoing a state change of one sort or another has much to recommend it", and that "the simultaneities and sequences of such mode-shifts could presumably be measured by outside observers, providing, in principle, a unique and determinate sequence of contents attaining the special mode."

But this is still the Cartesian theatre if it is claimed that the real ("absolute") timing of such mode-shifts is definitive of subjective sequence. The imagery is different, but the implications are the same. (Dennett 1991, 166)

This calls for a slight clarification. What is it, after all, that Dennett cannot accept? He seems to admit that, after all, a unique and determinate set of conscious contents could be found. However, he does not accept that the externally observed sequence of such contents corresponds to the subjectively experienced sequence, because time in the brain is represented in the brain by something else than simply the time of the occurrences of brain states. To put it simply, if two brain-states simultaneously reach the threshold of consciousness, it does not follow that they are experienced as simultaneous. Accordingly, if one brain-state reaches the threshold of consciousness following another, it does not follow that they were experienced as subsequent. Thus, any brain state reaching consciousness might represent its time of happening in any given way: if A and B occur in truth simultaneously in the brain, they might nevertheless represent their time of occurring, e.g., so that A is experienced after or before B. That is, the real sequences cannot be experienced and thus any sequence in experience is based on representation of sequence, not sequence itself.

It seems to me that this is just another way of saying that no real, definitive stream of consciousness exists, since it becomes rather empty to designate some brain-states as conscious if they were not experienced at that time but only represented their time of experiencing as, e.g., "10 years from now" and thus resulted in no subjective experiences right there and then. If the state-changes that presumably reflect unconscious contents becoming conscious do not correspond to subjective experience, we are in the paradoxical situation that we can – from the outside – designate any state-change in the brain as possibly the state-change from unconscious to conscious, since we have no way of confirming or disconfirming that this is so. If the subject's willful behaviour is not taken to reveal the real temporal and other contents of his conscious states, then it is difficult to anchor conscious experience to anything going on in the brain. It leads us back to the ontology of the Multiple Drafts model, according to which there is no single, definitive stream of consciousness, only a parallel stream of conflicting and continuously revised contents.

As far as I can judge the controversies between Dennett's and Damasio's models of consciousness, I conclude that Dennett's thinking is deeply buried in his peculiar philosophy and ontology. It should not be expected that neuroscientists who have primarily been concerned with empirical work, would embrace such a philosophy, because it is grounded on disputable problems in the philosophy of mind. Although empirical researchers like Damasio and Young agree with Dennett about some points (see the Commentaries in Dennett and Kinsbourne 1992) I predict that Dennett will have a hard time persuading cognitive neuroscientists to accept that no definitive conscious contents (intrinsic intentionality) exist and that the distinction between conscious and unconscious is always arbitrary inside the brain. Unfortunately, the ontological and philosophical implications are well hidden in Dennett's theory, and some empirical scientists might not realize what kind of an ontology they are in fact accepting if they welcome the

Multiple Drafts model.

Thus, I suggest that the Multiple Drafts model is the first to go down the drain. Damasio's model preserves the most important arguments against centered theories without carrying too much philosophical burden with it. Next, I must contrast this model with the consciousness-centered models and see who leaves the battleground alive.

4.4. Is consciousness central and unified or fragmentary and multiregional?

A pivotal question about which the different models disagree is whether consciousness is realized in some sort of centralized and unifying system or as a property of distributed neural activations. Baars's and Schacter's models are clearly "central", whereas Dennett's and Damasio's are not. Both views seem to be backed by a rather massive amount of empirical evidence. How to decide, then, which course to take on this matter?

As we remember, attention has the important role of elevating activation levels above the critical level of consciousness in Damasio's theory. The experiences themselves happen wherever the primary modality-specific representations reside – the information is not carried around and combined in the system. The convergence-zones code the connections and supply the feedback which is necessary for a coherent set of representations to be reached. In contrast, Baars's and Schacter's models describe – at least implicitly – the system as composed of unconscious modules, which then deliver their products to the conscious system. Furthermore, Baars argues that neurophysiology is compatible with and suggestive of a common system for consciousness.

Now, we must remember that all of these models are based on almost completely different empirical approaches. Damasio's evidence comes from functional neuroanatomy and neuropsychology. Baars is mostly concerned with cognitive psychology, but also neurophysiology and physiological psychology. Schacter's model is built on the phenomena of implicit knowledge and anosognosia (unawareness of deficit) in neuropsychological syndromes. Thus, we should expect, rather, to find a common core to all this than to choose one theory and forget the rest. If there are any core truths to be found concerning consciousness, these complementary theories should show at least a glimpse of them.

The fundamental point, according to Baars (1988), is how the enormously complex, fast, and parallel neural activity can, in consciousness, reduce to a serial and slow level of functioning. Neuroscientists are mostly working with the former system, and psychologists the latter. In order to combine these views, we should find some structure in the brain which can carry out the functions postulated for the Global Workspace system of Baars's theory.

This system should be associated with conscious functions like wakefulness, focal attention, and orienting responses; on the input side, many systems should have access to it, and different inputs should be able to co-operate or compete when accessing the global workspace. On the output side, it should be able to distribute the activity and information to many other parts of the brain, presumably practically everywhere.

Baars (1988) proposes that this kind of global neural workspace in the brain consists of the Reticular Formation of the brain stem and midbrain, the outer shell of the thalamus, and the set of neurons projecting upward diffusely from the thalamus to the cerebral cortex. This system he calls the Extended Reticular-Thalamic Activating System (ERTAS).

We can therefore suggest that the ERTAS underlies the "global broadcasting" function of consciousness, while a selected perceptual "processor" in the cortex supplies the particular *contents* of consciousness to be broadcast. ... These conscious contents, in turn, when they are broadcast, can trigger motor, memory, and associative activities. There is independent evidence that cortical activity *by itself* does not become conscious. ... We would suggest that any cortical activity must trigger ERTAS support in a circulating flow of information before it can be broadcast globally and become conscious. (Baars 1988, 126)

Thus, Damasio and Baars both agree that the content of a conscious state resides in the cortex, but for Baars, this information content must be "broadcast" across the system, whereas Damasio explicitly denies such transfer of representations. Does Damasio agree with Baars that cortical activity does not by itself become conscious? Apparently he does, because "attention" – whatever it is – is needed in Damasio's model to boost the level of activity.

The concept of attention is remarkably obscure in Damasio's theory. However, it is precisely the most critical process, the functioning of which it is necessary to understand if we want to know why some contents become conscious and others remain in the dark. It is a mysterious mechanism which operates in the twilight zone between the neural fragmentary representations and the mental, conscious experiences. Furthermore, Damasio gives no account of the limited capacity of consciousness. His theory does not prevent every single representation being conscious at the same time – provided their activity levels are boosted in the same time-window.

Damasio (1989b, 49) mentions that "attention depends on numerous factors and mechanisms", which is of course true, but patently unhelpful. Nevertheless, he emphasizes that the state of the perceiver and the context of the process also play important roles in determining the levels of activations and that "the reticular activating system, the reticular complex of the thalamus, and the limbic system mediate such roles under partial control of the cerebral cortex."

It seems that we can, at last, settle for some agreement between the different theories. Our interpretation is that both theories postulate the interaction of the ERTAS system with the cortical representations as a necessary condition for conscious contents to occur. It is unclear whether the information content should be thought of as moving in the system, as Baars suggests, but perhaps such an assumption is not indispensable. Anyway, the global workspace or some such system is needed to explain the limited capacity and seriality of conscious processes. Also Schacter et al. (1988) would agree, since they say that conscious processes require the *involvement* of a mechanism different than the modular discrimination systems.

There is, nonetheless, one critical point in the neuropsychological data which seems to challenge Damasio's theory. If the existence of implicit knowledge even in some cases is the result of normal cortical activation, as seems to be the case judging from normal implicit performance, then it cannot be a matter of simple activation that is at stake. In other words, the interaction that is missing brings something qualitatively new into the process, not just more activation, since normal activation per se seems not to help the patients possessing implicit knowledge to become conscious of that knowledge.

In sum, to have consciousness of some specific content C, we necessarily need the representation of C in the relevant cortical module. But to have any kind of consciousness at all, we need the global workspace which can somehow access these contents. If we imagine consciousness as always arising from the interaction between these two systems, the conflict between consciousness-centered and fragmentary theories begins to fade. The contents are based on fragmentary representations but the critical interaction comes from some sort of general-purpose system. It depends on the nature of this interaction whether representations are actually transferred in the system or whether they simply undergo state-changes right where they are. This question is empirical and thus out of the reach of our present speculations.

4.5. Jackendoff and the ghost in the computational machinery

Ray Jackendoff's theory suffers from certain pretheoretical commitments which lead to serious difficulties later on and question those commitments. As you may or may not recall, Jackendoff's starting point is computationalism. He states that every phenomenological distinction has a corresponding computational distinction, but only computational states are causally efficient. In other words, consciousness is, according to this model, causally inert. This also means that consciousness has no functions at all: it is epiphenomenal.

The other models we have encountered have all presumed that consciousness is useful, functional and central. As a further contrast to them, Jackendoff thinks that consciousness is somehow projected from modular-level representations. Conscious contents are sharply distinguished by modality and must, therefore, be based on a modality-specific level of processing. Thinking is a central, functional and modality-free process, whereas consciousness is intermediate-level, epiphenomenal and modality-specific.

We think that Jackendoff's model is unacceptable for several reasons. Consciousness is a completely useless entity in this model; a true ghost in the machine. And the mechanism by which consciousness is enigmatically "projected" from computations remains a complete mystery. In addition, it is rather counterintuitive to separate thinking from consciousness – in this model, all thinking could happily go on without a trace of consciousness.

It seems to us that Jackendoff's computationalism drives him to accept these questionable postulations. As he admits (1987, 18) "it is completely unclear to me how computations, no matter how complex or abstract, can add up to an experience." So he must "project" conscious experience from computations. And if we want to have a computational theory of intentional thought, we must separate it from our theory of consciousness, because we do not really have the latter. Consequently, we end up with an epiphenomenal consciousness which has nothing to do with thought processes.

Jackendoff succeeds only in showing the inadequacy of computationalism as a basis for a theory of consciousness. But what would be an alternative and why has he not considered it?

I find it every bit as incoherent to speak of conscious experience as a flow of information as to speak of it as a collection of neural firings. (Jackendoff 1987, 18)

My view is, as also expressed in previous chapters, that computationalist theories of consciousness are difficult if not impossible to incorporate into the natural order of other sciences, for philosophical and conceptual reasons. The alternative is, I suggest, a neurobiological theory of consciousness, which is not, in principle, impossible. We have even made some progress in the course of this article in understanding what the possible neural mechanisms involved in conscious contents are: they are properties that presumably emerge from an interaction between cortical representations and a global workspace system.

It seems that no matter how we twist and bend computations, no experiences emerge. However, this is not the case with matter. The universe itself has twisted and bent matter into a multitude of different systems with different properties, and we should expect consciousness to be one property like the others in nature. Perhaps the pessimism concerning neurobiology as a possible solution to the problem stems from the intuition that it is impossible to *see* anything remotely conscious in neural matter. Anyhow, we should not even expect to see it, since most of what scientists usually see through their instruments are dots of light or measurements of quantities. We need to *infer* that behind the observable neural surface there are different subsystems with different properties, among them a conscious one.

4.6. Reflections on Baars's and Schacter's theories

4.6.1. The limits of unconscious processing

In what follows, I will try to combine the ideas of Schacter's and Baars's models and see what kinds of empirical developments could increase our knowledge of the relationship between the conscious and the unconscious in human information processing. The merit of neuropsychological data is that it shows that a host of processing can be done without consciousness. In other words, it tests our hypothesis concerning the sufficient conditions of consciousness. Baars's theory contains a list of necessary conditions of consciousness that must all be fulfilled before information becomes conscious. I will be concerned especially with face processing and language comprehension and I will suggest some ways of combining Baars's hypothesis with the neuropsychological data. Finally, I will propose some future directions for these models based on the most recent empirical findings.

Baars (1988) lists five necessary conditions that any conscious event must, according to his theory, fulfill. Now had any of these necessary conditions been unfulfilled, you would not have had the experience. Here we can start to relate Baars's theory to the cognitive neuropsychology of awareness and especially to implicit knowledge. So far work in cognitive neuropsychology has concentrated on the unconscious specialist processors that are involved in the processing of different kinds of information. Now, however, it is possible to investigate what neuropsychological patients can tell us about the necessary conditions of conscious processing.

Patients possessing implicit knowledge of certain features of the world show that unconscious processing of stimuli can proceed further than previously was assumed. We may ask, what are the necessary conditions of conscious processing that have been violated in neuropsychological patients possessing implicit knowledge? In other words, why is the knowledge they possess only implicit and not conscious?

How to relate the implicit/explicit dissociations to Baars's framework? What kinds of empirical findings are evidence of true dissociation between unconscious special systems and a conscious system and what kinds of dissociations can be explained in different ways? This much is clear: whenever information is processed only implicitly, it must lack at least one of the necessary properties of conscious processing. But which ones? Baars's idea of conscious processes was that first information from modules must spread globally and activate contexts, then it must be global for a certain time and it must also be informative. How to reconcile this with the idea of a "disconnection from the conscious mechanism"? Schacter et al. (1988) develop the idea of disconnection a little further:

Note also that the idea of 'disconnection' as used here need not imply a disconnection of fibre tracts that link various brain structures. ... Rather, our use of disconnection refers more generally to a failure of a processor or module to gain access to a conscious mechanism, and does not make any assumptions about the nature of the neurological disruption that produces the access failure. (Schacter et al. 1988, 270)

It seems that we can treat "failure of a processor or module to gain access to a conscious mechanism" as equivalent with "a message lacking at least one of the necessary properties of consciousness." Implicit knowledge in neuropsychological patients fulfills at least the requirement of informativeness, and it seems to evoke an unconscious context, although this context cannot interact with the conscious message. I propose that, e.g., in implicit recognition, knowledge of the activated context cannot get access to global broadcasting and thus it cannot interact with the percept which, subsequently, remains stripped from meaning. When this percept-context interaction is absent, mere activation of the context cannot become the content of consciousness, because it would result in an inconsistent interpretation of the percept. For example, prosopagnosic patients who see a face and experience it as unfamiliar – because of lacking context-percept interaction – cannot become conscious of the activated context, since it is a competing, not a complementary interpretation of the percept. One processor is saying (because of disconnection) that no context is available – thus the unfamiliarity. The activated context is trumpeting "recognized!" through the indirect pathways, but in vain. The recognition message could win the competition only through the damaged pathway but, to the global workspace, the only message is silence, and thus the default interpretation "unfamiliar" remains.

I suggest, then, that implicit knowledge remains unconscious (in recognition impairments) because first, the principal route for percept-context interaction is disconnected, and second, because the unconsciously activated context, consequently, competes with the conscious one, and cannot gain access to consciousness through any other pathways. I will elaborate these ideas further in the light of the empirical findings.

4.6.2. Unconscious face recognition and language processing: Theoretical considerations

It seems to me that by combining ideas from Baars's framework and implicit knowledge we can theorize about the frontiers of unconscious processing. Let us consider auditory language comprehension. There is a certain processing chain in which the physical signal is converted to a meaningful word or sentence. It includes at least identification of phonemes, identification of words, and activation of the semantic content. The two first phases presumably reside exclusively within the auditory input system, whereas the third necessarily entails some sort of global spreading of information.

Let us imagine that we have a patient who does not explicitly understand spoken words. What would be evidence of an unimpaired input-system that is disconnected from consciousness? First, we would have to show that the patient can explicitly differentiate words from non-words: that would be proof of an intact auditory lexicon. Second, he would have to be unable to match spoken words with their written, pictorial or other representations: the words would lack meaning for him. If he nevertheless showed cross-modality priming effects, interference, or learning facilitation, it would be evidence of widespread effects of the input and activation of the relevant contexts. Then it would be the case that the input processor has functioned at least near-normally and the information has activated appropriate connections across other parts of the nervous system, and yet the knowledge is unconscious.

What exactly does it mean to consciously understand the meaning of an auditorily presented word? Phenomenologically, we are conscious of the phonological image (cf. Jackendoff 1987) – how the word *sounds* to us – and at the same time we have easy access to a large body of semantic information of the referent. Reflect on hearing the word "strawberry". It almost immediately evokes visual imagery of a red berry, you can almost feel the taste of it in your mouth, you might remember how it feels in your hand or in what situations you have encountered it last summer. At the same time, a massive amount of related information is activated and you have some kind of a "feeling of knowing" that you understand what a strawberry is. By contrast, a neuropsychological patient who cannot consciously understand the word presumably hears only the phonological image which brings nothing at all to consciousness, except, perhaps, a "feeling of not-knowing". Damasio (1989b) describes concepts in the brain in the following way:

In my perspective, the basis for a concept is a collection of simultaneous reconstructions of sensory and motor representations that have a high probability of being triggered by the same non-verbal or verbal stimulus. ... The neural basis for the reconstructed representations is the activation of many separate neural population ensembles, distributed in various cortical regions. They constitute a related set because the activations occur within the same time-window and are co-attended. (Damasio 1989a, 24–25)

But if the patient is conscious of the phonological image of the word, does that not imply that, after all, there is no disconnection between awareness and the auditory word recognition system? It seems that the patient can hear a word but not *as* any specific word, just as the prosopagnosic patient can see faces, but not faces *as* faces of familiar people. What is the difference between these cases and those in which the whole modality or realm of representation is totally blank for the patient as in e.g., blindsight or hemineglect? In the former, a modality-specific representation is sent to consciousness, but it fails to activate the relevant context; in the latter, no modality-specific message ever reaches consciousness. Implicit knowledge in these cases is, respectively, different in quality: in blindsight, no information gets to the Conscious Awareness System and yet is manifested implicitly; in the latter, a percept is stripped of its familiarity because it fails to interact with the context where it belongs. This context is, however, activated, but the activation is not consciously accessible.

Do these cases represent fundamentally different levels of disconnections from awareness? I suggest not: the disconnection itself is of a similar nature, although that which is disconnected is a different kind of processor in these cases. In the case of face processing, it has been suggested that

Recognition of a familiar face involves a match between the products of structural encoding and previously stored structural codes describing the appearance of familiar faces, held in face recognition units. Each recognition unit contains the description of the face of a known person, and the recognition unit will signal to a decision system the extent to which the seen face resembles its stored description. Activation of the recognition unit indicates that the seen face seems familiar. The face recognition unit can then access semantic information about the person seen via a person identity node, and finally the person's name. The person identity node would also be accessible from other types of input such as the voice or the written or spoken name. (Young 1988, 89–90)

In implicit face recognition, it has been suggested, the face recognition units continue to operate normally, but their outputs fail to reach consciousness, and thus the patient's mental state does not have the content: "I know this face!" However, the face recognition units are supposed to have routes other than to consciousness: the processing going on spreads automatically and is expressed in physiological measures and as response interferences or biases (for a review, see Bruyer 1991). It seems that a conscious feeling of recognition is a necessary condition for the "person identity nodes", that is, semantic knowledge about the person, to be activated into consciousness. However, these person-identity nodes seem to get their share from the automatic activation, since Young et al. (1988) have shown that priming effects can spread cross-modally both in normal subjects and in a prosopagnosic patient (from faces to names) who did not overtly recognize the primes. But what then *is* the difference between the activation in the face recognition units and in the identity nodes? The former is supposed to be disconnected from consciousness, but the latter certainly is not, since the semantic information can be consciously activated by showing some other stimulus than the face. But then we must raise the possibility that perhaps the activation in face recognition units is also only automatic, and the real disconnection is between structural encoding and recognition units. This means that we must postulate two different connections from the structural encoding to recognition units, and only the one allowing automatic activation is spared. It seems to be difficult to test empirically whether the recognition units function normally or only "automatically". The alternative remains that the recognition units do not function normally and thus there would be two different processing modes within the processor itself. At least it seems clear that there must be two modes of functioning in the person identity nodes, which themselves are spared but can be activated either automatically, through face stimuli, or in addition, consciously through other stimuli.

If we use the model of face processing proposed by V. Bruce and A. W. Young (1986; see also Young 1988), the interpretation of implicit face recognition seems to be as follows. First, the structural encoding functions normally and its outputs are usable in directed visual processing and consciousness. The structural encoding also sends its outputs to the face recognition units, but its output-route to consciousness is blocked. However, it has certain other output-routes which are able to cause automatic activation in the next stages of processing and also in physiological reactions. This automatic activation is, by itself, not sufficient for subsequent conscious processing to happen. Thus, to activate the "semantics" of a familiar face, it is necessary to send the output of the recognition units consciously. The mental state of the prosopagnosic patient is either like: (structural encoding) "This is a face" & (face recognition units) "This face is not familiar" & (person-identity nodes) "This face is not the face of any of the persons I know" or like: "This is a face" & "This is a familiar face" & "This is the face of person Y"; but never like: "This is a face" & "This face is not familiar" & "This is the face of person Y." Another way to interpret why automatic activation of semantic content does not suffice for recognition is to say that the resulting conscious message would be internally inconsistent and not able to become conscious as a whole.

Now we have come to a satisfactory interpretation of implicit recognition in prosopagnosia: it definitely seems to involve the disconnection of the face recognition units from consciousness. How could we construct a corresponding model in the case of language comprehension?

S. Franklin (1988) and D. Howard and Franklin (1988) distinguish different levels of comprehension impairment. In *word sound deafness* the patient is unable to identify word sounds. In *word form deafness* the patient can distinguish phonemes but is unable to access the word form correctly: he mixes words (and non-words) with similar sounding words and non-words. These two lowest levels of impairment may be compared to an impairment in the structural encoding of faces: in both cases, the patient is confused in categorizing certain external objects as objects belonging to a certain category, that is, as a word (or as a face). These patients seem, then, to have distorted or impaired perceptions of faces or words.

The more interesting cases in face processing, however, were found at a higher level of impairment. Thus, the most interesting level of impairment might be that of *word meaning deafness*, in which the patient can correctly access the word form, but nevertheless has no idea of the meaning of the word. If the deficit is modality specific, it reflects an inability of getting from the auditory input lexicon to the semantic system. If it infects all modalities, it suggests a semantic disorder.

In the case of word meaning deafness the patient hears the word as we do, but it simply does not ring a bell for him. But then, does this not mean that, after all, there is access from the lexicon to awareness? Here we have no "word recognition units" in addition to the word forms. How could the correct form of the word fail to evoke the right semantics, since, presumably, nobody has anything else with which to reach semantics? If it is the case that the input lexicon is intact, the semantic system is intact and the perception of the word is intact, it seems that an additional processor must be postulated, corresponding to the function of the face recognition units. This processor would perform a preliminary semantic analysis and its function would be necessary to cause full-fledged, cross-modality semantic processes. Another hypothesis would be that in fact nothing even could be disconnected from awareness in word comprehension, but it is simply the case that hearing the right form of a word is just not sufficient for the meaning to arise. Another route from the lexicon to cross-modality semantics exists which is unfunctional.

It is counterintuitive to claim that conscious messages would not produce activation of the relevant semantics, but we have no evidence that some sort of conscious message would be lacking. Fortunately, it is an empirically testable question whether there is an extra processor that is disconnected from awareness or just an automatic connection to semantics which is cut. In the case of the former, implicit semantic knowledge is possible, in the latter it is not. So, if we find cross-modality semantic activation in the absence of explicit understanding, there must be some additional processor disconnected from awareness or semantics. By contrast, if we find no implicit access to semantic knowledge, we may assume that the normal route to semantics is blocked and that this normal route is automatic or at least the normal route needs both the conscious message coupled with the automatic activation.

In the case of *general semantic deficit* we may assume that the spreading of conscious messages or the ability to respond to them has been disturbed, if implicit semantics nevertheless occurs.

The concept of "semantics" seems to be rather vague in neuropsychology and we must be careful not to misunderstand it. We should distinguish it from semantics as understood in linguistics, logic or philosophy, and we should also make certain observations of what semantics actually is or should be in neuropsychology. In the former disciplines, semantics is usually understood as defining the truth-conditions for expressions in some, usually artificial language. However, a useful distinction inside semantics has been made by W. V. O. Quine: semantics can be thought of as comprising two disciplines. The first is a theory of *reference*, which is interested in looking at the relations between symbols and the world. The second would be called a theory of *meaning*. The meaning of symbols must be distinguished from their referents, since we can depict some external object in more ways than one, thus having the same referent but different meanings. Now, neuropsychology seems to be interested in how our brains construct meaning, not what the denoted objects behind those constructions are. The "semantic system" so often encountered in neuropsychology is that system which combines information from different knowledge sources and allows us to, e.g., see an object *as* a specific object. Thus, agnosia patients whose percepts are said to be "stripped of meaning" are lacking the normal activation of multimodal associations and information; partly into consciousness and the rest easily accessible to consciousness.

Here it is useful to remember Damasio's characterization of concepts in the brain, which works also as a characterization of meaning in the brain:

> It is rather a potential set of representations activated from a dormant memory state, each of which has a high probability of being triggered by a given stimulus and of occurring together with the others. (Damasio 1989a, 25)

So, if there are two different ways of triggering meaning, in the case of generalized semantic deficit, the conscious way is defective, but the automatic one might nevertheless work. If no evidence of implicit semantics can be found, the hypothesis of two different activation paths must be abandoned. It must be remembered, however, that there might not be two different paths but only different degrees of activation. Since the semantic system as well as the representation of meaning is not localized, it is difficult to say what exactly is the output of such a system. Probably it is the co-activation of a coherent set of representations which then gains access to consciousness. If this coherence cannot be achieved, semantic disturbances might occur.

As we have noticed, it is by no means a simple task to interpret the different kinds of recognition impairments and relate them to models of consciousness. Nonetheless, it is, I believe, exactly what has to be done if we want to grasp what it is to consciously understand something. I will return to this matter briefly and suggest a model for conscious semantics.

4.6.3. Do we have to assume one common consciousness system?

There seems to be uncertainty about whether the empirical data, after all, are sufficient to support the hypothesis of one general consciousness system. As we noted above, it is necessary to reconcile the fact that perceptual representations are fragmented with what implicit knowledge and phenomenology tell about consciousness. However, not all neuropsychologists agree that implicit knowledge should be interpreted in terms of one consciousness system:

In addition, we have argued that the pattern of preserved performance is more easily considered as reflecting disconnection from awareness than impairment to perceptual mechanisms per se. Our reservation concerning Schacter et al.'s hypothesis is that we are not yet convinced that it is necessary to think in terms of one, centralized conscious mechanism. It seems to us equally likely that there may be multiple systems responsible for different aspects of awareness, which could mean that the complete pattern of possible disconnections might be very complicated. This is, of course, an empirical question, to be settled by further investigations. (Young and DeHaan 1990, 44)

Schacter (1990) reminds us that implicit memory in amnesics can usually if not always be explained by referring to different memory systems rather than to dissociations between conscious and unconscious systems. Thus skill learning and priming effects in amnesics only reveal activation outside the episodic memory system, which itself is presumably damaged. In the case of amnesia, we would have to show

... preserved implicit memory for the very global contextual attributes that are normally accessed explicitly and provide the underlying informational basis for an aware re-experiencing of a prior episode. (Schacter 1990, 168)

The point is to get evidence of an intact episodic memory system whose outputs are disconnected from awareness. Conclusive evidence about such disconnections has not been produced yet in the case of amnesia. However, if all the cases of implicit knowledge could be explained by postulating one implicit and one explicit system, the point of postulating a common system for explicit and conscious knowledge would, perhaps, quickly be lost:

Thus dissociations in blindsight would be interpreted in terms of two different visual systems, a conscious, explicit system that is impaired and an unconscious, implicit system that is preserved; dissociations in prosopagnosia would lead to the postulating of two different facial recognition systems; dissociations in

Wernicke's aphasia would be explained in terms of the two different comprehension systems; dissociations in amnesia would require postulation of two separate memory systems; and so on. (Schacter, McAndrews and Moscovitch 1988, 268)

Prima facie, this approach leads to an unacceptable multiplicity of different processing systems. And the final solution would only be postponed, since then we would have to ask, by virtue of which common property are all the explicit systems capable of producing conscious experience and how are those distributed conscious processes united into a cohesive phenomenology. Also the limited capacity of conscious processing would remain unexplained, if there is no common system underlying different conscious contents.

We do have, then, certain good pretheoretical reasons to believe that an approach which postulates multiple conscious systems is less satisfactory than an explanation which refers to a common system. Unfortunately, pure pretheoretical arguments are seldom sufficient in empirical sciences and, consequently, we would need to find even more convincing evidence than before: e.g., disconnections which provide evidence that a certain processing module or knowledge representation is intact, as revealed by implicit tests, but nevertheless *the very same information* is not or cannot be represented consciously and expressed explicitly.

It would also suffice to find cases where the module is perhaps somewhat damaged but implicit knowledge is expressed, if in such cases it would be highly suspicious to postulate a separate mechanism for implicit knowledge. As Schacter et al. (1988) point out, pure disconnections are presumably rare, and many cases will involve both disconnection and damage at the modular level. In addition, different degrees of disconnection between the conscious and unconscious mechanisms are conceivable: interaction is not all or none.

Recently, some reports concerned with implicit knowledge have suggested that, in many cases, there is not necessarily evidence of disconnection from awareness, but rather evidence of two different processing systems, one of which is able to work – and also normally works – completely automatically and is not able to produce consciousness. For example, Schacter, L. Cooper and S. Delaney (1990) showed that implicit memory for unfamiliar objects is functionally independent of explicit memory. Implicit memory was measured by using the priming paradigm and the results indicated that priming effects can be manifested also when there is no pre-existing memory-representation of the target items. They propose that these priming effects are based on a structural description system which is separate from, but interacts with, a semantic system. In addition, Schacter et al. (1990) showed that the priming effects in a letter-by-letter reader occur at the visual word form system. Schacter, Cooper and Delaney (1990) suggest that so-called perceptual representation systems play a crucial role in implicit memory. They are concerned with knowledge form and structure – but not semantics – in various input domains. Young et al. (1989) tested a patient who was suffering a semantic memory impairment: he could not overtly determine the category membership of living things. However, in a visually presented lexical-decision (priming) task, seeing the correct category before the target word facilitated the decisions as to whether or not the target was a word.

In all these cases, it seems that the implicit capacities are based on processing systems that are functionally different from those that cause explicit performance. That is, a different kind of information is needed for executing the explicit task, not only that the implicit knowledge would be disconnected from awareness. Young et al. (1989) comment on their findings in this way:

Certainly the presence of priming from related category labels demonstrates that M.S. achieves implicit access to information which can represent the structure of semantic categories in some way. We suspect, however, that much of this structure is associative and forms part of the word recognition system, where it exists for the reason neatly described by Fodor (1983) as allowing a stupid system to appear smart. (Young et al. 1989, 203)

This means that the activated implicit semantic knowledge is not the same semantic knowledge which forms the basis of conscious understanding of, e.g., a word. The multiple systems hypothesis, thus, remains a possibility: perhaps conscious understanding is the property of a different system, which truly *is* damaged, and it is not the case that the observed semantics is just *disconnected* from consciousness. We would need to show that the same system which normally produces conscious understanding can be, at the same time, both unimpaired and disconnected from consciousness. If such a situation is impossible, then consciousness must be the property of that system when it is intact.

Schacter (1990) prefers to interpret these kinds of cases in a manner consistent with the existence of a common consciousness system, calling the manner of explanation a "second-order" theoretical account. It is a sufficient explanation in most cases: the disturbance is in gaining access to some sort of domain specific information that is normally associated with, or provides a basis for, an experience of awareness in a particular domain. For example, implicit skill learning can be explained by separating the procedural memory system (which is intact) from the episodic memory system (which is impaired). In this case, the multiple-systems hypothesis says that consciousness is, in fact, a *property* of the episodic system, whereas Schacter's second-order theoretical account claims that the outputs from the episodic system to the conscious awareness system are badly degraded or non-existent, which prevents conscious re-experiencing. By contrast, Schacter's "first-order" account postulates a deficit at the level of the awareness system or a disconnection of that system from other systems. In other words, an otherwise perfect output from some module or processing system just cannot get into the conscious awareness system.

A second-order account of an awareness disturbance is not inconsistent with the idea that some sort of general-purpose, cross-domain awareness mechanisms exist; it merely indicates that one need not appeal to disruption of such mechanisms every time an awareness deficit is observed. (Schacter 1990, 157)

How do these considerations relate to implicit language comprehension? W. Milberg and S. Blumstein (1981), Blumstein, Milberg and R. Shrier (1982), and Milberg, Blumstein and B. Dworetzky (1988) have found priming effects from Wernicke's aphasics in visual and auditory tasks, on the basis of which they propose that semantic organization is normal, although access to this semantic information is severely defective. However, the "semantics" in question is presumably a reflection of similar perceptual representation systems like priming effects found in amnesics manifesting implicit memory. It has yet to be shown that information processing in Wernicke's aphasia can proceed also to the genuine semantic system, which operates cross-modally and in which the representations normally function as a basis for conscious understanding of meaning. It is difficult to see how this kind of system could be disconnected from consciousness, since it is hardly a module: rather, it is global in nature. Perhaps, in investigating the workings of this system, we are not so much concerned with global messages as in perception, but rather activation of conceptual contexts, the only output of which is a feeling of understanding the content or meaning of a percept.

4.7. Proposal for a model of conscious semantics

On the basis of the foregoing discussions, I sketch a model of what it is to consciously understand the meaning of any stimulus. Our example will be the understanding of a spoken word, but the same principles should apply for all modalities.

What do we mean by "understanding" a word? It means, roughly, that on hearing a word we get conscious access to some recalled properties of the referent, and a large amount of other related information becomes activated and, thus, it is easily brought to consciousness if needed. We must emphasize that understanding always requires knowledge in many different forms, e.g., lexical, visual, autobiographical knowledge.

Now, we must ask, how does this all work? How does the relevant set of representations become activated and in what form are those conscious experiences when we have them? A model of auditory input for speech usually includes at least three levels: a phoneme or speech sound level, a phonological or word form level, and a semantic or word meaning level. The varieties of impaired auditory word comprehension (word deafness) correspond to these levels: word sound, word form, and word meaning deafness (Franklin 1988; Howard and Franklin 1988).

A patient with word meaning deafness is able to reach the word form level: that is, he can tell which sound-patterns are real words and which are non-words. He can also tell which words rhyme and which do not. Thus, the phonological image of auditorily presented words seems to reside in the word form lexicon. There, phonologically closely related words tend to be associated with each other (look-cook-book), but no semantic relations are represented. Thus, here "cat" and "hat" have a link with a high-activation value, whereas "cat" and "mouse" have a link with very low activation value. We can think of this system as a PDP-network (Rumelhart et al. 1986). This is the level that has direct access to consciousness when we hear a word. Although I rejected Jackendoff's theory of consciousness in general, he makes this important observation in his book:

Now let us ask, What linguistic structures most closely correspond to the phenomenological form of linguistic images? Examining each of the levels, we find that the most appropriate units of form seem to come from *phonological structure.* ... As has been remarked for centuries, the meaningfulness of an utterance cannot be found anywhere in its palpable (that is introspectively available) form. The difference lies only in the presence or absence of conceptual structure hidden behind the scenes. (Jackendoff 1987, 288–289)

In addition to the word form lexicon, we must postulate a semantic lexicon, in which the semantic relations between word forms are represented. Thus, in this lexicon the connection between "cat" and "mouse" has a high activation value, whereas that between "cat" and "hat" does not. However, this semantic lexicon cannot yet be the true basis of understanding, since it only represents relations between *words*, not how those words connect to other things in the experienced world. Knowing that a word is semantically related to some other words forms only a thesaurus of items which in themselves lack meaning: it is like the Oxford Dictionary of English in the hands of someone who does not know any English at all. So, after all, this is a stupid system that mimics real understanding and, as such, can at best be only a precursor of true understanding.

Real semantics is always based on cross-modality associations (in addition to inter-modality associations). For example, upon hearing the word "strawberry", the following happens: First, it is analyzed to word form level. In the word form lexicon, the representation of [strooberi] gets the highest activation, and the words straw [stroo] and strawmark [stroomaak] are also highly activated. Second, the most activated word form then gains access to consciousness, resulting in an experienced phonological image of the form "strooberi". Meanwhile, the activation goes automatically to the semantic lexicon, resulting in the activation of a network of related words, e.g., blueberry, raspberry, gooseberry, blackberry, blackcurrant, cherry, etc. The highest activation is again in the word "strawberry".

Through cross-modality routes, the information that "strawberry" is the most activated item is sent to multiple sites, in which other networks are activated. Hence, in the visual modality, the object recognition units receive information, which activates the representation of a small red fruit with tiny yellow seeds on its surface and, on top of the berry, a green stalk with small leaves arranged in a star shape. In the taste modality, a sweet and fresh taste of strawberry is activated. In the episodic memory, recall of strawberry-related happenings in the past is facilitated. None of these activated pieces of knowledge may in fact become the contents of consciousness, but there is a certain *feeling-of-knowing* that we know the meaning of the word, which would be lacking were nothing at all activated beyond the word form level. If necessary, we can express that we understand the word by drawing a picture, telling about the taste or the memories, or classifying objects as closely or remotely related to strawberries.

In sum, necessary conditions for conscious understanding or semantics are: (1) Activation of the modality specific store mirroring real semantics; (2) Activation of a cross-modality semantic network; (3) Knowledge of a semantic match (feeling of understanding) and easy conscious access to the activated cross-modality information (see Fig. 11).

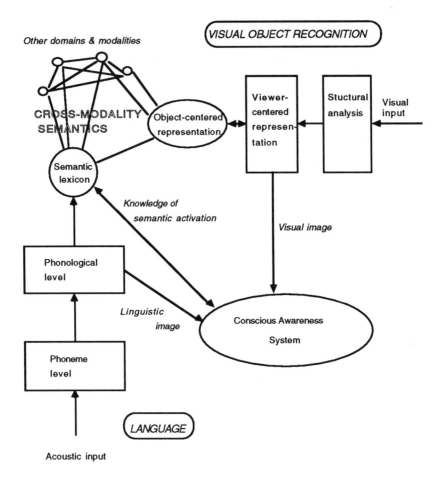

Fig. 11. A model of cross-modality semantics. On hearing a word, the most activated phonological representation has access to consciousness, but the interpretation of this experience is dependent on the activated cross-modality network of related representations and knowledge of this activation.

An important question is whether the cross-modality semantics can be activated implicitly, that is, without the subject's knowledge. As we noted above, most of the previous studies confirm only a modality specific semantic activation, which means that those representations that are needed in conscious understanding have presumably not been activated. However, the study of Young, Hellawell and DeHaan (1988) with a prosopagnosic patient revealed that the representation of names could be accessed implicitly from the representation of faces that remained unrecognized. If further research supports the hypothesis that cross-modality semantics can be activated without the patient's conscious understanding, then we must assume that cross-modality semantics can be activated through routes other than the conscious system or global workspace. If, however, only modality specific semantics can be found (e.g., semantic priming in lexical decision from word primes to word targets but never from word primes to picture targets) then we can hypothesize that the cross-modality activation necessarily needs the damaged route and the lack of understanding reflects the inaccessibility of cross-modality semantics.

On the model I propose, the "genuine semantic system" simply consists of the connections of the structural items across modalities. It is an empirical question whether a pattern can be activated in this system without thus accessing consciousness, or does accessing consciousness simply consist of such an activation.

We would like to suggest, however, that implicit activation of cross-modality semantics is possible. Let us assume that a patient cannot understand the word strawberry, but there is a priming effect both inter- and cross-modally to other related items. In addition, he can immediately access the semantics consciously when, e.g., he sees a strawberry or tastes it. Thus, the cross-modality network in itself cannot be damaged, but it seems that the subject does not receive any information of the semantic activation through the lexical presentation. (This case would correspond to the prosopagnosic case of Young, Hellawell and DeHaan 1988.) It would seem that in a case like this the modality specific system that contains the intramodal semantic network (relations to other words) cannot communicate with the rest of the cognitive system to tell that a semantic match has been found. The lack of this interaction does not prevent the cross-modal activation, but it prevents the subject from using it in his behaviour, since he believes that no semantics for the word exists.

4.8. Synthesis of theories

Perhaps we are now, after all these considerations, arguments and speculations, ready to summarize those postulates, which, I propose, form the core for future theories and research of consciousness. I argued against

Dennett's and Jackendoff's models and concluded that, whatever the science of consciousness will be, it should not be built on those theories. Instead, I think that the rest of the reviewed theories, that is, those of Schacter, Baars, and Damasio, could be combined and seen as complementary rather than as competitors.

From Schacter's model (Schacter 1990; Schacter et al. 1988) and from empirical findings connected with implicit knowledge in general, we learned the following points. One common system that operates above the level of modular systems is involved in all conscious processing. This assumption is the most general and parsimonious one that can be made in order to explain the existence of implicit knowledge in neuropsychological syndromes. Although the evidence is not yet unequivocal, that is, it does not force us to assume only one conscious mechanism, this assumption nevertheless seems to be the most advisable choice. The competing interpretation, according to which there might be several consciousness systems, has to explain what do those systems have in common, how the limited capacity of consciousness is explained, and why the theory must postulate such a multitude of conscious processors if only one would be enough. However, some neuropsychologists (for example Young, 1992) support the hypothesis of multiple conscious mechanisms, which means that this matter is far from settled yet.

Baars's cognitive theory of consciousness offers further evidence about the existence of one, general system for consciousness. His most important contributions concern the operating principles of this system and the relations between conscious contents and their unconscious contexts. He explains how a tiny portion of the massive amount of information that is processed unconsciously is selected for consciousness. The automatic specialist processors cooperate to bind separately processed features into coherent wholes. The coherent wholes then compete for access to the global workspace and the one which carries the most informative message with it will be selected through feedback from other parts of the nervous system. After a message gains global distribution and maintains that state for a minimum time, the contents of the message become conscious and interpreted through the contexts that are currently unconsciously activated. The neural substrate of the system necessary for consciousness is not to be found from the cortex, but instead from the reticular activation system and thalamus. Baars's model was found to be consistent with recent findings concerning the neurophysiological base of attention – e.g., Näätänen (1990) has found certain brain potentials which presumably are connected with the access to conscious perception and which possibly are the foundation of the competition between different messages in the nervous system.

Damasio's theory reminds us about the complexity and distribution of the processing going on in the sensory cortices. The feedback and feedforward connections there are compatible with what Baars thinks about the unconscious specialist processors: the neural architecture allows multilevel processing to take place in order for the different specialists to co-operate and compete. We resolved the controversy between Damasio's and Baars's theory by leaving it open whether or not the information is transferred from the specialist processors into the global workspace. Baars suggests that the concrete representation is *distributed* throughout the global system. In the light of Damasio's theory, we should conceptualize the story the other way around: the information is *not transferred anywhere*, but the global network gains access to those parts of the fragmentary representations that are activated. Anyway, the core idea in all these theories under consideration is that an interaction from other than modular or cortical levels, presumably from the reticular-thalamic level, is necessary for any cortical activity to become conscious.

There should be nothing philosophically problematic in this kind of theory of consciousness. It involves no infinite regresses, no inner eyes or homunculi. It only postulates one new theoretical construct into the flowchart of mind. This subsystem preserves enough of our initial ideas about consciousness for us to call it the Conscious Awareness System (Schacter 1990) or something similar. This subsystem has one unique property: the information in it is *experienced by the subject* – it is part of his experienced world. This property makes it possible for the organism to use this information in its subsequent *adaptive behaviour* – whatever its output mode may be. In other words, if any information that is normally available to conscious experience becomes unavailable for any reason, then it also ceases to be available for adaptive behaviour.

Future research has several interesting paths to take in investigating consciousness. Cognitive neuropsychology can further clarify the nature of disconnections from consciousness. Which disconnections are really between consciousness and a module and which ones reflect the involvement of two different processing systems, one implicit, the other explicit. Cognitive and neurophysiological research on attention (Näätänen 1990) will have fascinating stories to tell us about the relations between automatic, unconscious and controlled, conscious processing. Cognitive theories should not forget to take into account the research going on in functional neuroanatomy, since the actual architecture of the brain is, after all, the system in which the human mind is created.

If these educated speculations concerning the direction of research turn out to be correct, there will be one extremely critical point of research. We would like to know what is so special in the interaction of cortical modules and the reticular-thalamic network that it generates consciousness. It seems to us that current ways of brain-imaging do not provide us with this kind of information, simply because they cannot depict the relevant level of description. Most electrophysiological measures, like electroencephalography (EEG), event-related potentials (ERP) and magnetoencephalography (MEG) are confined to telling us only about the activity of the cortex. Positron emission tomography (PET), computerized tomography (CT) and magnetic resonance imaging (MRI) can picture also deeper structures and PET also their neurochemical activity, but there is no technique that could show us on-line how processing in a certain module on the cortex relates to processing in the reticular formation and thalamus when we are conscious of the content stored in the cortex. So, we need not only new theories of consciousness, we also need new equipment to reveal the relevant level of organization.

4.9. Philosophical commitments

Any theory of consciousness is at least implicitly committed to accept some philosophical views and to reject others. I want to make explicit some of those commitments that I am ready to make and that go naturally with the advocated view. After all, the philosophical ideas should provide the most fundamental insights into questions concerning consciousness.

4.9.1. Rejection of eliminative materialism

To begin with, I found the arguments for the elimination of consciousness from science baseless. At the moment, nothing is further from the truth than the claim that consciousness is at the end of its journey as a scientific concept. The number of articles and books published on this subject alone during the last 5 or 10 years is simply baffling. And a lion's share of this accumulating literature is not the isolated philosopher's somber meditation, but, by contrast, empirical or theoretical research in the cognitive sciences – the chapters we have just wandered through together should provide substantive evidence for that. The last straw for the eliminativist should be that since 1992 a new international journal, called *Consciousness and Cognition* (Academic Press) is published. It promises to "provide a natural-science approach" to consciousness and it will feature both empirical and theoretical research. What more do we need to show that consciousness is not futile for science?

Therefore, it is obvious that I want to be a "realist" in the question of consciousness. This means that I regard conscious phenomena as real, important and also necessary for any complete theory of mind.

4.9.2. The complementarity of the first- and the third-person views

Another significant commitment is that I accept the complementarity of the first-person and third-person perspectives (cf. Velmans, 1991). From a strict third-person point of view, no experiences exist, and thus the "theories of consciousness" that can be formed from such a starting point could never distinguish between unfeeling zombies and conscious subjects. A good example of the consequences of adopting a rigid third-person philosophy is Dennett's philosophy of mind and consciousness. He ends up denying the existence of a subjective point of view, intrinsic intentionality, determined contents of consciousness, and qualia. Consciousness, beliefs, desires and other system-level properties exist only from the point of view of an external observer, never independently, inside the organism itself.

Such philosophical commitments, I believe, seriously misconstrue the whole matter. Theories based on such questionable principles never begin to capture what the problem of consciousness is, even less can they solve it. Thus, whatever the merits of the third-person view and the perils of the subjective perspective, the science and philosophy of consciousness will not survive without the latter.

4.9.3. The rejection of computationalism

Time after time, we have noticed the incapability of computationalism to account for consciousness. First, computationalism seems to presuppose an exhaustive third-person view on mental phenomena, since, as Searle has argued, computation involves syntax and symbols, and they entail an external observer, for whom a thing is symbolical or syntactical. There are no objects that are symbols in themselves, thus nothing is computation in itself. Computation names an observer-relative process, not a process of physics which would exist independently of us, the interpreters and users of computations. This is in grave disagreement with what I believe should be the starting point of an explanation of consciousness.

I see the world as a hierarchy of levels, each of which has its own systems and nomic connections. Consciousness comes into play at a specific level in this organization. I think that consciousness is ultimately something neurobiological, which is not to say that it can or should be reduced to neurobiology. All conscious phenomena share a certain property (or complex of properties), by virtue of which these phenomena are consciously experienced. This property is created in the interaction of cortical, feature-encoding systems with the deep reticular and thalamic structures. The determinate contents of conscious experience can in principle be agreed upon. Thus, we accept the notion of intrinsic intentionality, which means that understanding or aboutness can really take place only in our minds. That is, any perception in any modality can only be understood to mean or to be about something by connecting it with other representations in the subject's experienced world. Our brains can never reach out to the real world to see what is in the beginning of the causal chains and networks that generated the experience. Instead, the brain can combine simultaneously happening experiences by linking memories of them with association paths across modalities. We understand our perceptions because of the cohering relations with other experiences, not because of the correspondences with objects in the external reality.

Consciousness could be a mereologically supervenient property of neural organization. To admit that consciousness is a neurobiological property is to deny that it is a computational property. Computations are not the stuff that the mind is or could be made of, if the mental is taken to be continuous with the natural world. I thus reject, like Searle (1990), computational accounts of consciousness and consider them only productions of our present stage of ignorance of neurobiological details.

One further example of the unsuccesfulness of computationalism is Jackendoff's theory. He innocently supposes that computationalism is the starting point on which a theory of consciousness should be built. He does the best that anybody can, trying to combine consciousness with computations, but the results are, unfortunately, disastrous. He is driven, almost against his own will, to endorse epiphenomenalism:

I'm not too happy about this consequence: consciousness seems too important – too much fun – to conceive of it as useless. (Jackendoff 1987, 27)

He nevertheless stubbornly clings to computationalism. Well, I also share his conviction that consciousness is too important to be useless, and I am ready to sacrifice computationalism. Conceived of as a supervenient property at a certain level of the organization of nature, consciousness preserves its dignity and usefulness. An epiphenomenon hardly improves an organism's chances of survival or production of offspring. Thus, computationalism is anti-biological and anti-evolutionary. As it stands, it is more than hard to believe that computationalism is of any use in the future science of consciousness, if the only things we can do with it is to deny consciousness, or make it an epiphenomenon.

4.9.4. Drawbacks and benefits

What kinds of merits and difficulties does this kind of view bring with it? To start with the good news, it preserves our intuitions about what consciousness is and it is compatible with the naturalization of consciousness. It avoids the liberalism and chauvinism that functionalism and identity theories have been accused of (Block 1978), since a supervenient property can be multiply realized within certain limits. It is compatible with current empirical evidence from multiple sources and it suggests that consciousness could be realized in some sort of neural network, but not in classical computational architecture.

The weakest point of my approach is that I am committed to the existence of somewhat mysterious subjective properties, which are supposed to be supervenient upon certain neural activity. Nonetheless, I think that this approach does not lead to difficulties even nearly as grave as those encountered by pure third person theories. An essential but mistaken assumption that many such theories seem to suffer from is that they consider science as somehow fundamentally unproblematic: the third-person point of view has worked so well in physics, chemistry, and biology that surely we should not give it up when we start considering psychology.

Unfortunately, even the Bedrock of Science, particle physics, is far from being unproblematic. After fifty years of frantic research, we still have no universally accepted interpretation of the microlevel events in quantum mechanics, where something odd seems to be going on. Therefore, we do not possess any solid and stationary cornerstones of science, on which we could build a tower of Babel from physics to economics. On the contrary, even the basics are confused and obscure and the levels of nature function all but unmysteriously. It is not advisable, thus, to praise the third-person view and to abandon everything else for it. It is much easier to believe that reality itself is so complex as to create subjectivity than to endorse the third-person view and reject that any mental phenomena as we subjectively understand them even exist.

I want to emphasize that consciousness cannot be treated separately as an object for scientific inquiry, and as a philosophical topic. So far a remarkable portion of philosophical work done on consciousness has proceeded without much awareness of the empirical results that are relevant for the matter. Vice versa, empirical researchers often speculate upon consciousness without much worrying about the philosophical consequences. I propose that both sides of the coin should be taken into account simultaneously, as I have tried to do in this study. Otherwise, no paradigm of research can be established.

It may be that we will never get any final answers to the problems of consciousness, but there are, after all, few questions to which we do get such answers in science. The existence of time, space, gravitation, laws and constants of nature etc. can only be explained up to a certain point. We can always ask, "But what is it really?" or "But why is it the way it is?" Anyhow, we believe that right now there is a good chance of making remarkable progress in the problem of consciousness, and that, I guess, is the most one can ever say about any scientific task. I hope that my evaluation of the problem and its current and especially future developments will turn out to be, if not exactly prophecy, at least premonition. Let me now close this discussion about the philosophical and scientific dimensions of consciousness, since a lot of work awaits to be done, if we expect one day to really see the future science of consciousness.

BIBLIOGRAPHY

Allport, A.: 1988, 'What Concept of Consciousness?', in: Marcel, A.J. and Bisiach, E. (eds.), *Consciousness in Contemporary Science*, New York: Oxford University Press.
Baars, B.J.: 1988, *A Cognitive Theory of Consciousness*, New York: Cambridge University Press.
Bauer, R.M.: 1984, 'Autonomic Recognition of Names and Faces in Prosopagnosia: a Neuropsychological Application of the Guilty Knowledge Test', *Neuropsychologia 2 2* (4), 457–469.
Bisiach, E., Luzatti, C. and Perani, D.: 1979, 'Unilateral Neglect, Representational Schema and Consciousness', *Brain 1 0 2*, 609–618.
Block, N.: 1978, 'Troubles with Functionalism', in Block, N. (ed.), 1980, *Readings in Philosophy of Psychology*, Cambridge, Massachusetts: Harvard University Press.
Block. N.: 1980, 'What Is Functionalism?', in Block, N. (ed.), 1980, *Readings in Philosophy of Psychology*, Cambridge, Massachusetts: Harvard University Press.

Block, N.: 1990, 'Inverted Earth', *Philosophical Perspectives*: **4** , 53–80.

Blumstein, S.E., Milberg, W. and Shrier, R.: 1982, 'Semantic Processing in Aphasia: Evidence from an Auditory Lexical Decision Task', *Brain and Language* **1 7**, 301–315.

Bowers, J.S. and Schacter, D.: 1990, 'Implicit Memory and Test Awareness', *Journal of Experimental Psychology: Learning, Memory, and Cognition* **1 6** (3), 404–416.

Bruce, V. and Young, A.: 1986, 'Understanding Face Recognition', *British Journal of Psychology* **7 7**, 305–327.

Bruyer, R.: 1991, 'Covert Face Recognition in Prosopagnosia: A Review', *Brain and Cognition* **1 5**, 223–235.

Cermack, L.S., Bleich, R.P. and Blackford, S.P.: 1988, 'Deficits in the Implicit Retention of New Associations by Alcoholic Korsakoff Patients', *Brain and Cognition* **7**, 312–323.

Cermack, L.S., Talbot, N., Chandler, K. and Wolbarst, L.R.: 1985, 'The Perceptual Priming Phenomenon in Amnesia', *Neuropsychologia* **2 3** (5), 615–622.

Churchland, P.M.: 1979, *Scientific Realism and the Plasticity of Mind*, Cambridge: Cambridge University Press.

Churchland, P.M.: 1981, 'Eliminative Materialism and Propositional Attitudes', *Journal of Philosophy* **7 8**, 78–90.

Churchland, P.M. and Churchland, P.S.: 1981, 'Functionalism, Qualia, and Intentionality', *Philosophical Topics* **1 2** (1), 121–145.

Churchland, P.S.: 1983, 'Consciousness: The Transmutation of a Concept', *Pacific Philosophical Quarterly* **6 4**, 80–95.

Churchland, P.S.: 1986, *Neurophilosophy: Toward a Unified Science of the Mind-Brain*, Cambridge MA: MIT Press.

Churchland, P.S.: 1988, 'Reduction and the Neurobiological Basis of Consciousness', in Marcel, A.J. and Bisiach, E. (eds.), *Consciousness in Contemporary Science*, New York: Oxford University Press.

Crick, F. and Koch, C.: 1990, 'Towards a Neurobiological Theory of Consciousness', *Seminars in The Neurosciences* **2**, 263–275.

Damasio, A.R.: 1989a, 'Concepts in the Brain', *Mind and Language* **4**, 24–28.

Damasio, A.R.: 1989b, 'Time-Locked Multiregional Retroactivation: A Systems-Level Proposal for the Neural Substrates of Recall and Recognition', *Cognition* **3 3**, 25–62.

Damasio, A.R.: 1990, 'Synchronous Activation in Multiple Cortical Regions: A Mechanism for Recall', *Seminars in The Neurosciences* **2**, 287–296.

Damasio, A.R., Damasio, H. and Van Hoesen, G.W.: 1982, 'Prosopagnosia: Anatomic Basis and Behavioral Mechanisms', *Neurology* **3 2**, 331–341.

Dennett, D.C.: 1969, *Content and Consciousness*, London: Routledge and Kegan Paul.

Dennett, D.C.: 1978, 'Toward a Cognitive Theory of Consciousness', in Dennett, D.C., *Brainstorms*, Brighton: Harvester.

Dennett, D.C.: 1982, 'How To Study Human Consciousness Empirically or Nothing Comes to Mind', *Synthese* **5 3**, 159–180.

Dennett, D.C.: 1987, *The Intentional Stance*, Cambridge MA: MIT Press.

Dennett, D.C.: 1988, 'Quining Qualia', in Marcel, A.J. and Bisiach, E. (eds.), *Consciousness in Contemporary Science*, New York: Oxford University Press.

Dennett, D.C.: 1990, 'The Myth of Original Intentionality', in Mohyeldin Said, K.A., Newton-Smith, W.H., Viale, R. and Wilkes, K.V. (eds.), *Modelling the Mind*, Oxford: Clarendon Press.

Dennett, D.C.: 1991, *Consciousness Explained*, Boston: Little, Brown.

Dennett, D.C. and Kinsbourne, M.: 1992, 'Time and the Observer: The Where and When of Consciousness in the Brain' (with Commentary), *Behavioral and Brain Sciences*, 1 5, 183–247.

Edelman, G.M.: 1989, *The Remembered Present: A Biological Theory of Consciousness*, New York: Basic Books.

Ellis, A.W. and Young, A.W.: 1988, *Human Cognitive Neuropsychology*, Hove and London: Lawrence Erlbaum.

Finney, J.: 1978, *Invasion of the Body Snatchers*, New York: Sphere Books.

Fodor, J.A.: 1983, *The Modularity of Mind*, Cambridge MA: MIT Press.

Franklin, S.: 1988, 'Auditory Comprehension Impairments in Aphasia', in Scherzer, E., Simon, R. and Stark, J. (eds.), *First European Conference on Aphasiology*, Vienna: Austrian Workers' Compensation Board.

Gabrieli, J.D.E., Milberg, W., Keane, M.M. and Corkin, S.: 1990, 'Intact Priming Patterns Despite Impaired Memory', *Neuropsychologia* 2 8 (5), 417–427.

Glisky, E.L., Schacter, D.L. and Tulving, E.: 1986, 'Computer Learning by Memory-Impaired Patients: Acquisition and Retention of Complex Knowledge', *Neuropsychologia* 2 4 (3), 313–328.

Glisky, E.L. and Schacter, D.L.: 1988, 'Long-Term Retention of Computer Learning by Patients with Memory Disorders', *Neuropsychologia* 2 6 (1), 173–178.

Glisky, E.L. and Schacter, D.L.: 1989, 'Extending the Limits of Complex Learning in Organic Amnesia: Computer Training in a Vocational Domain', *Neuropsychologia* 2 7 (1), 107–120.

Gordon, B.: 1988, 'Preserved Learning of Novel Information in Amnesia: Evidence for Multiple Memory Systems', *Brain and Cognition* 7, 257–282.

Graf, P. and Schacter, D.L.: 1985, 'Implicit and Explicit Memory for New Associations in Normal and Amnesic Subjects', *Journal of Experimental Psychology: Learning, Memory, and Cognition* 1 1 (3), 501–518.

Graf, P., Squire, L.R. and Mandler, G.: 1984, 'The Information That Amnesic Patients Do Not Forget', *Journal of Experimental Psychology: Learning, Memory, and Cognition* 1 0 (1), 164–178.

Graves, R.E. and Jones, B.S.: 1991, ''Blindsight' and 'Neglect' in Normal Subjects' (abstract), *Journal of Clinical and Experimental Neuropsychology* 1 3 (1), 76–77.

Hobson, A.J.: 1988, *The Dreaming Brain*, New York: Basic Books.

Howard, D. and Franklin, S.: 1988, *Missing the Meaning? A Cognitive Neuropsychological Study of the Processing of Words by an Aphasic Patient*, Cambridge MA: MIT Press.

Hubel, D.H. and Wiesel, T.N.: 1962, 'Receptive fields, binocular interaction and functional architecture in the cat's visual cortex', *Journal of Physiology* 1 6 0

(London), 106–154.

Jackendoff, R.: 1987, *Consciousness and the Computational Mind*, Cambridge MA: MIT Press.

Karnath, H.O. and Hartje, W.: 1987, 'Residual Information Processing in the Neglected Visual Half-Field', *Journal of Neurology* 2 3 4, 180–184.

Kim, J.: 1984, 'Concepts of Supervenience', *Philosophy and Phenomenological Research* XLV, 153–176.

Kim, J.: 1990, 'Supervenience as a Philosophical Concept', *Metaphilosophy* 2 1, 1–27.

Lockwood, M.: 1989, *Mind, Brain and the Quantum*, Oxford: Basil Blackwell.

Marcel, A.J. and Bisiach, E. (eds.): 1988, *Consciousness in Contemporary Science*, New York: Oxford University Press.

Marr, D.: 1982, *Vision*, San Francisco: Freeman.

Marshall, J.C. and Halligan, P.W.: 1988, 'Blindsight and Insight in Visuo-Spatial Neglect', *Nature* 3 3 6, 766–7.

McAndrews, M.P., Glisky, E.L. and Schacter, D.L.: 1987, 'When Priming Persists: Long-Lasting Implicit Memory for a Single Episode in Amnesic Patients', *Neuropsychologia* 2 5 (3), 497–506.

McGinn, C.: 1983, *The Subjective View*, Oxford: Clarendon.

McGinn, C.: 1989, 'Can We Solve the Mind-Body Problem?', *Mind* XCVII (391), 349–366.

McGinn, C.: 1991, *The Problem of Consciousness*, Oxford: Basil Blackwell.

Milberg, W. and Blumstein, S.E.: 1981, 'Lexical Decision and Aphasia: Evidence for Semantic Processing', *Brain and Language* 1 4, 371–385.

Milberg, W., Blumstein, S. and Dworetzky, B.: 1988, 'Phonological Processing and Lexical Access in Aphasia', *Brain and Language* 3 4, 279–293.

Musen, G. and Treisman, A.: 1990, 'Implicit and Explicit Memory for Visual Patterns', *Journal of Experimental Psychology: Learning, Memory, and Cognition* 1 6 (1), 127–137.

Nagel, T.: 1974, 'What Is It Like to Be a Bat?', *The Philosophical Review* 8 3, 435–450.

Nagel, T.: 1979, 'Subjective and Objective', in Nagel, T., *Mortal Questions*, London: Cambridge University Press.

Nagel, T.: 1986, *The View from Nowhere*, Oxford: Oxford University Press.

Neely, J.M.: 1977, 'Semantic Priming and Retrieval from Lexical Memory: Roles of Inhibitionless Spreading Activation and Limited Capacity Attention', *Journal of Experimental Psychology: General* 1 0 6 (3), 226–254.

Newcombe, F.: 1985, 'Neuropsychology of Consciousness', in Oakley, D.A. (ed.), *Brain and Mind*, London: Methuen.

Newcombe, F., Young, A.W. and DeHaan, E.H.F.: 1989, 'Prosopagnosia and Object Agnosia without Covert Recognition', *Neuropsychologia* 2 7 (2), 179–191.

Nissen, M.J., Willingham, D.W. and Hartman, M.: 1989, 'Explicit and Implicit Remembering: When Is Learning Preserved in Amnesia?', *Neuropsychologia* 2 7 (3), 341–352.

Näätänen, R.: 1990, 'The Role of Attention in Auditory Information Processing as

Revealed by Event-Related Potentials and Other Brain Measures of Cognitive
   Function', *Behavioral and Brain Sciences* 1 3, 201–288.
Paillard, J., Michel, F. and Stelmach, G.: 1983, 'Localization without Content: a
   Tactile Analogue of Blind Sight', *Archives of Neurology* 4 0, 548–551.
Penrose, R.: 1989, *The Emperor's New Mind: Concerning Computers, Minds, and
   the Laws of Physics*, New York: Oxford University Press.
Renault, B., Signoret, J.L., Debruille, B., Breton, F. and Bolgert, F.: 1989, 'Brain
   Potentials Reveal Covert Facial Recognition in Prosopagnosia',
   Neuropsychologia 2 7 (7), 905–912.
Revonsuo, A.: in press, 'Is There a Ghost in the Cognitive Machinery?',
   Philosophical Psychology.
Rizzo, M., Hurtig, R. and Damasio, A.R.: 1987, 'The Role of Scanpaths in Facial
   Recognition and Learning', *Annals of Neurology* 2 2, 41–45.
Rorty, R.: 1982a, 'Comments on Dennett', *Synthese* 5 3, 181–187.
Rorty, R.: 1982b, 'Contemporary Philosophy of Mind', *Synthese* 5 3, 323–348.
Rowlands, M.: 1990, 'Anomalism, Supervenience, and Davidson on Content-
   Individuation', *Philosophia* 2 0, 295–310.
Rowlands, M.: 1991, 'Towards a Reasonable Version of Methodological
   Solipsism', *Mind and Language* 6, 39–57.
Rumelhart, D.E., McClelland, J.L. and the PDP research group: 1986, *Parallel
   Distributed Processing*, Vols. 1 and 2, Cambridge MA: MIT Press.
Schacter, D.L.: 1987, 'Implicit Memory: History and Current Status', *Journal of
   Experimental Psychology: Learning, Memory, and Cognition* 1 3 (3),
   501–518.
Schacter, D.L.: 1990, 'Toward a Cognitive Neuropsychology of Awareness:
   Implicit Knowledge and Anosagnosia', *Journal of Clinical and Experimental
   Neuropsychology* 1 2 (1),155–178.
Schacter, D.L., Cooper, L.A. and Delaney, S.: 1990, 'Implicit Memory for
   Unfamiliar Objects Depends on Access to Structural Descriptions', *Journal of
   Experimental Psychology: General* 1 1 9 (1), 5–24.
Schacter, D.L., McAndrews, M.P. and Moscovitch, M.: 1988, 'Access to
   Consciousness: Dissociations between Implicit and Explicit Knowledge in
   Neuropsychological Syndromes', in Weiskrantz, L. (ed.), *Thought without
   Language*, Oxford: Oxford University Press.
Schacter, D.L., Rapsack, R.Z., Rubens, A.B., Tharan, M. and Laguna, J.: 1990,
   'Priming Effects in a Letter-by-Letter Reader Depend upon Access to the Word-
   Form System', *Neuropsychologia* 2 8, 1079–1094.
Searle, J.R.: 1979, 'What Is an Intentional State?', *Mind* 8 8, 72–94.
Searle, J.R.: 1980, 'Minds, Brains, and Programs', *The Behavioral and Brain
   Sciences* 3, 417–457.
Searle, J.R.: 1984a, 'Intentionality and Its Place in Nature', *Synthese* 6 1, 3–16.
Searle, J.R.: 1984b, *Minds, Brains and Science*, Cambridge MA: Harvard
   University Press.
Searle, J.R.: 1987, 'Minds and Brains Without Programs'. in Blakemore, C. and
   Greenfield, S. (eds.), *Mindwaves*, Oxford: Basil Blackwell.
Searle, J.R.: 1988, 'The Realistic Stance', *Behavioral and Brain Sciences* 1 1,

527–529.
Searle, J.R.: 1989, 'Consciousness, Unconsciousness, and Intentionality', *Philosophical Topics* 1 8, 193–209.
Searle, J.R.: 1990, 'Consciousness, Explanatory Inversion and Cognitive Science', *Behavioral and Brain Sciences* 1 3, 585–642.
Shallice, T.: 1988, *From Neuropsychology to Mental Structure*, New York: Cambridge University Press.
Shallice, T.: 1991, Précis of *From Neuropsychology to Mental Structure* (with Commentary), *Behavioral and Brain Sciences* 1 4, 429–469.
Shoemaker, S.: 1982, 'The Inverted Spectrum', *Journal of Philosophy* 7 9, 357–381.
Sloman, A.: 1991, 'Why Consciousness Is Not Worth Talking About?', *Paper presented at The Second International Colloquium on Cognitive Science*, San Sebastian, Spain.
Squires, E.: 1990, *Conscious Mind in the Physical World*, Bristol and New York: Adam Hilger.
Stich, S.P.: 1983, *From Folk Psychology to Cognitive Science*, Cambridge MA: MIT Press.
Tranel, D. and Damasio, A.R.: 1985, 'Knowledge without Awareness: An Autonomic Index of Facial Recognition by Prosopagnosics', *Science* 2 2 8, 1453–1454.
Tranel, D. and Damasio, A.R.: 1988, 'Non-Conscious Face Recognition in Patients with Face Agnosia', *Behavioural Brain Research* 3 0, 235–249.
Tulving, E.: 1987, 'Multiple Memory Systems and Consciousness', *Human Neurobiology* 6, 67–80.
Van Gulick, R.: 1988a, 'A Functionalist Plea for Self-Consciousness', *The Philosophical Review* XCVII (2), 149–181.
Van Gulick, R.: 1988b, 'Consciousness, Intrinsic Intentionality, and Self-Understanding Machines', in Marcel, A.J. and Bisiach, E. (eds.), *Consciousness in Contemporary Science*, New York: Oxford University Press.
Van Gulick, R.: 1989, 'What Difference Does Consciousness Make?', *Philosophical Topics* XVII (1), 211–230.
Velmans, M.: 1990, 'Consciousness, Brain, and the Physical World', *Philosophical Psychology* 3, 77–99.
Velmans, M.: 1991, 'Is Human Information Processing Conscious?' (with Commentary), *Behavioral and Brain Sciences* 1 4, 651–726.
Volpe, B.T., LeDoux, J.E. and Gazzaniga, M.S.: 1979, 'Information Processing of Visual Stimuli in an Extinguished Field', *Nature* 2 8 2, 722–724.
Weiskrantz, L.: 1980, 'Varieties of Residual Experience', *Quarterly Journal of Experimental Psychology* 3 2, 365–386.
Weiskrantz, L.: 1987, 'Residual Vision in a Scotoma: A Follow-Up Study of 'Form' Discrimination', *Brain* 1 1 0, 77–92.
Weiskrantz, L.: 1988, 'Some Contributions of Neuropsychology of Vision and Memory to the Problem of Consciousness', in Marcel, A.J. and Bisiach, E. (eds.), *Consciousness in Contemporary Science*, New York: Oxford University Press.

Wilkes, K.V.: 1984, 'Is Consciousness Important?', *British Journal for the Philosophy of Science* **3** 5, 223–243.

Wilkes, K.V.: 1988, ' —, Yíshí, Duh, Um, and Consciousness', in Marcel, A.J. and Bisiach, E. (eds.), *Consciousness in Contemporary Science*, New York: Oxford University Press.

Wilkes, K.V.: 1989, 'Mind and Body', *Key Themes in Philosophy: Royal Institute of Philosophy Lecture Series* **2** 4, 69–83.

Young, A.W.: 1988, 'Functional Organization of Visual Recognition', in Weiskrantz, L. (ed.), *Thought without Language*, Oxford: Oxford University Press.

Young, A.W. and DeHaan, E.H.F.: 1990, 'Impairments of Visual Awareness', *Mind and Language* **5** (1), 29–48.

Young, A.W.: 1992, 'Neuropsychology of Awareness', *Paper presented at the International Symposium on Consciousness*, University of Turku, Finland.

Young, A.W., Hellawell, D. and DeHaan, E.H.F.: 1988, 'Cross-Domain Semantic Priming in Normal Subjects and a Prosopagnosic Patient', *The Quarterly Journal of Experimental Psychology* **4 0 A** (3), 561–580.

Young, A.W., Newcombe, F., Hellawell, D. and DeHaan, E.: 1989, 'Implicit Access to Semantic Information', *Brain and Cognition* **1** 1, 186–209.

Zeki, S.: 1990, 'Colour Vision and Functional Specialization in the Visual Cortex', *Discussions in Neuroscience* **6**, 11–61.

Zohar, D.: 1990, *The Quantum Self*, London: Fontana, Flamingo Paperbacks.

PART II

COGNITIVE SCHEMATA

COGNITIVE SCHEMATA

This part addresses methodological and philosophical questions involved in cultural anthropology, utilizing the recent developments in cognitive studies. Cognitivism, conceived as a general approach in cultural anthropology, aims at explaining behaviour by means of the processes of cognitive systems. Two explanatory strategies may be distinguished: intentional explanation of behaviour, and structural explanation by means of cognitive schemata. Of these two strategies, the structural explanation is of vital interest in cultural anthropology, and accordingly it is treated more extensively here. The notion of rationality will play a central role in both explanatory strategies. Intentional explanation assumes that the system's dynamics are lawful and intelligible; structural explanation assumes that the schemata involved in steering the dynamics are built upon some simple rules.

5. INTENTIONAL EXPLANATION

Cultural anthropology, and especially its subdiscipline cognitive anthropology, is ultimately based on folk psychology. It construes human behaviour as a product of a cognitive system that consists of interacting cognitive states (cf. Dougherty 1985; Holland and Quinn 1987). Cognitive states like beliefs and desires are compound entities made up of psychological modes and mental representations. Cognitive processes are interactions among cognitive states. Cognitive states are identified on semantic grounds, that is, their propositional contents are identified on the basis of what they refer to (in some possible world). Cognitive states are thus intentional in the classic phenomenological sense. It is common to call the explanations that refer to cognitive states "intentional explanations". Intentional explanations hypothesize that the cognitive states of persons and of other cognitive systems interact causally to produce behaviour. Another explanatory strategy that exploits the model of the cognitive system is structural explanation. It aims at the identification and reconstruction of clustered mental representations, or cognitive schemata (D'Andrade 1990; Shweder 1991).

Let us look at the intentional strategy first. In cognitive and cultural anthropology, economics and history, to explain why a person did X it suffices to refer to his cognitive states: he did X because he believed that it would help him to attain something he desired. Or to explain why a person believes that P: he had two more beliefs, "Q" and "Q supports P", and these two beliefs interacted to produce the belief that P. The interplay of desires exemplifies so-called practical reason, and the latter exemplifies theoretical reason. Practical reason starts from given beliefs and desires and terminates in new desires or action intention, whereas theoretical reason operates on given beliefs to produce new beliefs. This terminology of "theoretical and practical reason" is common in cognitivist philosophy, whereas in cognitive and cultural anthropology and psychology, it is more common to talk about "representational and operational rules" instead. In any case, the commonsense model of the cognitive system that lies behind the various branches of cognitivism can be depicted as follows:

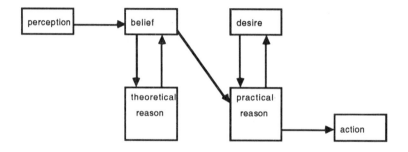

Fig 1. The commonsense model of cognitive system.

In this figure the psychological modes of perception, belief, desire and action are represented, as well as the two varieties of reasoning. The arrows stand for the flow of ideas, or mental representations. This is the paradigmatic model of intentional explanation. As we move towards the microstructure of cognition, and open up the mechanisms hidden in the black boxes of the above model, the intentional explanation loses its intuitive appeal. We shall make a short digression into sub-personal cognition. The intuitive difference between the personal and the sub-personal levels is that within the former, there is conscious access to the representations, whereas in the sub-personal level such access is missing. Moreover, locating psychological modes in the sub-personal level is always bound to be more or less metaphorical. Sub-personal units "understand" or "desire" only in some metaphorical sense since they do not experience anything. How are these personal and sub-personal levels of cognitive systems related? The accepted view is that the personal level complex system can be analyzed into a collection of sub-personal processors or production rules. We will return to the problem of analytical explanation in Chapter 8.

Intentional explanation is paradigmatically used in explaining personal level actions and cognitive dynamics, mainly beliefs and valuations. Intentional explanation is rarely seen as an independent or useful explanatory strategy in cultural anthropology. This is because it spells out what is assumed to be true in any case, namely, that people have beliefs and desires and they act in accordance with prudence and rationality. However, intentional explanation is typically present in every cultural anthropological account, even though it is not clearly stated. An ethnographic description of a society, for example, which aims at documenting most of its cultural entities and social activities, assumes that the people in that community have shared beliefs, normal desires, and are able to perform proper cost/benefit calculations. Or, a historical account of some past society assumes that the members were intelligent and reasonable enough to survive for a certain period of time. There are cases of exotic, apparently irrational beliefs and actions, and these cases question the sufficiency of the intentional explanation. By the same token, they point towards the structural explanation. Exotic minds are found both in anthropology and neuropsychology.

5.1. Exotic minds in anthropology

The tough cases for intentional explanation can be put into different groups according to their respective levels of exoticness. Exoticness is assumed to be relative to some categorization K (presumably ours) that cuts the world into entities.

> *Mildly exotic beliefs*. The informant has a belief concerning a mechanism which does not exist in the categorization K, but the type or kind of which could exist. For example, he believes that one's health status results from the balance of hot and cold substances in the body. Here the anthropologist can easily identify (and begin to understand) the cognitive state in question since he can picture what the object of belief would look like and act like.

> *Drastically exotic beliefs.* The informant has a belief concerning a type of entity which could not exist in the categorization K. For example, he believes that a spirit residing in a plant cured his headache.

In cultural anthropology, the cases of drastically exotic beliefs are indeed common. Intentional explanation is not sufficient for most cases. What is needed is the construction of the functional roles of the belief in question. That is, the target belief is related to the surrounding system of beliefs, desires and other cognitive states. The functional network becomes the vehicle of explanation. There is a methodological rule in cultural anthropology: a belief, exotic or not, should be contextualized into a larger system. Prima facie, there should not be such things as unexplainably exotic beliefs. This strategy applies also to the mildly exotic beliefs – their meaning is determined by means of identifying the surrounding cognitive states. That is, they are related to a structure of other beliefs, and by the same token we have moved into structural explanation. Another point worth noting is that human communities can afford more exotic theories than exotic practices. There are no canoe-using communities that make a hole in a canoe before they go canoeing. The common sense world is common to all humans (Smith 1991).

> *Exotic reasoning.* The informant forms his beliefs by means of inductive rules that deviate from the rule of high probability; or the informant does not utilize experimental manipulation in order to find out the causal dependencies. The exotic pieces of reasoning could be identified by means of treating them as if they were black boxes and relating them with their inputs and outputs. Thus the anthropologist's task of understanding the exotic could go on.

> *Exotic rationality.* The informant's behavior is irrelevant with respect to true beliefs, nourishment and cost/benefit calculations. A cognitive system of this type would cease to exist in any dynamic environment. The minimum requirements of rationality are assumed to prevail universally. There are no lasting irrational human communities (cf. Rescher 1988).

Another set of problematic cases for intentional explanation contains sub-personal oddities where the ascription of beliefs or other normal cognitive states is questionable.

5.2. Exotic minds in neuropsychology[1]

In neuropsychology, we encounter peculiar minds, the function of which has been distorted in some strange way after brain damage. In some of these cases, intentional explanation of the patient's behaviour becomes problematic, which challenges certain presuppositions embedded in the "intentional stance" (Dennett 1987). Here we shall be concerned with two different kinds of patients: those possessing a so-called "split-brain", and those exhibiting implicit knowledge in their behaviour.

The cerebral hemispheres of split-brain patients have been separated from each other by sectioning the corpus callosum and other commissures that normally combine the hemispheres. Usually this has been done in order to tame an unbearably violent epilepsy. After the operation the patient usually recovers well and nothing unusual can be noticed in his everyday behaviour.

However, in controlled laboratory tests split-brain patients manifest surprising dissociations of mental processes. A standard experimental setting is something like this: the patient is asked to fixate his gaze onto the center of a screen. After that, two words are briefly flashed on the screen so that one of them is to the left of the patient's fixating point, and the other is to the right. The exposure time is so short that it is impossible for the subject to scan the words with several fixations. Thus, it is ensured that from the left visual field, information goes only to the right hemisphere and from the right visual field, to the left – the projection areas are always in the contralateral sides of the brain (Gazzaniga and LeDoux 1978).

Let us suppose that the flashed words were PINE-APPLE. Now, if the subject is asked what he saw, he answers that he saw the word APPLE. The language-production mechanisms are in most people exclusively in the left hemisphere – hence, that hemisphere has only seen APPLE. No matter how you question him, you get no answers which would reveal that he had any awareness whatsoever about PINE or PINEAPPLE. Nonetheless, if the patient is asked to point with his left hand – which is exclusively controlled by the right hemisphere – to what he saw, he will point to a picture of a pine-tree, if the other choices are apple and pineapple. It seems then, that we have one subject fully aware of the concept of apple, one fully aware of the concept of pine, and no subject who has seen the word pineapple (Marks 1981).

Some patients do have crude linguistic capacities also in their right hemispheres. When the separated hemispheres were asked the same questions, they did not give identical answers. One patient, when asked which job he

---

[1] This section was contributed by Antti Revonsuo.

would choose, responded with his left hemisphere "draughtsman", but, by contrast, the right chose "automobile race". Findings like this have led to controversy concerning the unity of mind, and it has been suggested that the patients possess two independent conscious minds, although competing interpretations also exist, counting the patient's minds differently (Gazzaniga 1988; Gazzaniga and LeDoux 1978; LeDoux et al. 1977; Gazzaniga et al. 1977; Marks 1981).

A different kind of neuropsychological curiosity is so-called implicit knowledge. Since we have given a rather extensive treatment of this matter in Chapter 3, we will only briefly remind ourselves of the basic principles. In general, neuropsychological patients are typically unable to perform certain cognitive operations, although some others might be spared. Thus, we may have patients who are selectively impaired in recognizing objects (agnosia), understanding speech (Wernicke's aphasia), visual perception (cortical blindness), facial recognition (prosopagnosia), awareness of the left side of space (neglect), remembering recent events (amnesia), and so on.

Therefore, when asked to use his impaired function, the patient fails disastrously. Also his everyday behaviour reflects his inabilities. Nevertheless, when the same impaired cognitive operations are tested implicitly, that is, in a way which requires indirect use of the impaired function, some of the patients perform surprisingly well, sometimes normally. The patient's performance, his reaction times, electric brain potentials or skin conductance reveal that despite the overt inability and loss of ability, the required information does anyhow reside somewhere inside the brain.

Now, we may ask, how can we apply intentional descriptions to the behaviour of these patients. It seems that both the split brain patient and the one with implicit knowledge behave in ambiguous ways, from the point of view of the interpreter. It seems that at time t, we have an intentional system S, which contains two further intentional systems, S* and S#. The former system believes that or has the mental content p, whereas the latter believes or has the mental content not-p. How to resolve this problem?

We have two opposite solutions. There are those, most notably Dennett (1987), who think that intentional explanation is all in the eye of the beholder. Interpreting intentional behaviour is, for Dennett and other instrumentalists, not like finding out an absolute truth about which we could be right or wrong. There simply is no truth about what a system really believes; there are no beliefs inside the head which we have to discover. We can choose to interpret its beliefs in any way we want, since the beliefs only have an existence in our interpretations of the system, not in the system itself. Interpreting the mental contents of systems is, according to this view, like watching clouds: no fundamental problems appear if you see a cloud as a face, somebody else as an aeroplane or a dolphin. We do not have to ask the ontological question "how can one and the same thing be a face, an aeroplane and a dolphin", because the cloud of course really is none of them but just an ordinary cloud. Analogously, the intentional system – in this case the neuropsychological patient – really believes nothing: the patient has no unambiguous mental content independently of our interpretations.

For a realist, however, the matter cannot be brushed under the carpet quite so straightforwardly. It sounds, to say the least, rather counterintuitive to claim that people in general do not have any definitive mental contents independently of intentional interpretations. For a realist, there must be one description which corresponds to the true mental state that the person is entertaining. In these problematic cases, then, we must have some principled way to tell what these patients are really experiencing. It seems to us that we can designate consciousness as that property which distinguishes between the real, ongoing mental states from other outputs of the organism which can be interpreted as having mental contents, but which, in reality, totally lack them.

This strategy can easily be applied to patients with implicit knowledge, since in such cases it is quite clear which outputs are the consequences of willful, adaptive behaviour and which just reflect some automatic processes going on in the brain. The case of the split-brain patient calls for a more unconventional solution. It seems obvious that both hemispheres, when observed in isolation, are capable of "willful" and adaptive behaviour, and as their responses seem to be based on conceptual and cross-modality, conscious understanding, we are left with the hypothesis that we really have two independent intentional and conscious systems, which can entertain separate and genuine mental states simultaneously, independently of each other. Only if it were shown that one hemisphere is totally unconscious could we determine a single mental content, but as it stands, we must allow for two.

These cases involve, once again, the controversy between intrinsic and as-if intentionality. However, they illustriously demonstrate that intentional interpretation is based on common sense functionalism, which carries with it certain assumptions concerning the rationality and the unity of the person. It would be quite consistent with the data to claim that, in fact, neuropsychological patients are only suffering from a strange syndrome of untruthfulness, in other words, that they are all pathological liars! They just want to confuse the poor researchers with their malevolent stories of not seeing or being able to recognize the stimuli. They also become ingenious actors, and they can hardly contain their laughter when the fool neurologists buy it all. After all, one of the first studies of implicit knowledge in prosopagnosia was carried out using the so-called Guilty Knowledge Test – the same technique that is sometimes used in criminal investigations, where involuntary physiological signs are sought for when stimuli related to the crime are presented (Bauer 1984). Another way of interpreting these cases against folk-psychology would be to say that, well, those guys can just believe two opposite things at the same time, and that's it. Or that they can keep many separate thought-streams going on in their consciousness simultaneously; no problem.

So, it seems that we do not want to give up folk psychology, since we know from our own case that believing opposite beliefs simultaneously is extremely difficult, in fact, it is impossible. We also know that a multitude of streams of consciousness has not occurred in our own mind and it is difficult to even imagine, how it could be the case for anybody. Neuropsychologists, on the other hand, would have a hard time trying to explain all those diverse forms of brain-injury by referring to sudden pathological untruthfulness and brilliant abilities to act as though suffering from real deficits.

The existence of these cases calls into question the division of the intentional system into the system-level and the sub-personal level. It seems, namely, that not all the sub-personal parts are as devoid of mental contents as others. For example, the Conscious Awareness System (Schacter 1990; see above, Chapter 3) is a sub-personal system, the functioning of which is the necessary and sufficient condition for conscious experience to occur. Thus, the property of consciousness is manifested at the sub-personal level and not only at the personal level.

6. STRUCTURAL EXPLANATION

The object of explanation in intentional explanations is typically a type of action (that he did X) or a single cognitive state (that he believes that P and Q). Explanations of basic actions and of mental acts like judgments or occurrent beliefs have served as exemplars of intentional explanation thanks to their simple structure and prominence in the personal level of psychological modes and conscious access. Yet in cultural and cognitive anthropology, it is typically a piece or a pattern of exotic behaviour, a system of beliefs, a text or some other cultural entity that requires explanation. In these cases neither theoretical nor practical reason is utilized as the explanatory ground. Reference to a processor or rule does not suffice either. Instead, a structured collection of representations functions as the explanatory premise. A structured collection is a system of representations. The terms "cognitive schema", "belief system", "cognitive map", "script", "cognitive model", "frame", "cultural model", and "mental model" have been used to designate this systematic collection of interrelated representations. We shall assume the term "cognitive schema" and name the corresponding explanation structural explanation (see also Casson 1983).

Structural explanation utilizes three, usually complementary, strategies, the first of which is structural explanation proper, while the other two are general systematization tools applied along with the first one:

> *Explanation by design*: Whenever the object of explanation is a complex entity consisting of multiple parts (a system), look for a design or a model (another system) which is isomorphic with the explanandum. This other system is the cognitive schema. The isomorphism is not usually one-to-one, but rather the schema is an abstraction or a formal representation of the object of explanation.

> *Integrative explanation*: Whenever the object of explanation appears to be a part of a larger structured whole, look for those relations that make up this larger whole.

> *Analytical explanation*. Whenever the object of explanation is a complex entity, open up its structure and try to identify its components.

Cultural entities like texts, buildings, jokes, human behaviour, beliefs, and belief systems are good candidates for structural explanation. In any reasonable theory of culture, the existence and individuation of cultural entities is dependent upon some cognitive phenomena – mental representations and their systems, or cognitive schemata, for short. In what follows we will have mainly the explanation by design in mind when talking about structural explanation. Integrative and analytical explanations are widely used in various fields of research – they are the general tools of cognitive systematization, and thus they are not confined to the study of cognitive schemata. Indeed, the example of analytical explanation discussed in Chapter 8 will be an explanation of rationality.

Structural explanation shares some domain with three other important theoretical strategies in cultural anthropology: textualization, hermeneutics, and structural anthropology (see Piaget 1970). Textualization is an explanatory strategy in which all cultural entities are treated as if they were texts, that is, created things with syntactic structure (or grammar) and semantic interpretation. Textualization enables the anthropologist to read the whole cultural material without having to distinguish between first-hand texts (for example, written samples or interviews) and second-hand texts (for example, rituals or visits to a supermarket). Textualization formalizes cultural entities in the sense that it substitutes their abstract properties for them. Such a procedure is of course one step towards identifying a mental model. In paradigmatic cultural studies (folkloristics, literary theory), textualization or formalization as such is a respectable explanatory goal. Formalization aims at spelling out the meaning of the text (or rather, one of various meanings implicated in the text). Hermeneutics is traditionally known as the general method of identifying and decoding meanings. The process of interpretation, in which we start with the text and end up with its meaning, is guided by a set of hermeneutic rules. Thus hermeneutics steers the formalization (assuming that the species of meaning we are looking for is the one accessible by means of this method). To put it in general terms, formal interpretation works on an entity that has (consensually agreed-upon) properties P_1, P_2, ... , P_n. Formalization aims at characterizing a group of higher-order properties F_1, F_2, ... , F_m, each of which is a function of some group of P_i's. Thus a formal interpretation of an entity quantifies over its base properties, generating a family of higher-order properties. These, in turn, can be quantified over, producing a more abstract or formal interpretation. The base properties P_i are typically apparent or evident to all the members of the social discourse in question, whereas the higher-order properties are accessible to a chosen few only. Accordingly, the meaning of the entity is accessible only to those who can recognize correct higher-order properties. Cultural entities themselves pose very few restrictions upon their interpretation: anything complex enough can be interpreted to mean anything else. The entity must have enough base properties for a sensible quantification to take place. Cultural studies textbooks contain numerous references to the hermeneutic principles of interpretation, yet they are seldom explicated. Symmetry, opposition, repetition, containment, boundedness, beginning, ending, substance, attribute, relationship, and so on, are among the most often quoted hermeneutic principles. A promising working hypothesis is that principles of interpretation are reducible to claims concerning the composition and structure of cognitive schemata.

Structural anthropology (Lévi-Strauss 1963) aims at identifying the formal properties of cultural entities, most notably of myths. In the first volume of his *Mythologiques, The Raw and the Cooked* (1969), Lévi-Strauss gives us a convenient list of those formal properties, or principles of interpretation, that he employs in the study of myths: transformation, analogy, contrast, congruence, non-congruence, identity, difference, isomorphism, to name a few. These properties are assumed to exist in the myths as well as in the human minds that generated the myths in question.

In structural explanation, the explanandum is inferred from the schema by utilizing only a minimal amount of processing rules. The burden of explanation in the structural strategy is on the structured cognitive schema, not on the devices that process or manipulate the schema and its constituents. Thus, structural explanation differs significantly from intentional explanation, in which the representations themselves can be quite simple and the burden of explanation is on the processing rules.

As was noted above, at times structural explanation consists solely in identifying an abstract or formal structure in the explanandum. The schema is assumed to exist (or rather subsist) in the Platonic realm of pure forms, and a successful schema-identification (or interpretation) confirms the assumption concerning the abstract way of being of formal structures. This is particularly true of humanistically oriented cultural studies. Cognitivism, on the contrary, locates the cognitive schemata in the minds of individual human beings and in the social reality of interacting individuals. It is worth noting, as an aside, that the Platonic realm of ideas is not radically different from what is called social or cultural reality. The latter notion assumes that concepts cannot exist without sentient organisms, whereas the former does not make this assumption.

7. THE COGNITIVE SCHEMA

Thus far, we have argued for the hypothesis that structural explanation of cultural entities makes use of formal structures. Let us now proceed to examine the question of whether these formal structures are collections of representations. That is, we need to know if there exists a meeting point for two species of cognitive schemata; those that reside in cultural entities, especially texts, and those that reside in cognitive systems, most notably in culturally competent human beings. In order to answer this question we need first to investigate the role of cognitive schemata in cognitive systems. Mental representations are processed by the cognitive system. Processes take

place when the system executes the inferences that terminate in new
representations. In the case of the human cognitive system, some of these
representations are treated as perceptions, beliefs, desires, or actions. They are
manipulated in specific ways when they are within each of these different
psychological modes. It is reasonable to hypothesize that representations do
not operate in isolation from one another, but are clustered into systems of
representations, or cognitive schemata. At first sight, there are interesting
differences among these cognitive schemata. Some schemata are more stable
than others. Some are specific to an individual or to a situation, some are
culture-bound and shared by a group of people. Yet some are best seen as
universally shared cognitive schemata, species-specific clusters of
representations that are not relative to any historical context. What are the
functions of cognitive schemata? How do they manifest themselves? First of
all, they constrain the interactions between representations, since they are the
structures into which representations are hooked. Secondly, they constrain the
contents of some representations because they provide the Kantian
transcendental conditions of experience. Thirdly, they manifest themselves in
thinking and doing, in theoretical reasoning and practical action.

Characterizations of cognitive schemata abound in the current literature.
Before scrutinizing them, we will propose a preliminary characterization,
based on the assumption that cognitive schemata should fulfill the three tasks
above. A schema is a system of representations. Thus it is a mental entity,
and it is a system. As a system it has a composition (its parts) and a structure
(the relations that connect the parts together). A schema can be pictured as a
network in which the nodes stand for representations and the links stand for
relations. A schema can be incorporated into another schema, and a complex
schema can be partitioned into several subschemata. The schema interacts
with the cognitive system: the system (or its parts) processes the parts of the
schema, and the structure of the schema constrains the way this processing
actually happens. There is a trade-off between the complexity of the schema
and the complexity or the processing power of the system. The more complex
cognitive schemata are more self-steering, and the processors needed can be
less intelligent.

The cognitive schema is made up of mental representations, that is, of
mental entities that denote objects or "point beyond themselves". Mental
representations can be compared to linguistic representations like names,
predicate terms and sentences. Mental representations designate constructs like
individual concepts, predicates and propositions. These, in turn, refer to
extramental objects like things, properties, and situations. In cultural

anthropology it is a common and relatively harmless shortcut to treat representations and conceptual constructs alike. Yet, strictly speaking, representations are mental, that is, factual objects, whereas constructs are conceptual objects. The shortcut is not dangerous since each representation exemplifies a construct and constructs can be seen as classes of mental representations. We will endorse the anthropological tradition and view representations as tokens of constructs.

Now that we have a preliminary characterization of cognitive schemata available, let us proceed to formulate the questions that any account of cognitive schemata should address:

> *—The question of nodes*: What is the composition of cognitive schemata? Are mental representations concepts (individual concepts or predicates) or propositions, or can we leave the question open and just go on talking about representations? Do they refer to things, properties or situations, or just entities? Furthermore, do cognitive schemata involve pictorial representations (non-conceptual or non-propositional parts)?

> *The question of links*: What is the structure of cognitive schemata? What kinds of relations connect the representations into a system? The problem of links is predisposed towards a reductive answer, one that would provide a manageable, small set of links. The number of potential links is enormous – just think of the multitude of relations that is cognized by human beings.

These questions are of course interrelated, since the choice of composition affects the possible range of structures. The final answers are not given a priori, but certain choices must be made before the empirical study of cognitive schemata can even begin. These choices should be the grounds for reasonable hypotheses. Depending on the level of analysis and on the task in hand, the representations can be construed as concepts, propositions, or pictorial representations. The prima facie problem with pictorial (non-conceptual) representations is that they are difficult to connect with concepts and propositions that are the default form of linguistic representation. In other words, there are no suitable relations that could connect mental pictures with mental words. We will return to the problem of pictorial representations or image schemata later. The structure of cognitive schemata is made up of the relations that connect the representations into a system. The task that faces a theory of cognitive schemata is to characterize a set of basic relations. The various phenomena encountered in the field of cultural anthropology should be accounted for by means of these relations. That is, the data should be rendered intelligible in terms of the cognitive schemata that are constructible from the set of basic relations.

The set of distinct representations is not restricted. A representation may denote any conceivable entity whatsoever. The only restriction is that they should conform to specified formal conditions, that is, that they are individual concepts, predicates, or propositions. The most economic answer to the question concerning the composition of cognitive schemata is that the representations denote entities. It is an economic solution because we cognize the world in one way or another, that is, as entities. When the task is a specific one, for example, analyzing stories or interviews, it is more profitable to look for propositions, that is, units of mental representations that denote situations, and their interrelations. A specific task calls for a specific entity, for example, a situation. With regard to the second question, that of the structure of cognitive schemata, one may propose that the crucial theoretical figure is that of dependence. Entities are dependent upon other entities, and the principal task of model analysis is to find out how people cognize complex entities that consist of interdependent entities. Barry Smith and his collaborators have proposed dependence as the unique link between entities (Smith 1982). There is a trade-off between the amount of links and the amount of nodes. Limiting to one link only necessitates a large number of different types of entities: substances, attributes, relations, aspects, extensive parts, intensive parts or moments, and so on. Next we will look at some prominent characterizations of cognitive schemata and related concepts.

7.1. The structure of thought

William James gave a lucid description of cognitive schemata that shape experience. His fundamental idea was that thoughts make up a larger whole, the stream of thought, which gives a kind of frame of reference for the study of any individual thought. The stream of thought, or the fact that "thought goes on", is immediately given to our introspection.

First of all, thought is constantly changing. The thoughts and feelings that make up the stream of thought are in a sense unique; no state of consciousness "once gone can recur and be identical with what it was before" (James 1950 Vol. 1, 230; e.r.). Objects of thought can remain the same, but each time they are viewed in a slightly different context, from a slightly different viewpoint. Objects of thought are discrete and we have names for each of them, but the stream of thought puts the objects in contexts, in which their clear-cut boundaries are lost:

And the thought by which we cognize it is the thought of it-in-those-relations, a thought suffused with the consciousness of all that dim context. (James 1950 Vol. 1, 233)

As our experience accumulates, we change, and our thought cannot remain the same. In the quote above the crucially important point is that the objects of thought are not cognized as 'bare substantive things', but rather as nodes in networks, in which they are linked to many other things.

Secondly, thought is sensibly continuous. Even when interrupted by sleep or loss of consciousness, thoughts are experienced as continuous, as belonging to the same consciousness. This readily follows from the first characteristic – thoughts are personal. But the transitions between thoughts (of different objects) are smooth and continuous as well. Thoughts are linked to each other by means of mechanisms that constitute the stream of thought, that give consciousness its structure. James describes the experience of hearing a sound of thunder after a period of silence:

Into the awareness of the thunder itself the awareness of the previous silence creeps and continues; for what we hear when the thunder crashes is not thunder *pure*, but thunder-breaking-upon-silence-and-contrasting-with-it. (James 1950 Vol. 1, 240)

Thoughts are intertwined, mixed with each other. And since the world is experienced through the stream of thought, the world itself is cognized as a system of interconnected things. A thought never apprehends just one thing, but a multitude of items:

We name our thoughts simply, each after its thing, as if each knew its own thing and nothing else. What each really knows is clearly the thing it is named for, with dimly perhaps of thousand other things. (James 1950 Vol. 1, 241)

Things are thought of in the contexts in which they are linked with other things. Our thinking tends to concentrate on the substantial individual things, and tends to leave the relationships among individual things unnoticed. James proposes that there are mental entities for cognizing the relationships, too. The stream of thought contains two types of parts, substantive and transitive. The substantive parts know the individual, thingish objects, whereas the transitive parts know the relationships between objects. The transitive parts are responsible for the feature of thought discussed above, namely that objects are endowed with links that situate them in contexts. According to James, the substantive parts in the stream of thought have not been questioned in mainstream philosophy, but the transitive parts have rarely been acknowledged. Yet they play an important role in giving the object its context, and thought its experienced contituity. James claims that:

> If there be such things as feelings at all, then surely as relations between objects exist in *rerum natura*, so surely, and more surely, do feelings exist to which these relations are known. (James 1950 Vol. 1, 245; e.r.)

An instance of a transitive part of the stream of thought is the feeling of tendency, or fringe. The fringe of an object is the schematic structure of consciousness. The fringe "is part of the object cognized, – substantive qualities and things appearing to the mind in a fringe of relations" (James 1950 Vol. 1, 258, fn; e.r.). The fringe of an object furnishes our thought with

> ... the sense of its relations, near and remote, the dying echo of whence it came to us, the dawning sense of whither it is to lead. The significance, the value, of the image is all in this halo or penumbra that surrounds and escorts it. (James 1950 Vol. 1, 255)

A page later it is called "the halo of felt relations". Together with the substantive parts of the stream of thought this feature amounts to a beautiful system of nodes and links. Thus the very basic workings of the stream of thought are structured such that they assume the presence of cognitive schemata. The stream of thought is dominated by changing topics, with reference to which the cognitive schemata are constructed. The potential components (nodes) are integrated into the model or rejected from it on the basis of how their fringe, the halo of felt relations, suits the topic:

> Relation, then, to our topic of interest is constantly felt in the fringe, and particularly the relation of harmony and discord, of furtherance or hindrance of the topic. (James 1950 Vol. 1, 259)

A thought is accepted as a schema component in the stream of thought "provided we only feel it to have a place in the scheme of relations" (James 1950 Vol. 1, 259). It fits in, provided it is in harmony with the topic or the dominant thought: "The most important element of the fringes is ... the mere feeling of harmony or discord" (James 1950 Vol. 1, 261). Jamesian cognitive schemata are thus constructed of nodes and links so that their structure is constrained by the search for harmony and the avoidance of discord. The formal and functional nature of thought is emphasized by James. He compares the stream of thought with algebra, where the sequence of terms "is fixed by their relations rather than by their several values" (James 1950 Vol. 1, 271).

The constituents of cognitive schemata, as we will see, are endowed with meanings only in a larger whole: "It is *internodal* consciousness, giving us the sense of continuity, but having no significance apart from its mere gap-filling function" (James 1950 Vol. 1, 265, fn). The formal model is instantiated in the actually occurrent thought, the type is tokened, and the formal nodes are filled with rich representations: "the thinker in words must let his concluding word or phrase be translated into its full sensible-image-value, under penalty of the thought being left unrealized and pale" (James 1950 Vol. 1, 271).

James readily accepts that the stream of thought may contain both propositional and pictorial elements, or both words and images. But the question is: "Can the halo, fringe or scheme in which we feel the words to lie be the same as that in which we feel the images to lie?" (James 1950 Vol. 1, 260). The felt relations among the words are parallel to those among images:

... *qua* thought, *qua* sensations *understood*, the words have contracted by long association fringes of mutual repugnance or affinity with each other and with the conclusion, which run exactly parallel with like fringes in the visual, tactile and other ideas. (James 1950 Vol. 1, 261)

The fringe thus turns the object into a schema which consists of nodes and links. It is a part of the object cognized, which is a mental entity. Hence, James proposed that there are structures in experience. In modern cognitivist theories, these structures are called cognitive schemata, frames, models, scripts, and so on.

7.2. Frames

Marvin Minsky introduced the concept of frame in his influental paper 'A Framework for Representing Knowledge' (1975). He characterizes it as follows:

A frame is a sort of skeleton, somewhat like an application form with many blanks or slots to be filled. We'll call these blanks its terminals; we use them as connection points to which we can attach other kinds of information. (Minsky 1986, 245)

Frames are activated in perception, thinking, and in other cognitive activities, and they supply the cognizer with the context that surrounds the cognized object, or the cognized aspect of the object. For example, a chair-frame, a table-frame, and a person-frame are all activated when you get a glimpse of a person sitting behind a table. The frames bring it about that you expect him to be a normal person with two legs and all the rest, and also that he is sitting on a chair with so-and-so many legs, possibly armrests, and so on. Frames comprise default assumptions about the world; without structured and interrelated assumptions, or frames, "the world would simply make no sense" (Minsky 1986, 247). Minsky's frames are suitable for the analysis of experience. A person sitting in a chair is experienced as having legs, and so on.

7.3. Schemata in the perceptual cycle

Ulric Neisser (1976) proposes that schemata are involved in every aspect of human behaviour. Not only doing, but also perceiving and thinking utilize schemata. He defines the perceptual schema as follows:

> A schema is that portion of the entire perceptual cycle which is internal to the perceiver, modifiable by experience, and somehow specific to what is being perceived. The schema accepts information as it becomes available at sensory surfaces and is changed by that information; it directs movements and exploratory activities that make more information available, by which it is further modified. (Neisser 1976, 54)

In short, Neisser presents three points that are generalized to cover all cognition: schemata are mental entities, they are flexible, and they match their objects. He continues by comparing schemata with formats and plans. schemata resemble formats in that they constrain what is cognized – the incoming information must have a suitable form in order to become a meaningful part of cognition. Plans, on the other hand, guide activities. Analogously, schemata restrict the search for further information. Neisser continues:

> Real formats and plans incorporate a sharp distinction of form and content, but this is not true of schemata. The information that fills in the format at one moment in the cyclic process becomes a part of the format in the next, determining how further information is accepted. (Neisser 1976, 65)

There are two interpretations available. The first is that the schema as a mental entity has both formal and contentful properties, and these properties are interwoven. The interwovenness can be explicated as follows. The schema as well as the incoming information have both formal and contentful properties. The acceptance of a piece of information is based on its contentful properties, but as soon as it is there, its formal properties are there as well (a piece of information cannot exist without formal properties), and these affect the schema in a mechanical way. The end result is that the piece of information becomes a part of the schema. Another interpretation is that the "information" as well as "being part of the format" are both construed on the level of content only, and their formal properties are ignored. Thus, for example, an incoming piece of information that there are children in the yard would become a part of the schema by means of which the cognizer would then proceed to observe his surroundings. The information that there are children in the yard would function as a default assumption that would constrain the incoming information, for example, the information that a football just hit the window. These two interpretations are not incompatible, but rather complementary. The latter one leaves a thorny problem unanswered, namely, how this interplay of contents is possible, or how the schema/environment interactions are realized. The former interpretation goes a level deeper and proposes that the levels of form and content are partly isomorphic because the models and their constituent representations have a grammar, that is, they are formal systems that embody contents. The claim that schemata have a kind of dual nature (the schema types are abstract, their tokens-in-use are concrete), has been nicely formulated by Thorndyke:

A schema is a cluster of knowledge representing a particular generic procedure, object, percept, event, sequence of events, or social institution. This cluster provides a skeleton structure for a concept that can be "instantiated", or filled out, with the detailed properties of the particular instance being represented. (Thorndyke 1984, cited in Johnson 1987, 19)

Our example above concerning children, a football, and the window is perhaps not a suitable one for the purpose of assessing Neisser's ideas. The example, as well as our preliminary characterization of schemata, suggest that they give structure to our experiences in a quite straightforward way. When I see that there are children in the yard there is a schema in my head that is different from the schema I have when I wonder whether there are cats in the yard. Neisser, on the contrary, compares schemata with genotypes and the actual experience with phenotype:

It would be a mistake to identify the schema with what is perceived, just as it is a mistake to identify any gene with a definite characteristic of an adult organism. (Neisser 1976, 56)

Here we encounter the question of levels again, this time in different guise. The experience, or "what is perceived", involves a content, a cluster of representations that are individuated by means of their objects. The underlying "genotypic" mechanism that enables such an experience processes parts of the

schemata, combining them into larger wholes. Our characterization of
cognitive schemata built them from representations, and the mechanisms
underlying experience were supposed to consist of representations and their
relations. An unrelated representation is not experienced. The minimal unit
of experience is a systemic cluster of representations. Thus, it seems that
Neisser's theory of schemata is not intended to cover experiences as such, but
rather the sub-personal mechanisms that make experiences possible. How
does Neisser answer the two questions concerning the nodes and links of
cognitive schemata? Since he defines the schema in functional terms by
relating it to a larger whole, the perceptual cycle, he does not bother with its
composition or structure. A schema is anything that fills the functional role
in the perceptual cycle. We do learn from him that schemata are structured
since they are analogous to formats. Their ultimate composition will be
found in physiological mechanisms.

7.4. Scripts

R. Schank and K. Abelson (1977) have given a widely cited characterization
of "script". In addition, they have suggested a set of links that structure the
cluster of representations into a cognitive schema. They write:

A script is a structure that describes appropriate sequences of events in a particular
context. A script is made up of slots and requirements about what can fill those
slots. The structure is an interconnected whole, and what is in one slot, affects
what can be in another. (Schank and Abelson 1977, 41)

A script is thus a schema that denotes a process, or a situation that
changes in time. The "slots" in this definition correspond to the nodes of the
network model and the requirements correspond to the links. The requirements
set some abstract conditions upon the slots. The slots are filled with concrete
information when the script is instantiated. In other words, a script that is not
in use consists of abstract representations that do not match the richness of
actual experience. When the script is activated, rich, concrete representations
are substituted for the abstract ones and the slots are filled, as in Thorndyke's
formulation above. Scripts are not as mutable as Neisser's schemata:

Scripts handle stylized everyday situations. They are not subject to much change,
nor do they provide the apparatus for handling totally novel situations. Thus, a
script is a predetermined, stereotyped sequence of actions that defines a well-
known situation. (Schank and Abelson 1977, 41)

Even unchanging cognitive schemata can handle a large variety of concrete situations, if the schemata are abstract enough. Still, the inflexibility of the Schank and Abelson scripts distinguishes them from Neisser's and other contemporary theories of cognitive schemata. The impressive part of their theory concerns the building blocks of cognitive schemata, that is, the nodes and links. We will present a simplified and partial version of their views (Schank and Abelson 1977, especially Chs. 1–2).

The reality they purport to represent is the everyday world of persons who think, talk, walk, learn folksongs, buy land, and drink tea. The basic entities in this reality are actors and objects. Both are variable entities in the sense that they can be in different states. Actors act upon objects and affect their states and locations. Thus, the basic nodes are actors, objects, and their states. The basic links that connect actors and objects are actions. They fulfill the action slots in cognitive schemata like

$$ACTOR \longrightarrow ACTION \longrightarrow OBJECT$$

Actions, in turn, can form causal links with actors, objects and their states, thus forming more complex cognitive schemata. An action is a kind of complex node that can be linked to other things.

Let us look at the causal links. Our everyday world that interests cultural anthropologists abounds with links that connect actors and objects. Therefore, the crucial task is to diminish the multitude of links into a compact and well-behaved set of basic links (the problem of links above). The basic links proposed below do not correspond one-to-one with the everyday verbs they purport to mimic, but only partially. That is, the everyday links (*analysandum*) used in the following examples can be said to involve the action links (*analysans*), or that the action links give a partial analysis of the everyday world. There are five types of causal links:

CL 1.   Actions can result in state changes.
CL 2.   States can enable actions.
CL 3.   States can disable actions.
CL 4.   States (or acts) can initiate mental states.
CL 5.   Mental states can be reasons for actions.

Let us look at a story that aims at explaining a case of illness. The story exemplifies a typical piece of raw data in cultural anthropology (for more of this data, see Kamppinen and Raivola ms). In the story the above links are exemplified:

For example, a young man had as if tuberculosis in his lungs. He was taken to a hospital but they could not cure him. So they took him to a witch, who said that the man had been bewitched by means of these small animals that burrow in the soil. His symptoms were as if he had tuberculosis, but it was not. It was that he had been done harm, because he had a woman, with whom he had had children, and he had been with another woman, and for this reason the first woman had done harm to him. And he died, yes he died. These small animals left his lungs after he died. The woman had harmed him by putting these animals into his lungs. These animals are insects, playacuros, three centimeters long.

Here the link between the "small animals" and the young man exemplifies the causal link type 1. The small animals bring about his deterioration. Also the actions of the man's wife result in state changes; her activity is a necessary condition for the episode to take place. The state of affairs that the man had been unfaithful enabled the woman's action in the first place, thus exemplifying link type 2. Of course the woman could have harmed the man without any unfaithfulness whatsoever, but that would have been another type of episode. The very same state of affairs initiated her mental state of revenge, which, in turn, motivated her. Thus, links 4 and 5 are exemplified. The man, being ill, was disabled from conducting his normal life, including his day-to-day actions, which exemplifies link type 3. We shall encounter similar reconstructions below, where some further anthropological applications of model theory are studied.

7.5. Connectionist models

The work of Rumelhart, McClelland and the PDP research group (1986) contains a detailed study of cognitive schemata. More precisely, they purport to give a fresh interpretation of the much-used concept of schema in terms of PDP or Parallel Distributed Processing models. The basic idea of connectionist models is that cognition is realized in networks of interrelated units. These units represent the features of an outside reality by becoming activated; their interconnections are responsible for the activation spreading across whole networks. Thus the activation as well as the accompanying representations are distributed over networks of connected units. The cognitive state of such a system is identified with the state of the network. The cognitive schema is not yet identical with such a network, since its functions are different. Rumelhart et al. (1986, 20) note that the cognitive schemata have apparently double roles: on the one hand, they are the structure of the mind, something that enables the mind to cognize its environment the way it does; on the other hand, they are mutable enough to fit almost anything. The answer they propose is that cognitive schemata are not "things" but emergent, systemic entities founded upon networks:

There is no representational object which is a schema. Rather, schemata emerge at the moment they are needed from the interaction of large number of much simpler elements working in concert with one another. Schemata are not explicit entities, but rather are implicit in our knowledge and are created by the very environment that they are trying to interpret – as it is interpreting them. (Rumelhart et al. 1986, 20)

Once they emerge, they are there. It is difficult to see why Rumelhart et al. deny the existence of cognitive schemata as representational objects. Is not a coalition, or a complex entity, an object?

Certain groups, or subpatterns of units tend to act in concert. They tend to activate one another and, when activated, tend to inhibit the same units. It is these coalitions of tightly interconnected units that correspond most closely to what have been called schemata. (Rumelhart et al. 1986, 20)

The denial of representational objects in general is a pervading theme in the PDP models. The PDP models do not view the cognitive system as a device that manipulates representations, but rather as a collection of networks whose activations coincide with the representational states.

John Holland et al. (1986) develop a theory of cognitive systems that is close to PDP models. Their fundamental building block is the production rule, IF (condition) THEN (action), and the network structure that is constructed from such rules is the bearer of representational states. The crucial difference between their view and the PDP models is that in PDP models, all cognitive activity is due to the strengthening and weakening of existing connections among the network units; no new connections are born, since the network is already hardwired in the system. In the theory of Holland et al., new production rules are generated as the cognitive system faces novel situations. Holland et al. (1986, 12) hold that the schema (as it is used by Schank and Abelson) is too inflexible a concept. They propose 'mental models' instead. In a mental model, several schemata can combine into one flexible structure that changes according to the situation. The characterization of mental models they give is strikingly similar to the PDP characterization of mental models given above:

[Mental models are] transient, dynamic representations of particular unique situations. They exist only implicitly, corresponding to the organized, multifaceted description of the current situation and the expectations that flow from it. (Holland et al. 1986, 14)

An interesting similarity between this characterization of mental models and the above one of cognitive schemata is that in both cases the multicomponent system, the network, from which the mental model or the schema emerges is inside the cognitive system itself. Yet in neither case is the schema identical with any part of the network. The schema supervenes on the network activity that is triggered by the environment.

How do these theories answer the questions of nodes and links? The received view of PDP models is that the units are activated or inhibited by their connections with other units and the environment. The units are sub-symbolic; they do not represent the commonsense features of our everyday world like cats, houses, and teapots, but rather so-called microfeatures, which are aspects (parts) of commonsense features. The connections are of two generic types, excitatory and inhibitory. The problem of nodes and links is not answered by this, since the schema is not identical with the structure consisting of units (presumably nodes) and interconnections (presumably links). D. A. Norman writes in the concluding chapter of the second PDP volume:

Schemata are not fixed structures. Schemata are flexible configurations, mirroring the regularities of experience, providing automatic completion of missing components, automatically generalizing from the past, but also continually in modification, continually adapting to reflect the current state of affairs. (Rumelhart et al. 1986, 536)

The importance of PDP and related (rule-based) models is not in casting light upon the structure of experience, but in proposing hypotheses about the microstructure of cognition. Activations or inhibitions on the sub-symbolic level are not experienced at all, but the higher-level cognitive schemata can serve for the analysis of experience, also. It is clear from the above quotation that treating cognitive schemata as transient, emergent entities, and not as identical with any collection of network building blocks, allows us to construct any cognitive schemata we might find useful. If cognitive schemata are deemed ontologically non-existent, there is no reason to worry about the details of their nodes and links.

7.6. Image schemata

The mainstream theories of cognitive schemata suppose that the nodes and links make up propositional entities with truth values. Another trend is the view that cognitive schemata are mental pictures, rich in details and representing their objects in the way real pictures do; they do not have truth values, but some kind of "conditions of satisfaction".

Mark Johnson (1987) is against both of these currents. He proposes a Kantian theory of what he calls 'image schemata' or 'embodied schemata'. Such a schema is neither a proposition nor a mental picture. What is it, then? As far as its structure is concerned, the schema "consists of a small number of parts and relations, by virtue of which it can structure indefinitely many perceptions, images, and events" (Johnson 1987, 29). The schema has to have a structure of a certain complexity in order to accomplish its tasks. Johnson gives the schema the classical Kantian role; our experience is founded upon transcendental foundations, without which it would not be sensible:

... in order for us to have meaningful, connected experiences that we can comprehend and reason about, there must be a pattern and order to our actions, perceptions, and conceptions. A schema is a recurrent pattern, shape, and regularity in, or of, these ongoing ordering activities. (Johnson 1987, 29; e.r.)

The example Johnson gives is the containment schema, or in-out orientation. According to Johnson, it exists preconceptually in our experience. Its preconceptual existence involves "separation, differentiation, and enclosure, which implies restriction and limitation" (Johnson 1987, 22). In spite of these conceptual properties, the containment schema is not a propositional entity. Yet its effects can be described propositionally since it has an internal structure complex enough to give rise to rational entailments and can constrain our experiences. The containment schema is exemplified in our experience in at least five different ways; that is, we experience the world of contained and containing entities in specific ways (Johnson 1987, 22).

(1)   Containment involves protection from, or resistance to, external forces.
(2)   Containment limits and restricts forces within the container.
(3)   The contained object gets a relative fixity of location.
(4)   The contained object becomes either accessible or inaccessible to the view of some observer.

(5)   Containment is transitive. That is, if A contains B and B contains
        C, then A contains C.

Containment is one example of a pervading schema that constrains our
experience both in practical life (filling a teapot) and in theoretical thinking
(conceptual frameworks as containers). We have utilized the containment
schema in the interpretation of illness stories in an earlier study (Kamppinen
1989).

Another example is the family of so-called force schemata: compulsion,
blockage, counterforce, diversion, removal of restraint, enablement, and
attraction. For example, the following story (from Kamppinen and Raivola
ms) depicts a situation that exemplifies these cognitive schemata. I had just
asked the informant about the origins of mal aire, a type of ethnic illness
believed to be caused by airborne spirits:

Well, sometimes you walk outside in the night-time without thinking that it is the
time for evil spirits, and for the souls of the dead who abound in the air. And then
you encounter one of these, they shock you when they pass by. And they can bring
illnesses to your children by means of contact.

Here, the human being, who walks outside during the night, is exposed to
evil spirits; he attracts them, and, without any restraint, the spirits will bring
about changes in the person by means of contact. The world where these
cognitive schemata are applicable is of course the world of actors who apply
force upon objects, and where the objects can suddenly turn into actors. The
types of force schemata exemplify links that connect actors and objects into
networks. The same goes for the containment schema and its entailments.
They link contained objects with containers. Thus Johnson's schema theory
provides an account of nodes and links. The reality from which these
schemata emerge is our commonsense world. More precisely, the cognitive
schemata

... emerge as meaningful structures for us chiefly at the level of our bodily
movements through space, our manipulation of objects, and our perceptual
interactions. (Johnson 1987, 29)

The embodied schemata stem from our biological constitution that
determines our bodily movements as well as our manipulation of objects. It
is worth noting that Johnson not only provides a theory of schemata – an
account of their structure, nodes and links – but he also gives an answer to
the Kantian question: Whence do the structures of our experience come?
Johnson's position is in the spirit of Martin Heidegger and Maurice Merleau-

Ponty: We experience our own body and our own being-in-the-world so profoundly that these experiences affect the rest of our cognition and action. The bodily and perceptual experience is the primary experience.

7.7. Further applications

Schema theory has not been the privilege of philosophers, computer-scientists and psychologists only, but has emerged as background theory in many personal level sciences of human beings, most notably in cognitive and cultural anthropology. Here we will glance through two examples, both purporting to be general purpose anthropological theories of cognition.

M. H. Agar and J. R. Hobbs (1985) build a schema theory for analyzing interviews. Although they refrain from crediting their schemata with cognitive reality, they are quite straightforward about the nodes and links of schemata: the nodes are propositions or blocks of propositions, and the links form a well-behaved set of relations that connect propositions or blocks with one another. The analysis of interview materials or stories readily invites us to construct the schema in this particular way. The natural units in a free discourse are propositions and their combinations, and their interrelations make up the schematic structure of stories. The links are grouped into three types (Agar and Hobbs 1985, 424):

Strong temporal relations like THEN, ENABLE, CAUSE.

Linkage relations like BACKGROUND, EXPLANATION.

Expansion relations like ELABORATION, SPECIFICATION, CONTRAST, PARALLEL.

Since these links are purported to be used in the analysis of interviews, and especially in order to explicate the informant's perspective, they cannot be constructed from God's point of view nor expressed in impersonal form. The first link, THEN, connects two propositions or two blocks of propositions, and indicates that the informant places the corresponding situations in temporal ordering. The ENABLE link and the CAUSE link are varieties of causal relations. The first link between two blocks indicates that one provides causal background for the other, whereas the latter is a stronger relation; the one block generates the other. Instances of CAUSE are instances of ENABLE, but not vice versa. BACKGROUND and EXPLANATION links indicate that the informant posits "logical" or rational connections between blocks of propositions (or between corresponding situations). Again, BACKGROUND is a weaker link than EXPLANATION. The expansion relations indicate some other conceptual operations upon propositions. ELABORATION means that the topic of one block is further elaborated in the next block, SPECIFICATION indicates that the elaboration done is a specifying one. CONTRAST stands for a situation where two blocks ascribe mutually contradictory properties to one entity, whereas PARALLEL indicates that in two blocks, analogous ascriptions are made. Let us take an example, an account of mal aire (from Kamppinen and Raivola ms):

> My daughter had vomiting and diarrhea, and I went to a healer and asked that he would cure my daughter. He sang some magic songs and prepared some liquid. He cured my daughter. [How did she encounter this illness?] I had to work late in a house in which I was cooking and cleaning. I had left her sleeping alone in my house. The patron did not let me go until it was very late. I was at home ten-thirty, eleven-thirty, and during this period she had encountered mal aire. My little daughter, four months five months of age, alone in the house. It is very bad for little children to be alone during the night.

First we number the propositions and place the relations between them.

1.   My daughter had vomiting and diarrhea,
      EXPLANATION
2.   and I went to a healer and asked that he would cure my daughter.
      THEN
3.   He sang some magic songs and prepared some liquid.
4.   He cured my daughter.

The rest of the story describes the BACKGROUND, prompted by the question: How did she encounter this illness?

5.   I had to work late in a house in which I was cooking and cleaning.
      EXPLANATION
6.   I had left her sleeping alone in my house.
      ELABORATION
7.   The patron did not let me go until it was very late.
      CAUSE
8.   I was at home ten-thirty, eleven-thirty,
      EXPLANATION

9.   and during this period she had encountered mal aire.
        ELABORATION
10.   My little daughter, four months five months of age, alone in the
        house.
11.   It is very bad for little children to be alone during the night.

Agar and Hobbs decline from locating these schematic structures in the minds of the informants. The status of schemata is that they make sense of the story. Yet if the claim concerning the informant's viewpoint is sustained, it is difficult to see why these structures should not be treated as properties of the informant's cognition that constrain her experiences.

O. Werner and G. M. Schoepfle (1987) have built a highly abstract schema theory they call the **MTQ** schema. It is an ambitious theory since it proposes to reduce the number of basic links to three: Modification (**M**), Taxonomy (**T**), and Queueing (**Q**). By means of these links one can construct taxonomies and plans; these structures account for most of cultural knowledge (Werner and Schoepfle 1987, 111–112).

The links **M** and **T** connect terms and they are complementary. Two terms A and B are connected by the Modification link, or A modifies B,

> (A) **M** (B),

when B's intension is increased by the addition of A's attributes. For example, the expression "oatmeal is healthy" involves a case of Modification

> (healthy) **M** (oatmeal).

Two terms A and C are connected by the Taxonomy link,

> (C) **T** (A),

when A's intension is included in C's intension and C's extension is included in A's extension. For example, the sentence "rolled oats are cereals" involves a Taxonomy link

> (rolled oats) **T** (cereals).

Taxonomies are constructed by means of **M** and **T** links so that a hierarchically higher term (or entity) A is modified by some additional attributes (or properties) B and the result is a hierarchically lower term (or entity) C.

Modification and Taxonomy links are apparently analogous with the ELABORATION and SPECIFICATION links of Agar and Hobbs, but these operate on the level of propositions (or blocks of propositions), whereas Modification and Taxonomy connect terms that can be understood as constituents of propositions.

Queueing or serial order **Q** is used in the construction of plans. For example, a sub-plan included in preparing oatmeal is "when the water boils, add salt", or

(water boils) **Q** (add salt)

Werner and Schoepfle distinguish two varietes of Queueing, immediate succession **Q1** and eventual succession **Q2**. The above links THEN, CAUSE and ENABLE all involve serial ordering, and thus they can be said to be partially reducible to the Queueing link.

Werner and Schoepfle (1987, 115) give examples of how to reduce other, more complex relations to the three basic links of their theory. The examples are the part/whole relation and the causal relation. The sentences "(B) is a part of (A)" and "(B) is a cause of (A)" are first paraphrased into "(B) is an (A)-part" and "(B) is an (A)-cause", and then put in their formal parlance,

(B) **T** ((part) **M** (A)), and
(B) **T** ((cause) **M** (A)).

Thus, for example, the sentence "envy generates illnesses" (and the corresponding cognitive state needed in uttering the sentence) would involve a structure:

(envy) **T** ((cause) **M** (illnesses))

The approach of Werner and Schoepfler is fruitfully treated as complementing the approach of Agar and Hobbs, since the basic three links (or at least two of them) connect sub-propositional nodes, whereas the level of analysis in Agar and Hobbs is that of propositions and blocks.

Anthropological schema theories aim at solving the problem of nodes and links by means of partial accounts, so to say. That is, they propose nodes and links that are aspects of everyday experiences, without providing exhaustive descriptions. Similarly, philosophical theories concerning the transcendental presuppositions of our experiences are content with providing necessary but insufficient conditions. Theories of cognitive schemata abound in psychology, philosophy and anthropology, and some authors are willing to employ it as an all-purpose device whereas others hold that it is too narrow, and accordingly introduce other structures (cognitive schemata, embodied schemata, etc.). What is missing in most theories is an account of conscious experience, how cognitive schemata shape it. Johnson's theory of embodied schemata as well as the tools of Agar and Hobbs provide means for analyzing experience, but the mainstream theories are interested in cognitive systems that may or may not experience something.

8. RATIONALITY AND HERMENEUTICS

Explanation by means of cognitive schemata supposes that the cognitive schemata are constructed in some sensible way. The basic types of nodes and links are typically backed up by folk ontological and folk psychological intuitions; these contain principles of reasonable and sensible interpretation, principles concerning what makes sense.

Once the building blocks have been chosen, the construction of schemata employs more specific principles. The constructive search for cognitive schemata follows a set of rules – the explanatory schema in both explanation by design and integrative explanation must make sense of the explanandum. This is the case especially in integrative explanation where the object of explanation is integrated into a larger whole so that its role as a node in a network explains its existence. And in explanation by design, the search for a sensible formal structure in the text is to look for a complex, patterned entity that possesses some special aesthetic qualities. The hermeneutic rules of interpretation circumscribe the admissible, sensible structures that can be identified in a text. The same holds for intentional explanation. Intentional explanations of human actions and cognitive states presuppose that the person functions in a certain manner. The rules of theoretical and practical reason hypothesized are not just any rules, but those of rationality. In the case of intentional explanation the requirement of rationality covers both theoretical and practical reason.

> *Theoretical rationality*: The person should (is supposed to) have truthful beliefs that are founded upon experience, common sense, or on general conceptions. Beliefs should be consistent with one another and they should be useful, that is, enhance problem-solving.

> *Practical rationality*: The person should have appropriate goals, should be capable of reasonable means/ends and cost/benefit calculations, and he should act efficiently.

When these requirements are not fulfilled, intentional explanation is in trouble, as was noted above. Usually we aim at saving the rationality assumption by gathering more information about the specific circumstances. We presume that, if we find out more about the beliefs and desires involved, the apparent irrationality will disappear. Structural explanation aims at constructing explanatory cognitive schemata that are sensible, or "beautifully" structured. The sensibility of structures involves: consistency, systemicity or complex and patterned structure, symmetry, contrast, repetition, exclusion, containment, distinction, beginning, end, boundary, negation, affirmation, continuity, causality, sequence, attraction, dependency, and so on. Schema analysis, especially in the humanities, is notoriously liberal about what makes sense. Of course the choice of building blocks affects the set of admissible structures, but since very basic types of nodes and links (for example, entities and dependency) are usually chosen, they do not give sufficient guidelines for actually composing a particular schema. What is sensible and what is not depends on rationality in a very broad sense. Thus, structural explanation presupposes rationality, too. The requirements that steer the construction of cognitive schemata are closer to theoretical rationality than practical. Perhaps the brand of rationality in question here could be termed "the hermeneutics of cognitive schemata".

Intentional and structural explanations presuppose rationality, which is a property of cognitive systems and of cognitive schemata. To conclude this part, we will apply analytical explanation in explaining rationality. Analytical explanation aims at explaining rationality by specifying the components of the system. It decomposes the responsible mechanism into subsystems; in the paradigmatic case, the personal level rationality is decomposed into sub-personal rational agents. The analytical explanation should end up with simple components whose functions require essentially less complexity and rationality than those of personal level systems.

The task of analytical explanation has been formulated, for instance, by Daniel C. Dennett (see Dennett 1969, 1978 and 1987). He draws a distinction between disciplines dealing with whole persons (personal level cognitivism) and disciplines dealing with the information processing parts of persons (sub-personal level cognitivism). Personal level Cognitivism takes an "intelligence loan" when it ascribes cognitive states to whole persons or constructs sensible cognitive schemata. It is the task of sub-personal cognitivism to pay back this loan. To paraphrase Dennett (1969, Ch. 2):

(1)   Personal level intentional and structural explanations presuppose rationality.
(2)   Rationality implies organization.
(3)   Organization is improbable in the contingent universe.
(4)   Therefore, since an improbable state of affairs is prima facie problematic, rationality needs explanation.
(5)   Rationality is not explainable at the personal level, since personal level cognitivism uses rationality as an explanation.
(6)   Therefore, rationality is explained at the sub-personal level through analytical explanation.

Explaining personal level cognitive phenomena by means of analytical explanation gets rid of full-blown rationality principles but preserves some cogency conditions. The piecewise explanation of rationality is possible because rationality admits of degrees. Analytical explanation lays bare the less rational subsystems, the parts of the molar system, and their action is explained by partial rationality principles. That is, by some cogency conditions. Yet, what the analytical explanation ends up with are as intentional as the original higher level explanandum. It is tempting to think of intentionality as a mass property, too, and as correlated with rationality: the more rational, the more intentional. But the intrinsic intentionality of cognitive states and of mental representations is an all-or-nothing affair – a thing either exemplifies intentionality or does not. It would make no sense to claim that the state "S believes that P", or the representation P included, is more or less intentional than some other semantically individuated state. Of course the intentional states of snails and of neuronal subsystems are less human (that is, their social significance is different) than the paradigmatic examples, but it will not make them less intentional. Robert Cummins has argued against conflating intentionality and rationality on similar grounds:

The simple move that works with intelligence won't work with intentionality, for, unlike intelligence, intentionality isn't a matter of degree. ... Intentionally characterized capacities can be explained by analysis into other intentionally characterized capacities. But the analyzing capacities will not be less intentional than the analyzed capacity. (Cummins 1983, 92)

The absolute character of intentionality accords well with the relative nature of rationality. When a system's fully intentional components (cognitive states or the representations that make up a schema) are inappropriately organized, it is less rational than a system with appropriately organized components. It follows that even though analytical explanation explains rationality, intentionality is not touched upon by this move. Analytical explanation brings to light the organization of components but it does not explain the essential properties of the components – the intentional properties.

Hence, what is the role of intentionality in analytical explanation? We apply a specific explanatory strategy suggested by Robert Cummins (1983). The strategy in question is for explaining properties by means of so-called nomic attributions. In the case at hand, rationality is the property to be explained, and intentionality functions as the nomic attribution. The explanation of properties is usually contrasted with the explanation of state transitions. In paradigmatic cases, the explanation of state transitions appeals to "causal laws" (loosely construed). The explanation of properties, in its turn, appeals to the lawful instantiation of properties and to the composition of the system under study. The explanation of rationality (or why a system S is rational) would go as follows:

(1)   The components of cognitive systems and of cognitive schemata are intentional.

(2)   Any system equipped with intentional components and an organization R is rational, that is, any system having an analysis A is rational.

(3)   The system S has analysis A.

(4)   Therefore, the system S is rational.

Each premise exemplifies a specific type of explanation (cf. Cummins 1983, 7 and 17–18). The first premise is a nomic attribution, that is, a predication, a lawlike statement to the effect that all x's have a certain property P. The second premise exemplifies an instantiation law, which is a lawlike statement "specifying how a property is instantiated in a specified type of system." The third premise is a composition law that specifies "the (or an) analysis of a specified type of system." To specify a composition law is to engage in analytical explanation.

The components of cognitive systems and of cognitive schemata (that is, the cognitive states and representations) are linked in specified ways because they are intentional. Thus, it seems plausible that an analytical explanation of rationality would construe the ascription of intentionality as a nomic attribution. Hence, the intentionality of cognitive states and of representations would be in a position that is analogous to other nomic properties. For instance, the statement that individuals tend to maximize the size of their offspring expresses a law that is a nomic attribution in evolutionary biology.

Analogously, the statement that cognitive states and their constituent representations are intentional expresses a law that is a nomic attribution in cognitivism.

BIBLIOGRAPHY

Agar, M.H. and Hobbs, J.R.: 1985, 'How to Grow Schemata out of Interviews', in Dougherty, J.W.D. (ed.), *Directions in Cognitive Anthropology*, Urbana: University of Illinois Press.

Bauer, R.M.: 1984, 'Autonomic Recognition of Names and Faces in Prosopagnosia: A Neuropsychological Application of the Guilty Knowledge Test', *Neuropsychologia* 2 2 (4), 457–469.

Casson, R.: 1983, 'Schemata in Cognitive Anthropology', *Annual Review of Anthropology* 1 2, 429–462.

Cummins, R.: 1983, *The Nature of Psychological Explanation*, Cambridge MA: MIT Press.

D'Andrade, R.: 1990, 'Some Propositions About the Relations Between Culture and Human Cognition', in Stigler, J.W., Shweder, R. and Herdt, G. (eds.), *Cultural Psychology: Essays on Comparative Human Development*, Cambridge: Cambridge University Press.

Dennett, D.C.: 1969, *Content and Consciousness*, London: Routledge and Kegan Paul.

Dennett, D.C.: 1978, *Brainstorms*, Brighton: Harvester.

Dennett, D.C.: 1987, *The Intentional Stance*, Cambridge MA: MIT Press.

Dougherty, J.W.D. (ed.): 1985, *Directions in Cognitive Anthropology*, Urbana: University of Illinois Press.

Gazzaniga, M.S., LeDoux, J.E. and Wilson, D.H.: 1977, 'Language, Praxis, and the Right Hemisphere: Clues to Some Mechanisms of Consciousness', *Neurology* 2 7, 1144–1147.

Gazzaniga, M.S. and LeDoux, J.E.: 1978, *The Integrated Mind*, New York: Plenum.

Gazzaniga, M.S.: 1988, 'Brain Modularity: Towards a Philosophy of Conscious Experience', in Marcel, A.J. and Bisiach, E. (eds.), *Consciousness in Contemporary Science*, New York: Oxford University Press.

Holland, D. and Quinn, N. (eds.): 1987, *Cultural Models in Language and Thought*, Cambridge: Cambridge University Press.

Holland, J.H., Holyoak, K.J., Nisbett, R.E. and Thagard, P.R.: 1986, *Induction: Processes of Inference, Learning, and Discovery*, Cambridge MA: MIT Press.

James, W.: 1950, *The Principles of Psychology*, Vols. 1 and 2 (First published in 1890.), New York: Dover Publications.

Johnson, M.: 1987, *The Body in the Mind: The Bodily Basis of Meaning, Imagination, and Reason*, Chicago: Chicago University Press.

Kamppinen, M.: 1989, *Cognitive Systems and Cultural Models of Illness: A Study of Two Mestizo Peasant Villages of the Peruvian Amazon*, Folklore Fellows' Communications 244. Helsinki: Academia Scientiarum Fennica.

Kamppinen, M. and Raivola, P.: ms, *Boundaries*.

LeDoux, J., Wilson, D.H. and Gazzaniga, M.S.: 1977, 'A Divided Mind: Observations on the Conscious Properties of the Separated Hemispheres', *Annals of Neurology* 2, 417–421.

Lévi-Strauss, C.: 1963, *Structural Anthropology*, New York: Harper & Row.

Lévi-Strauss, C.: 1969, *The Raw and the Cooked*, New York: Harper & Row.

Marks, C.E.: 1981, *Commissurotomy, Consciousness and Unity of Mind*, Cambridge MA: MIT Press.

Minsky, M.: 1975, 'A Framework for Representing Knowledge', in Winston, P. (ed.), *The Psychology of Computer Vision,* New York: McGraw-Hill.

Minsky, M.: 1985, *The Society of Mind*, New York: Simon and Schuster.

Neisser, U.: 1976, *Cognition and Reality: Principles and Implications of Cognitive Psychology*, San Fransisco: Freeman.

Piaget, J.: 1970, *Structuralism*, New York: Harper & Row.

Rescher, N.: 1988, *Rationality: A Philosophical Inquiry into the Nature and the Rationale of Reason*, Oxford: Clarendon Press.

Rumelhart, D.E., McClelland, J.L. and the PDP research group: 1986, *Parallel Distributed Processing*, Vols. 1 and 2, Cambridge MA: MIT Press.

Schacter, D.L.: 1990, 'Toward a Cognitive Neuropsychology of Awareness: Implicit Knowledge and Anosagnosia', *Journal of Clinical and Experimental Neuropsychology* 1 2 (1), 155–178.

Schank, R. and Abelson, K.: 1977, *Scripts Plans Goals and Understanding*, London: Lawrence Erlbaum Associates.

Shweder, R.: 1991, *Thinking Through Cultures: Expeditions in Cultural Psychology*, Cambridge MA: Harvard University Press.

Smith, B. (ed.): 1982, *Parts and Moments: Studies in Logic and Formal Ontology*, Munich: Philosophia Verlag.

Smith, B.: 1991, 'The Structures of the Common-Sense World', in Pagnini, A. and Poggi, S. (eds.), *Gestalt Theory: Its Origins, Foundations and Influence*, Florence: Olschty.

Thorndyke, P.W.: 1984, 'Applications of Schema Theory in Cognitive Research', in Anderson, J. and Kosslyn, S. (eds.), *Tutorials in Learning and Memory*, San Fransisco: Freeman.

Werner, O. and Schoepfle, G.M.: 1987, *Systematic Fieldwork*, Vols. 1 and 2, Beverly Hills: Sage Publications.

PART III

RELATIVISM AND COGNITIVISM

RELATIVISM AND COGNITIVISM

This part consists of two sections. Section A deals with direct access to reality, or the question of how representations could ever match reality. The conclusion arrived at in section A is that there is no access to reality that is not mediated by concepts, that is, conceptually relative. Section B starts its argument from that conclusion, and investigates the consequences of conceptual relativism. Different strategies in coping with the problem of relativism are assessed. The cognitivist strategy appears to be the most promising. Yet, in the final chapter, "Ultimate Relativism", we argue that not only is our access to reality conceptually mediated, but in addition, the basis of mediation imposes a severe restriction on how the reality is conceptualized. Section A will introduce several classic and modern philosophers to the reader, for example John Locke, George Berkeley, Bertrand Russell, and William James, some of whose ideas were already presented in Part II.

A. REPRESENTATION AND REALITY

9. INTRODUCTION: REPRESENTATION AND REALITY

9.1. Some concepts and problems

The fundamental problem of cognitive science and of the philosophy of mind was posed a long time ago by the Greek sceptics when they asked how a perception or idea in the mind can *represent* reality, be *about* reality. They argued that even if an idea did in fact represent reality, we could never know that it does, because we are directly aware only of our own sensations and not with the supposed reality beyond them. In what follows we try to show that this old problem is still alive in philosophy despite the efforts of many generations of philosophers.

The ancient problem can, however, be divided into the following three problems (that are difficult to keep apart). (1) The problem of representation: 'How can an idea X represent an object Y?' This is the most general problem of the three. It is the fundamental problem of such disciplines as semiotics, the theory of meaning and the theory of intentionality. Because of its generality, it is also the hardest one to answer. (2) The problem of certainty, 'How can I be certain that there is an object Y that my idea X represents?', is the basic problem of the traditional theory of knowledge. Although logically it is less fundamental than the previous one, historically it appears before it. (3) And finally a more recent problem, that of the experience of reality: 'Why do I experience some objects as being real?' This is a phenomenological problem, that is, a problem not about the "objective" world but about our own experiences. (Phenomenology is, roughly, the study of experiences from the viewpoint of the subject himself.)

To ask questions like (1)–(3), one has to have a technical vocabulary that contains words both for the things in the world and for their ideas or representations in the mind. These ideas or representations are admittedly rather strange entities, but we must postulate their existence unless we want to be naive realists. A naive realist believes that reality is faithfully reflected or copied by the mind, so that there is no difference between how things really are and how they appear to be, or between reality and appearance. But everyday experience is enough to show that naive realism is wrong: things are not what they seem. An oar partly under water is not bent though it appears to be; railway tracks seem to merge in the distance but they don't; on a cold day, the same porch that feels cold when going out feels warm when coming in; and so on.

It is questionable whether there has ever been a naive realist who has tried to back his views with philosophical arguments. Yet there are many more critical realists who have argued that not all of our ideas are reliable but there is a subclass of ideas that offer us, as it were, a direct and infallible access to reality. In other words, the naive realist relies on all ideas, whereas the critical realist accepts only a few as being wholly reliable. We will consider several such theories and try to show that none of them quite succeeds in proving that there can be such a direct access. After that we will sketch an alternative. But before that some explanatory notes on the concepts that we use.

Instead of 'ideas', we speak of 'mental acts'. By a mental act we mean any mental event whatever. For instance, seeing, hearing, remembering and fearing are mental acts. (The term 'mental act' is preferrable to 'idea' because it would be rather strange to call one's fear an idea.) A mental act need not be an activity, that is, something that we do; for example, an act of seeing a cat is rather something that happens to us than something that we do. Moreover, not all mental phenomena are mental acts (events); some are mental states. For instance, loving somebody is a mental phenomenon but it is not a momentary event but a lasting state, and so is knowing one's address. These states ordinarily remain latent but they may become actualized when, say, one sees one's beloved or is asked about one's address. For simplicity, we will concentrate on mental acts.

A mental act, then, is an event in one's stream of consciousness. In fact, a person's stream of consciousness is composed of successive mental acts (whose borders are not very clear, though). If we want to speak about our experiences or about other people's experiences, we must somehow distinguish these mental events from one another. In other words, we must somehow individuate them, single them out. There are two ways of individuating them: in terms of their objects and in terms of their contents.

The first way, the way of objects, is externalist: an act of seeing a tree, for example, is individuated by pointing out the object that has caused the experience, namely the tree itself. Thus an act of seeing a tree differs from an act of seeing a cat by having a different causal history. Individuation by means of objects can be done even by an external observer; therefore it is no wonder that scientifically-minded people (not to mention scientistically-minded ones) usually accept this alternative.

The second way, that of contents, is internalist. The individuation of the act is done from the viewpoint of the experiencing subject himself. Instead of assigning a cause to the experience (in the scientific fashion), the internalist individuates the mental act by describing it, by expressing its content in words. An act of seeing a cat is distinguished from an act of seeing a cow by the fact that the former has a cat-like content, whereas the latter has a cow-like content. This way is internalist because one does not have to go beyond the limits of one's mind to individuate mental acts.

Thus there is a controversy concerning the right way of individuating mental acts. The externalists hold that the only scientific way of doing it is to assign an object to the mental. The internalists, on the contrary, argue that the externalist account cannot be applied to all mental acts: for instance, the acts of imagining a centaur and hallucinating a pink rat cannot be individuated by their objects because there simply are no such objects; therefore, the only way of individuating such acts is the internalist way, that is, the way of describing their contents.

The difference between the object and the content of a mental acts is analogous to that between the referent and the meaning of a linguistic expression. For instance, the expressions 'the morning star' and 'the evening star' refer to the same thing, the planet Venus, which is their common referent. Yet these expressions have different meanings, roughly expressible as 'the bright star that can be seen in the morning' and 'the bright star that can be seen in the evening'. Therefore it would be wrong to translate 'the evening star' by 'Morgenstern', because these expressions clearly have different meanings. As can be seen from this example, meanings are abstract entities (that is, entities that are neither in space nor in time – neither in the external world nor in a person's stream of consciousness). Furthermore, these meanings are not tied to any particular language, but can be expressed in any language (at least in principle). It is true that these entities are strange, but they are needed to solve puzzles like the one above.

Similarly, the contents of mental acts are abstract entities. They are the "meanings" of those acts, and they can be expressed by linguistic means (words and sentences). We need contents in order to explain how two persons can have the same thought. Such a shared thought cannot be a part of either person's private stream of thought. If it could, then the other could not have it. Such an abstract thought is often called a proposition. A proposition is, then, the content of a mental act, but it is also the meaning of the sentence that expresses the content of that experience. A proposition is an abstract entity that can be expressed and grasped (understood), but it cannot be seen, heard or written. What one hears are sounds; what one sees or writes are letters. But those sounds and letters express the thought, the proposition, which is the content of the experience.

The currently used term 'representation' can be seen to have two distinct meanings. First, it can be used to refer to a mental act in a person's stream of consciousness (provided that that act really represents something and is not, say, a sudden burst of objectless fear). Second, it can refer to the abstract content of a particular mental act. These meanings should be kept apart, but unfortunately they are often confused.

To sum up, we give the following characterizations:

> *Mental act* ≈ An event in a person's stream of consciousness.
> *Object* ≈ The thing seen, heard, feared, etc.
> *Content* ≈ The abstract meaning of the mental act which is expressible by means of language.
> *Proposition* ≈ (1) The sort of a content that can be expressed by a sentence. (2) The meaning of a sentence.
> *Representation* ≈ (1) The abstract content of a mental act.

(2) Its concrete "copy" in a person's stream of consciousness.

9.2. The sceptics

Let us start our discussion of the problems of representation and of reality from classical Greece. There the sceptics doubted whether there is any objectivity in our perceptions and thoughts. For example, Sextus Empiricus, a later sceptic, defines scepticism (in his treatise *Outlines of Pyrrhonism*) as follows:

Scepticism is an ability, or mental attitude, which opposes appearances to judgements. ... By "appearances" we now mean the objects of sense-perception, whence we contrast them with the objects of thought or "judgements". (McDermott 1985, 326)

For instance, we are immediately aware that honey appears to be sweet, but when we judge that honey is sweet, we overstep the mere appearance or sensation in our mind and pass a judgement about the external world. This is a step that the sceptics are reluctant to take. Sextus goes on:

Those who say that "the Sceptics abolish appearances", or phenomena, seem to me to be unacquainted with the statements of our School. For ... we do not overthrow the affective sense-impressions which induce our assent involuntarily; and these impressions are "the appearances". And when we question whether the underlying object is such as it appears, we grant the fact that it appears, and our doubt does not concern the appearance itself but the account given of the appearance – and that is a different thing from questioning the the appearance itself. For example, honey appears to us to be sweet (and this we grant, for we perceive sweetness through the senses), but whether it is also sweet in its essence is for us a matter of doubt, since this is not an appearance but a judgement regarding the appearance. (McDermott 1985, 327)

Sextus's point can be put as follows. We can be sure that something appears to us, and that we have sensations. We cannot doubt the existence of our own sensations because they "induce our assent involuntarily", i.e., we automatically accept them as true or real in the sense that it is indubitable that we have them. But if we look at the matter more closely, we notice that those sensations may well be false in another sense, namely in the sense that there is nothing in the external world that corresponds to them. For instance, we have noticed that sometimes (e.g., during a sickness) honey does not taste sweet to us. Therefore we cannot judge that honey is sweet but only that it appears to be sweet. Thus the only judgement we are justified in making is about our sensations, not about the (alleged) real things in the external world.

The sceptics were criticizing dogmatists, that is, philosophers who maintained that they can know what is really there in the external world. For instance, the Greek atomists Leucippus and Democritus had dogmatically argued that the world consists of tiny atoms and the empty space between them. Nothing else really exists. All objects of everyday experience, such as cats and chairs, are just collections of atoms. The reason why the sceptics called them 'dogmatists' was that they give their "assent to one of the non-evident objects of scientific inquiry" (McDermott 1985, 327). By this they meant that the atomists have not the slightest evidence for their views; they are just speculating about things beyond any possible experience.

9.3. The atomists

The atomists argued that all atoms, the ultimate building-blocks of all things, are similar except for two qualities: shape and size. All perceivable differences between the qualities of things can be explained by differences in the atoms, their movements and their modes configuration. For example, the difference between coldness and hotness can be explained by saying that the atoms in hot bodies are in quicker motion than the atoms in cold bodies. But the atoms themselves are neither hot nor cold. And the difference in colour between a green and a red apple can be explained by the different configurations of the atoms on their surfaces.

The atomists also believed that they could divide the qualities of things into real and apparent ones. The qualities of the atoms are real whereas the qualities of the ordinary objects are for the most part merely apparent. For instance, shape, size and motion are real qualities, whereas redness, greenness, hotness and coldness are apparent qualities. Greenness and coldness are not real qualities because atoms, the only real things, do not have them. Democritus says of these apparent qualities that

... they have no existence in nature, but ... are affects of our sense organs as they undergo the alteration which brings into being what appears to us. ... An indication that the aforementioned qualities do not exist in nature is that things do not appear the same to all living creatures, but what is sweet to us is bitter to others, and to still others sour or pungent or astringent; and so with the rest. (McDermott 1985, 70–71)

Later on, when modern science came into existence, the "real" qualities were called *primary* and the "apparent" qualities *secondary*. It was thought that the primary qualities differ from the secondary ones in three important respects: (1) the primary qualities do really exist in nature, whereas the secondary ones are products of our sense-organs; (2) the primary qualities can be known more reliably than the secondary ones; and therefore (3) the primary qualities are the ones that science uses in its explanations.

9.4. John Locke

John Locke has perhaps given the best-known expression to the doctrine of primary and secondary qualities. In the age of such giants of science as Isaac Newton, it was, according to Locke,

... ambition enough to be employed as an under-labourer in clearing ground a little, and removing some of the rubbish that lies in the way to knowledge ... (Locke 1964, 58, Epistle)

And indeed, thanks to the discoveries of science, the doctrine of primary and secondary qualities seemed to have gained a scientific status that it lacked in Antiquity when it was a purely speculative dogma. Impressed by the achievements of science, Locke optimistically believed that through primary qualities science had found a safe, privileged epistemic access to reality, whereas the subjective secondary qualities of everyday experience remained in the dark.

Locke's list of primary qualities includes "solidity, extension, figure, motion or rest, and number" (Locke 1964, II 8 9). Note that the concepts of these qualities are the very concepts that the contemporary science used in its explanations. Secondary qualities, on the contrary, are subjective, not measurable and therefore unfit objects for science:

Not knowing ... what number of particles, nor what motion of them, is fit to produce any precise degree of whiteness, we cannot *demonstrate* the certain equality of any two degrees of whiteness; because we have no certain standard to measure them by, nor means to distinguish every the least real difference, the only help we have being our senses, which in this point fail us. (Locke 1964, IV 2 13)

The real difference between primary and secondary qualities is that

... the ideas of primary qualities of bodies are resemblances of [the qualities] ... but the ideas produced in us by these secondary qualities have no resemblance of [the qualities] at all. (Locke 1964, II 8 15)

Thus Locke believed that there is something similar between our idea of extension and an extended thing, e.g., a stone. But there is nothing similar between our idea of whiteness and milk. The explanation seems to be the same as in Democritus: milk is composed of atoms none of which is white, but a stone is an extended thing composed of extended atoms. In short, our ideas of primary qualities are objective and have a firm foundation in reality; but the same does not hold true of our ideas of secondary qualities.

Nevertheless, Locke held that even the ideas of secondary qualities are not produced in a quite random way: for example, the characteristic configuration of atoms in milk always produces the same sensation of whiteness in a normal perceiver. And yet science teaches us that there is nothing white in milk itself. Therefore Locke says that the ideas of secondary qualities are "constant effects" of "something in the things themselves" while the ideas of primary qualities are "exact resemblances" of that something (Locke 1964, II 30 2).

To summarize: According to Locke, all our perceptual ideas are caused by the qualities of external objects. Some of these ideas resemble their causes, some do not. The ones that do are ideas of primary qualities, and the rest are ideas of secondary qualities.

9.5. George Berkeley

It is the great achievement of George Berkeley to have exposed Locke's doctrine for what it is: a version of a rather naive realism holding that the human mind has a safe and privileged access to reality through the ideas of primary qualities; and these ideas happen to be the concepts used by contemporary science. Berkeley's critical question is simple: How can we ever prove that the ideas of primary qualities are more reliable and more objective than the ideas of secondary qualities? And his answer is equally simple: We can never do that.

Berkeley was a rigorous empiricist who did not want to indulge himself in idle speculations. In philosophy, as in science, one should never go beyond experience. Therefore, we should never speculate about the hidden ("occult") causes of our experiences but be content with what experience gives us here and now: our own ideas. As he put it: "It is evident to any one who takes a survey of the objects of human knowledge, that they are ... ideas..." (Berkeley 1972, 113; Principles # 1).

Locke, too, was an empiricist in this sense. He had said that "the mind in all its thoughts and reasonings hath no immediate object but its own ideas", and therefore "it is evident that our knowledge is only conversant about them" (Locke 1964, IV 1 1). The difference between Locke and Berkeley was that Berkeley was the more consistent empiricist of the two. He argued that Locke abandoned his empiricism and strayed into mere speculation when he maintained that the ideas of primary qualities are more reliable and objective than the ideas of secondary qualities. He put forward several arguments to disprove Locke's view.

(1) The talk about "resemblance" between an idea and its object does not make any sense. An idea can never resemble any material object, not even its "own" object; the qualities of ideas and objects are so totally different. As Berkeley himself put it: "An idea can be like nothing but another idea" (Berkeley 1972, 117; Principles # 9).

In fact, Berkeley is right. The idea of an extended object is not itself extended. It cannot be, because it is in the mind and it does not make sense to ascribe physical properties to mental ideas. Just consider the idea of a horse: Does it have four legs? How much does it weigh? Does it neigh? It seems obvious that an idea is neither four-legged nor does it neigh or weigh more than half a ton. It does not have these properties; it just represents them. Therefore it is useful to distinguish between having properties and representing them.

Because an idea may represent physical properties without having them, there need be no resemblance at all between the representation and the thing represented. It is true that a photograph can be said to resemble a person, but this is because they are both physical things. A mental representation, on the contrary, cannot be said to resemble its physical object because they belong to entirely different ontological categories ("ideas" and "things", respectively); and yet there is a relation representation between them.

A defender of Locke could argue that Locke's word 'resemblance' could be translated into a more modern idiom by using the term 'representation'. Thus, instead of saying that the idea of a horse resembles the horse itself, one should say that the idea of a horse represents the horse. The relation of representation between an idea and its object does not require any sameness of properties between the two terms of the relation: it is not necessary that the idea of a horse and the horse itself share a single property; it is enough that the idea represents its object. Thus there need be no resemblance between the representation and the thing represented.

But does all this help Locke? Perhaps a little, but the fundamental difficulty remains. If one is committed to empiricism, as Locke is, one cannot go beyond one's own experiences or ideas to see whether they resemble their objects or whether they correctly represent their objects. In order to perform that feat, one should be able to compare one idea with an external object, but that is what strict empiricism forbids. Therefore the doctrine of primary and secondary qualities is not compatible with the basic tenets of empiricism.

(2) Berkeley argues that our habit of dividing things into "objective" and "subjective" is unfounded. For instance, there is nothing in experience to justify the claim that hotness really is in the fire but the pain caused by a prickle is not in the pin:

> Since ... you neither judge the sensation itself occasioned by the pin, nor anything like it to be in the pin; you should not ... judge the sensation occasioned by the fire, or anything like it, to be in the fire. (Berkeley 1972, 208–209; 1st Dialogue)

We do think that sometimes pins cause experiences of pain and fires cause experiences of warmth, but we do not think that the pain is in the pin in the same way as the warmth is in the fire. But why do we think like this? Is it warranted by anything in our immediate experience? Does experience justify our naive belief that a fire is warm in itself but a pin is not painful in itself? Berkeley has asked a very good question. (Those who disagree are invited to consider the following questions: Is a laser beam warm in itself? Is it painful in itself? Is it more like a pin or fire?)

(3) Berkeley further doubts whether there is anything in our immediate experience that justifies the belief that primary qualities, such as extension and shape, are in the external world while secondary qualities, such as colours, are only in the mind. He asks: "But do not colours appear to the eye as coexisting in the same place with extension and figures?" (Berkeley 1972, 235; 1st Dialogue). If we do not go beyond experience, we must answer in the affirmative, for if we are committed to empiricism and if colours are seen to be in the same place as extension and figure, there is no reason whatever to say that, for example, the greenness of a green apple is in the mind whereas the shape of the same apple is in the apple itself, that is, in the external world.

9.6. Conclusion

It seems that after Berkeley's criticism there are two possibilities: either we reject empiricism or the doctrine of primary and secondary qualities. Locke wanted have them both, but that is not possible. In fact, Berkeley pointed out that nobody can consistently accept all of the following theses:

(1)   The real objects of experience are our own ideas.
(2)   In science and philosophy one should not make hypotheses that go beyond all possible experience.
(3)   Primary qualities are more real and more reliable than secondary

qualities.

Locke tried to accept all three, Berkeley pointed out that (1) and (2) are incompatible with (3), and therefore he rejected (3).

We do not suggest that the classical empiricism of Locke (or even its more consistent version in Berkeley) is a philosophical doctrine that everybody in his right mind should accept. We have only tried to show that the doctrine of primary and secondary qualities is incompatible with the basic tenets of classical empiricism. In what follows we trace some modern theories that share Locke's optimism about the possibility of finding a direct access to reality. They have not found that access in the ideas of primary qualities but in such things as acquaintance, indexical experiences and *de re* acts.

10. ACQUAINTANCE

10.1. The meaning of 'acquaintance'

The theory of acquaintance can be seen as an attempt to pursue the epistemological project of achieving absolute certainty. While the Greek sceptics and Berkeley argued that we can be absolutely sure only of our sensations or ideas, the acquaintance theorists, most notably Bertrand Russell, hold that the sphere of certainty can be extended to the objects of acquaintance. Indeed, Richard L. Gregory argues that Russell's distinction between knowledge by acquaintance and knowledge by description can be seen as a modern version of Locke's distinction between primary and secondary qualities (Gregory 1981, 352). He is right inasmuch as both the ideas of primary qualities and knowledge by acquaintance are claimed to have a direct access to reality.

To put it in the terminology of acquaintance, Locke thought that we are "acquainted" with the external objects through the ideas of primary qualities, whereas Berkeley held that we are "acquainted" only with our own ideas. We believe that Russell's theory of acquaintance is just as vulnerable to criticism as was Locke's theory to Berkeley's devastating arguments. However, before we start to examine and criticize Russell's views it is useful to have a look at what the term 'acquaintance' means in ordinary language and in philosophical jargon.

The first thing to be noticed is the fact that the dictionary definition of the word 'acquaintance' has little to do with the technical sense given to the term by philosophers, especially by Russell. For instance, *The Oxford*

Minidictionary gives the following succint definitions:

> *Acquaint* v.t. make known to, *be acquainted with*, know slightly.
> *Acquaintance* n. slight knowledge; person one knows slightly.

When philosophers speak of acquaintance, they have a totally different thing in mind. For instance, D. W. Smith's article 'Acquaintance' begins as follows:

Acquaintance is *direct awareness*, what the medievals called 'intuitive cognition' (*cognitio intuitiva*) and later philosophers called simply 'intuition'. More precisely, acquaintance is a *singular* awareness of a particular object *in one's presence*. The paradigm is perception, where the subject is in a causal contact with the object of awareness ... (Smith 1991, 15)

The difference between the ordinary and the technical senses is clear: (1) In ordinary speech we say that we are acquainted with a person who is not present at the moment, e.g., 'I am acquainted with the President'. But if the term 'acquainted' is used in its technical meaning of 'direct awareness of a particular in one's presence', it cannot be said that a man is acquainted with his wife if she is out of sight! (2) The "slight knowledge" involved in the everyday concept of acquaintance involves the ability to recognize or re-identify the thing one is acquainted with. But the philosophers' concept of acquaintance does not require any such ability: I may now be acquainted with a thing that I cannot recognize five minutes from now. All that is required by the technical concept of acquaintance is a direct perceptual contact with the object here and now.

10.2. James's acquaintance

It was William James who introduced the concept of acquaintance into philosophy. His concept, however, still bore traces of its origin in everyday language. James noticed that many languages have two different verbs for two different types of cognition: German has 'kennen' and 'wissen', French has 'connaître' and 'savoir', and so on. In a translation of a sentence like 'I know him but I don't know whether he is such-and-such' the French and the Germans would use two different verbs. James tried to avoid this deficiency of English by introducing the terms 'acquaintance' and 'knowledge about' to designate these two types of cognition. (For simplicity, we will speak of 'knowledge' and 'acquaintance' when dealing with his views.) James points out that acquaintance presupposes very little knowledge about its object. It is as if acquaintance could do its job independently of knowledge. He writes:

I am acquainted with many people and things, which I know very little about except their presence in the places where I have met them. I know the color blue when I see it, and the flavor of a pear when I taste it! ... but about the inner nature of these facts or what makes them what they are, I can say nothing at all. I cannot impart acquaintance with them to any one who has not already made it himself. I cannot describe them, make a blind man guess what blue is like. ... At most, I can say to my friends, Go to certain places and act in certain ways, and these objects will probably come. (James 1950 Vol. 1, 221)

It is clear from this passage that James held the everyday view that acquaintance involves some kind of ability to re-identify the thing one is acquainted with. Thus, for him, to be acquainted with X is to be able to tell X from other things. Or, to put it differently, to be acquainted with X is to perceive X as something that one is already familiar with. This ability does not, however, presuppose the ability to define X or to give a complete description of X.

In fact, it seems that James's acquaintance is an instance of non-propositional knowledge, that is, knowledge that cannot be expressed by sentences; whereas his "knowledge about" belongs to propositional knowledge or knowledge involving whole sentences and expressible through them. At least James says that the difference between acquaintance and knowledge is reflected in the structure of a sentence so that the subject stands for the object of acquaintance while the predicate gives (propositional) information about the object. In other words, acquaintance is the first act in the cognitive process; it creates the connection between the mind and its object; and then comes "knowledge about" and ascribes properties to the object. So, the task of acquaintance is to identify (or re-identify) the object and the task of knowledge is to predicate properties of it. In James's own words:

What we are only acquainted with is only present to our minds; we have it, or the idea of it. But when we know about it, we do more than merely have it; we seem, as we think over its relations, to subject it to a sort of treatment and to operate upon it with our thought." (James 1950 Vol. 1, 222; e.r.)

The following is maybe the clearest passage where James describes the non-conceptual character of acquaintance. Note especially two things: (1) how the "meaningless" demonstratives 'this' and 'that' work as means of getting acquainted with a thing, and (2) how James explicitly mentions re-identification as an essential feature of acquaintance:

Any fact, be it a thing, event, or quality, may be conceived sufficiently for purposes of identification, if only it be singled out and marked so as to separate it from other things. [1] Simply calling it "this" or "that" will suffice. To speak in technical language, a subject may be conceived by its *denotation*, with no *connotation*, or a very minimum of connotation, attached. [2] The essential point is that it should be re-identified by us as that which the talk is about; and no full representation of it is necessary for this. ... Most of the objects of our thought, however, are to some degree represented as well as merely pointed out. (James 1950 Vol. 1, 462–3)

To sum up, James's basic point is that there are two modes of cognition, non-propositional acquaintance and propositional "knowledge about", and in acquaintance we have a direct access to reality. It was this idea that was taken over and further developed by Russell.

10.3. Russell's acquaintance

With Russell, 'acquaintance' breaks all ties with ordinary language and becomes a purely technical term. In his theory, acquaintance does not require the ability to re-identify the object one is acquainted with. His basic idea is that in knowledge by acquaintance we have a direct, immediate, non-conceptual access to the external object. He defines 'acquaintance' in a way that was later to become the official definition of acquaintance (cf. D.W. Smith's definition above):

I say that I am *acquainted* with an object when I have a direct cognitive relation to that object, that is when I am directly aware of the object itself. (Russell 1986, 16)

In another context he further adds that the direct awareness of an object (i.e. acquaintance) takes place "without the intermediary of any process of inference or any knowledge of truths" (Russell 1967, 25). That is to say, acquaintance with an object does not require any propositional knowledge about that object. I may be acquainted (in the Russellian sense) with an object about which I know no truths at all. Therefore acquaintance does not presuppose conceptual or propositional knowledge. The opposite of knowledge by acquaintance is knowledge by description. Russell defines it in the following way:

I shall say that an object is 'known by description' when we know that it is '*the* so-and-so', that is when we know that there is one object, and no more, having a certain property ... (Russell 1986, 20)

For instance, I may believe that the richest man in town votes the Conservative Party without being acquainted with that man, indeed even without knowing who he his, because I hold the general belief that all rich people support the Conservative Party. This is a general belief and not a belief about any person in particular. It involves both a "process of inference" ('All rich people vote Conservative; therefore the richest man in town votes Conservative') and "knowledge of truths" ('Rich people generally vote Conservative').

Therefore the essential difference between knowledge by acquaintance and knowledge by description lies in the fact that knowledge by acquaintance is direct while knowledge by description is mediated by descriptions (or concepts, as we would like to say).

Russell further argues that knowledge by acquaintance is the basic form of knowledge without which all other knowledge would be impossible. He writes: "All our knowledge ... rests upon acquaintance as its foundation" (Russell 1967, 26). This means that if there were no acquaintance, there would be no knowledge by description either, for all knowledge presupposes acquaintance. (This is a new formulation of Hume's thesis that ideas must be reducible to impressions.)

In another place he emphasises that knowledge by acquaintance is not an inferior kind of knowledge. Quite the contrary, there is nothing that it lacks:

When you have acquaintance with a particular, you understand that particular itself quite fully, independently of the fact that there are a great many propositions about it that you do not know, but propositions concerning the particular are not necessary to be known in order that you may know what the particular itself is. It is rather the other way round. In order to understand a proposition in which the name of a particular occurs, you must already be acquainted with that particular. (Russell 1972, 59)

Therefore the dictionary definition of acquaintance as "slight knowledge" does not apply to Russell's concept of acquaintance. There is nothing slight about the kind of knowledge he meant when he spoke about knowledge by acquaintance.

There is a curious thing about Russell's concept of acquaintance that should be mentioned in passing, even if it will be charitably forgotten afterwards. It has to do with the nature of the objects that we are acquainted with. Russell says that sense-data are the only objects of acquaintance:

When we ask what are the kinds of objects with which we are acquainted, the first and most obvious example is *sense-data*. ... among the objects with which we are acquainted are not included physical objects (as opposed to sense-data), nor other people's minds. (Russell 1986, 17 and 19)

He himself is not able to stick consistently to this stipulation. He constantly lapses into speaking about our being acquainted with things in the external world. There are, then, two interpretations of acquaintance: the subjective one according to which we are acquainted with our sense-data only, and the objective one that holds that we are acquainted with ordinary physical things. Because the subjective interpretation is too weak for Russell's purposes and because the followers of Russell have all accepted the objective interpretation, we also do so.

10.4. Proper names and acquaintance

The difference between knowledge by acquaintance and knowledge by description is reflected in language: we use proper names (Russell speaks simply of 'names') to refer to objects with which we are acquainted and descriptions to refer to other objects.

The difference between names and descriptions is not primarily a linguistic but an epistemic one. If one just sees or hears a linguistic sign, one cannot know whether it is a name or a description. Only when we get to know that the user of the sign is acquainted with the referent of the sign can we be certain that it is a proper name. It follows that the word 'Socrates' is a name for Plato, who was acquainted with Socrates, but for us, who have only read descriptions about him, this same word is only a description, no different in this respect from expressions like 'the teacher of Plato', 'the drinker of the hemlock', etc. Thus, as Russell puts it:

We are not acquainted with Socrates, and therefore cannot name him. When we use the word 'Socrates', we are really using a description. Our thought may be rendered by such phrase as, 'The Master of Plato', or 'The Philosopher who drank the hemlock', or 'The person whom logicians assert to be mortal', but we certainly do not use the name as a name in the proper sense of the word. (Russell 1972, 56)

Strictly speaking, only demonstrative pronouns are Russellian logical proper names: "The only words that one does use as names in the logical sense are words like 'this' or 'that'" (Russell 1972, 56). What is peculiar about demonstratives is that they do not seem to have any descriptive meaning at all: there is nothing in common among all the objects that can be referred to by using the word 'this' (except for the fact that they are in the speaker's immediate vicinity; but that is not a real descriptive property). The same does not hold true of the descriptive word 'horse' since all horses have some common equine features on account of which they are (correctly) called horses.

In short, the function of a proper name (like that of acquaintance) is just to pick out an individual, and the function of the rest of the sentence is to predicate a property of it. (This is just what James said.)

10.5. "Propositions of acquaintance"

Only people who are acquainted with the thing they are speaking about use its name as a proper name, while for the rest of us it is a mere description. When Plato asserted Socrates to be mortal, he meant something totally different from what we say when we use an apparently identical statement. According to Russell, the difference between Plato's assertion and ours is that, while Socrates himself occurs as a constituent of the proposition which Plato asserted, only a description of Socrates occurs in our proposition. He writes:

For the name itself is merely a means of pointing to the thing, and does not occur in what you are asserting, so that if one thing has two names, you make exactly the same assertion whichever of the two names you use, provided they are really names and not truncated descriptions. (Russell 1972, 103)

When Plato said 'Socrates is mortal', he expressed what could be called a "proposition of acquaintance". Its structure is:

$$S\ [\ is\ M\ ]$$

But when we utter the same sentence, our utterance expresses an ordinary proposition which has an entirely different structure:

$$[\ S\ is\ M\ ]$$

Here the items inside the square brackets belong to the non-physical, i.e., conceptual realm. The difference between Plato and us is that while Plato made an assertion about the relationship between a particular and a concept, we make an assertion about the relationship between two concepts. (In fact it makes sense to say that Socrates is a mere concept for us because we have never been acquainted with him.)

Thus Socrates himself as a physical object is a constituent of the proposition that Plato asserted. But only the individual concept of Socrates occurs in what we assert about him. Another way of expressing of what we take to be Russell's point is to say that there are two kinds of propositions, complete and incomplete. (The idea comes from John Perry whose views on indexicality we will examine later on.) A complete proposition consists of conceptual elements only whereas an incomplete proposition consists of an empty place, which can be filled by an object, and a concept. Pictorially:

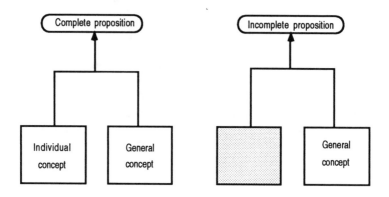

Fig.1.

When we have added an object to an incomplete proposition, we get a genuine Russellian hybrid proposition consisting of a concrete object and an abstract concept.

10.6. Frege's criticism of Russellian propositions

Russell quite clearly holds that if we are acquainted with a thing and if we say something about it, then that thing itself is a constituent of the proposition that we express. Taken literally this is, of course, nonsense. If we distinguish between concrete and abstract entities, i.e. entities that are in space and time and those that are not, then we must say that concepts and propositions are abstract entities. And abstract entities cannot have parts that are concrete entities. In particular, an abstract proposition cannot have a concrete thing as its constituent.

To repeat what was said at the beginning, a sentence is a concrete entity – sounds in the air or marks on the paper – but the meaning of a sentence is something different; it is an abstract entity that cannot be located in space and time. But it can be expressed by a sentence (or by several sentences). For instance the proposition that the dog is dead can be expressed by the following sentences: 'The dog is dead', 'Le chien est mort', 'Der Hund ist tot', etc. And what makes each of these sentences true is the fact (the actual state of affairs) that the dog is dead.

Thus we have three different kinds of entities: (1) concrete sentences, (2) their meanings or propositions and (3) facts or actual states of affairs. A corresponding distinction can be made in the case of a word: (1) the word itself (e.g., 'dog'), (2) its sense or meaning (the one that is expressed by an entry in a dictionary) and (3) its referent (the animal itself).

Russell was extremely reluctant to accept propositions or meanings. He tried to get along without them. In private correspondence, Gottlob Frege tried to make Russell see the absurdity of the view that concrete particulars could figure as constituents of propositions. Frege, using the distinction between referent and sense, argued that the concrete referent of a name is the wrong sort of an entity to be a constituent of an abstract proposition; only the sense of a name can be such a constituent. Frege wrote:

... [1] Mont Blanc with its snowfields is not itself a component part of the thought [i.e. proposition] that Mont Blanc is more than 4,000 metres high. ... [2] The sense of the word 'moon' is a component part of the thought [i.e. proposition] that the moon is smaller than the earth. ... [3] We can nevertheless say: 'The moon is identical with the heavenly body closest to the earth'. ... The identity is not an identity of sense, nor of part of the sense, but of denotation [i.e. referent]. (Frege and Russell 1988, 56)

Frege makes here the following points:

(1)   A concerete particular (i.e. a referent of a word) cannot be a constituent of an abstract proposition.
(2)   But an abstract meaning (i.e. a sense of a word) can well be a constituent of an abstract proposition.
(3)   When we make a true identity statement, e.g., 'Cicero is Tully', we do not assert that the senses of the words 'Cicero' and 'Tully' are identical (they clearly are not) but that their referents are identical, that is, that the two words refer to one and the same thing that is called by those two names.

Russell could not accept Frege's solution because he held that there are no such things as meanings (senses, propositions and the like). Therefore he just repeated his view in his reply:

... I believe that in spite of its snowfields Mont Blanc itself is a component part of what is actually asserted in the proposition 'Mont Blanc is more than 4,000 metres high'. We do not assert the thought, for this is a private psychological matter: we assert the object of thought ... in which Mont Blanc is itself a component part. (Frege and Russell 1988, 57)

It would take us too far afield to correct all the unclarities in Russell's reply. Instead, let us try to see whether a Russellian position can be defended against the Fregean attack. And since attack is the best defence, the Russellians argue that Frege cannot give a proper explanation of the phenomenon of indexicality.

11. MENTAL INDEXICALITY

11.1. Indexicality: the here-and-now of cognition

Our main interest in this section will be mental indexicality. But since it is a difficult topic, we start with linguistic indexicality. Indexical words, such as 'I', 'this', 'here' and 'now' have a peculiar feature: they refer to different objects in different contexts of utterance, whereas non-indexical words, such as ordinary proper names, always refer to the same object. For instance, if I use the word 'I', I refer to myself, but if you use the same word, you refer to yourself. But if I use my proper name and you use the same proper name, we both refer to the same object, namely me. In short, the refence of indexical words is context-sensitive, that is, depends on their context of utterance, while the reference of non-indexical words is not context-sensitive. Therefore we may characterize indexical words as follows:

> *Indexical words* are words that pick out different objects in different contexts.

This characterisation of indexicality applies only to single words. But by using the concept of proposition (i.e. the meaning of a sentence) it can be broadened so that it is also applicable to sentences:

> *An indexical sentence* is a sentence that expresses different propositions in different contexts.

In other words, if a sentences contains an indexical expression, for example 'this' or 'I', then its context of utterance determines which proposition is expressed. Just like the pronoun 'I' picks out, or refers to, different individuals when used by different persons on different occasions, so the sentence 'I am hungry', uttered by different people, expresses different propositions on each context of use. For instance, if I say: 'I am hungry' and you you say: 'I am hungry', we use the same words to express different propositions: I say something about myself and you say something about yourself. Or if I say today: 'I am hungry', and if I utter the same words again next week, then I express different propositions on these two occasions. Thus the context of utterance (who utters the words and at what time etc.) determines which proposition has been asserted.

To sum up, if a sentence contains at least one indexical word, then it is context-sensitive, which means that the context of its utterance determines which proposition has been uttered. But if the sentence does not contain any indexical elements, then it is context-insensitive: it expresses the same proposition on all contexts of utterance. In short, in the case of indexicals, *context determines proposition*. (However, it would be more accurate to say that the context *co-determines* the proposition because the meanings of the non-indexical words of the sentence do most of the determination, after all.)

11.2. Frege on indexical propositions

Indexicality has a close connection to acquaintance. Russell's examples of logically proper names were 'this' and 'that'; and they are indexical expressions. He further held that 'this' and 'that' do not really occur in the propositions in which they seemingly occur; instead, their referents occur in them. Thus there are two different kinds of proposition (or this is how we interpreted him): (1) ordinary propositions consisiting of concepts and (2) what we have called "propositions of acquaintance" consisting of an object and a concept. And it is precisely the existence of such hybrid propositions that Frege denied. He argued that concrete object cannot be constituents of abstract propositions.

Frege's basic view of indexical expressions is rather simple. It is, to use Perry's expression, that *indexicals are communicative shortcuts*. That is, if we distinguish sentences from propositions, then it does not make sense to ask whether propositions contain indexicals or not; for indexicals belong to the level of sentences, not to that of propositions. In other words, there are no indexical elements in propositions. All apparent indexicals can always be eliminated. Thus, according to Frege's view, *there are no essential indexicals*. Recalling that propositions are also contents of experiences, this means that there are no mental indexicals, either.

Frege's grounds for his view are as follows. He maintains that we cannot understand a sentence containing an indexical expression unless we know the context of its utterance. He seems to think that an indexical sentence is somehow incomplete, and we, as it were, fill in the empty spaces left by the indexical sentence when we understand or grasp it. For instance, if we hear the sentence 'I am hungry' from the next room, without recognizing the speaker, we do not know which proposition has been uttered. But if we see (and recognize) the utterer, we know which proposition was uttered. In Frege's own words:

> In all [indexical] cases the mere wording, as it can be preserved in writing, is not the complete expression of the [proposition]; the *knowledge* of certain *conditions accompanying the utterance*, which are used as means of expressing the [proposition], is needed for us to *grasp* the [proposition] correctly. (Frege 1988, 40; e.a.)

In what sense, then, are indexicals "inessential"? There are two answers: (1) They are inessential because they are eliminable. Any indexical sentence can be translated into a non-indexical sentence. For instance the indexical sentence 'That is a cow' can be translated into the non-indexical sentence 'The animal that GF is pointing at on 23 June 1908 in Jena at 11:34 is a cow'. (2) The second answer can be found in two passages in Frege. He says that (i) knowledge of the context of utterance "is needed for us to *grasp* the [proposition] correctly" (Frege 1988, 40); and that (ii) "[a] property of a [proposition] will be called inessential if it consists in, or follows from, the fact that this [proposition] is *grasped* by a thinker" (Frege 1988, 54; e.a.). It follows from (i) and (ii) that the indexical elements of a proposition are inessential.

It seems that Frege is arguing here that a proposition, if it really is a proposition, is always complete, but its *expression* is not always complete. This is quite understandable, for ordinarily the speaker does not want to bore the hearer with the details about the context which the latter can grasp as a matter of course. For instance, it would be rather odd if the speaker would tell the hearer the time and place of the utterance, his own name, etc. (The hearer may have to mention these things when he reports what the original speaker said.)

Nevertheless, the problem of mental indexicality is not solved by Frege when he says that all indexical expressions can be eliminated. Even if all linguistic indexicality were eliminable, it is still an open question whether there is such a thing as mental indexicality or indexicality-in-the-mind. And it does seem that there are indexical experiences in every human being's stream of consciousness, for everybody has the "feeling" of being "here-and-now" and of being "the subject of this very experience". These are fundamental experiences that are (presumably) shared by all humans. (John Perry defends the existence and ineliminability of such experiences against Frege. We turn to his views in a moment.)

On the other hand, a supporter of Frege could argue that if there are such indexical experiences, why don't we simply say that there is something in common among all those people who have the feeling of being here-and-now? That something would be an abstract indexical content that can be expressed by such words as 'here' and 'now'. (This standpoint has been adopted by D. W. Smith, whose views on indexicality we will examine later on.)

Thus there seem to be three possible attitudes to mental indexicality:

(1)   Indexicality is a merely linguistic phenomenon. There is nothing of the kind in the mind. This is Frege's view.

(2)   There are indexical experiences in a person's stream of consciousness, but there are no abstract indexical contents ("thisness", "hereness", etc.) that could be shared by different people. This is Perry's view.

(3)   There are both concrete indexical experiences in a person's stream of consciousness and abstract indexical contents that can be shared by several people. This is D. W. Smith's view.

11.3. Perry and essentially indexical propositions

John Perry claims that Frege was wrong in holding that the indexical elements of language cannot be found in what language expresses, i.e., in propositions. Perry argues that the correct view is that non-indexical sentences express complete propositions, whereas indexical sentences (i.e., sentences containing indexical words) do not. In other words, Perry holds that *all propositions containing indexicals are by nature incomplete.* He makes this point by distinguishing between 'sense had' and 'sense expressed': "The sense *had* is incomplete; the sense *expressed* on a given occasion will be the result of completing that sense, with some sense completer available from the context of utterance" (Perry 1990, 54).

Perry seems to accept the Russellian view of the proposition, for he says that a complete proposition (or "thought") is composed of an object and of an incomplete sense : "To have a thought [i.e., proposition] we need an object and an incomplete sense" (Perry 1990, 67). Such propositions are hybrids like Russell's "propositions of acquaintance". Perry admits that Frege would not have accepted such hybrid propositions that have concrete objects as their constituents: "The idea of individuating thoughts [i.e., propositions] by objects, or sequences of objects, would be particularly out of place in his [Frege's] system" (Perry 1990, 70).

In a later paper, Perry calls these incomplete propositions *relativised propositions*. According to him, relativised propositions are "abstract objects corresponding to sentences containing indexicals" (Perry 1988, 97). To illustrate his point, Perry tells us an autobiographic story about how once in a supermarket he was searching a shopper who was making a mess with a leaking bag of sugar until he realised that he himself was that person. He argues that to believe 'I am making a mess' is a totally different thing than to believe 'The shopper with a leaking bag of sugar is making a mess', for first Perry believed merely the second sentence and only later the first one, and there was a dramatic change in his mental state when he came to accept the first one.

Perry seems to deny the possibility of abstract indexical contents because he says that many shoppers who all have a leaking bag of sugar may simultaneously accept the sentence 'I am making a mess' without being in the same belief state: "What the members of [this group] have in common is not what they believe. There is no de dicto [i.e . complete] proposition that all the ... shoppers ... believe" (Perry 1988, 97). But there is something that they share, namely the incomplete proposition '_____ is making a mess':

We are clearly classifying the shoppers ... corresponding to what we have been calling "relativized propositions" [i.e. incomplete propositions] – abstract objects corresponding to sentences containing indexicals. (Perry 1988, 97)

And insofar as they accept the same relativised proposition, they can be said to be in the same belief state. But there is no complete proposition that they all accept because they do not "believe the same thing of the same object." (Recall that Perry's propositions are Russellian hybrid entities.)

It seems that this incomplete sense is precisely the Russellian hybrid proposition *minus* the object. In other words, an incomplete proposition contains an empty place that can be filled by an object. A complete proposition does not contain any empty places: it consists of conceptual elements only. Therefore, the meaning of a non-indexical sentence is a complete proposition, whereas the meaning of an indexical sentence is an incomplete proposition.

Thus, going beyond Perry, it could be argued that there are three kinds of proposition-like entities:

(1)   Ordinary Fregean propositions that consist only of conceptual elements. (They are the meanings of non-indexical sentences).

(2)   Incomplete Perrian propositions. (They are meanings of indexical sentences and they contain an empty place.)

(3)   Complete Russellian propositions. (They are incomplete propositions whose empty place has been filled by an object, therefore they are hybrid propositions).

To put the point of Perry's story of several messy shoppers in our new terminology:

(a)   All the messy shoppers have the same partial belief state, expressible in each case by 'I am making a mess'. This means that they all accept the same incomplete Perrian proposition.

(b)   They do not believe the same Fregean proposition, because every one of them has a different individual concept of himself, an *Ichvorstellung*, as a constituent of the proposition.

(c)   They do not accept the same complete Russellian proposition, because every one of them is a constituent of the proposition that he believes. In other words, they do not believe "the same thing of the same object".

It is important to notice that the Perrian proposition is so incomplete that it cannot be used to individuate any individual shopper's belief from the similar beliefs of the other messy shoppers: they all accept the same incomplete proposition. But the Fregean and the Russellian propositions can be used to individuate their beliefs, because they all accept different Fregean or Russellian propositions. (The difference between them is that the Fregean proposition does the individuation in an internalist way, while the Russellian proposition does it in an externalist way.)

11.4. The experience of indexicality

We believe that Russell and Perry are wrong if they postulate strange hybrid propositions consisting of concrete objects and abstract meanings in order to explain the phenomenon of indexicality. But it is quite another question whether there is such a thing as mental indexicality. Frege firmly maintains that there isn't, but simple reflexion seems to suggest that there is something in everybody's stream of consciousness that corresponds to the indexical expressions of language.

The point can be put as follows: if there were nothing in our experience that corresponds to indexicals, then we would be viewing the world from a quite impersonal viewpoint. Thomas Nagel has called such a view the centerless view. He describes it beautifully:

Merely being TN isn't good enough for me: I have to think of myself as the world soul in humble disguise. ... the same thought is available to any of you. You are all subjects of the centerless universe. ... Essentially I have no particular point of view at all, but apprehend the world as centerless. As it happens, I ordinarily view the world from a certain vantage point, using the eyes, the person, the daily life of TN as a kind of window. (Nagel 1986, 61)

The objective self that I find viewing the world through TN is not unique: each of you has one. Or perhaps I should say that each of you is one, for the objective self is not a distinct entity. (Nagel 1986, 63)

A stream of consciousness without any experience of indexicality would be a world soul that, unlike Nagel's world soul, cannot look at the world from any particular point of view. It would be totally objective and totally detached. It is hard to think of such an entity.

But let us turn to something less breathtaking, namely Hans Reichenbach's and D. W. Smith's hierarchies of indexicality. In his book *Elements of Symbolic Logic*, Reichenbach argues that all indexical words (or 'token-reflexive words' as he calls them) are definable by means of 'this token':

It is easily seen that all these [i.e. indexical] words can be defined in terms of the phrase 'this token'. The word 'I', for instance, means the same as 'the person utters this token'; 'now' means the same as 'the time at which this token is uttered'; 'this table' means the same as 'the table pointed to by a gesture accompanying this token'. We therefore need inquire only into the meaning of the phrase 'this token'. (Reichenbach 1966, 284)

It is questionable whether 'I' really means the same as 'the person uttering this token', but what is important about Reichenbach's analysis is his insight that all indexical words are reducible to one basic form of indexicality, namely the self-reference of the expression 'this token'. This idea has been applied to the mental sphere by D. W. Smith in his book *The Circle of Acquaintance*. (Smith does not mention Reichenbach, but Russell who developed similar ideas at the time. See Russell 1980, Ch. 7.) Smith writes:

Roughly, the phrase "this experience" is fundamental, and the other indexicals are defined so that:

> "now" means the same as "the time of this experience";
> "I" means "the person now having this experience";
> "here" means "the place where I am now";
> "this [object]" means "the object now here visually before me."
> (Smith 1989, 206; Smith's square brackets)

What is new in Smith is, besides the application to the mental sphere, the idea of order among indexicals. Whereas the earlier theorists thought that there are several unclearly related indexicals, and Reichenbach thought that all indexicals all definable in terms of 'this token', Smith says that indexicals form a clear hierarchy in such a way that first comes 'this experience', second 'now', third 'I', fourth 'here', fifth 'this', etc.

What has that to do with the question as to the existence of mental indexicals? It shows that it is not necessary to explain all varieties of indexical experience; it is enough to explain the nature of the indexicality of 'this experience'. But this is a difficult task, indeed. We suggest that this basic form of indexicality is closely related to the fact that our conscious experiences are conscious of themselves and therefore self-referential.

11.5. The self-reference of some experiences

Indexicality is a form of self-reference, as Reichenbach pointed out. And, within the mental sphere, self-reference means just the fact that an experience refers to itself, that it is *conscious*. What is common to all mental phenomena is their intentionality, the feature that they are experiences about something. This means that in every experience we are aware of the object of that experience. But if it is a conscious experience, then we are also aware of the experience itself. It is as if there were two rays of consciousness: one directed to the object and one directed back to the act itself. Yet they are not two distinct experiences but only one. It seems that consciouness is just this self-monitoring activity of the human mind. We do not claim that this indexical aspect is very prominent in every experience. In fact, most often it is in the background, but it can be brought to the foreground in what philosophers call reflection.

When one says that animals do not have consciousness, one is saying, among other things, that animals cannot learn the use of indexical expressions. Consequently, an animal could be said to be conscious to the extent that it masters the use of indexicals. And it seems that one of the reasons why animals cannot learn the use of indexical expressions is that they do not have indexical experiences: they are not aware of 'now', 'here', etc., since if they were, they would also be aware of their opposites: 'then', 'there', etc. In other words, the experiential world of animals is wholly here-and-now but they do not know it, because that knowledge would presuppose the ability to be aware of there-and-then, too. As Aristotle put it, "Knowledge is of opposites".

It is important to notice that what is first in the logical order of indexicals (namely, "this experience") is not the first one to be learned. On the contrary, it seems that the order of learning is more or less the reverse of the logical order. Thus only an animal which has learnt the use of 'I' or 'now' can be called a fully conscious being. 'This' and 'that' are not enough.

Now we have gone so deep into the mysteries of indexicality that it is impossible for us to go any further. We conclude that if there are indexical contents, then there is no reason to suppose that indexical or context-sensitive mental acts should have a special direct access to reality. We believe that all acts are equal in this respect. We will return to the experience of indexicality after having examined one more version of alleged direct access to reality: so-called mental acts *de re*.

12. MENTAL ACTS *DE RE*

12.1. The de re/de dicto *distinction*

Acquaintance and indexicality are closely connected with so-called mental acts *de re*. Unfortunately there is no consensus as to what such acts are. John Searle writes in desperation that he has "never seen a clear and precise statement of what exactly the *de dicto/de re* distinction as applied to propositional attitudes is supposed to be" (Searle 1983, 208). And D. W. Smith has found three different interpretations of the distinction:

Quite different distinctions have been drawn under the terms "*de re*" and "*de dicto*": (i) that between singular and non-singular forms of intentional state; (ii) that between intentional states that are veridical (of a "*res*", or real object), and hence "relational", and those that have a content (are of a "*dictum*"), and hence are "notional", but are not necessarily veridical, or relational; (iii) that between context-dependent, or "indexical", relational attitudes and those that are merely notional. (Smith 1989, 188–9, fn 1)

To make things still worse, let us take just one short quote in which two additional features are added to the three mentioned by Smith. It comes from Richard L. Gregory's *Mind in Science*:

Russell distinguished between propositional and non-propositional knowledge ... For Russell, direct awareness ('acquaintance') is *de re* (non-propositional) rather than *de dicto* (propositional). (Gregory 1981, 353)

Thus we have the following characteristics that are used in drawing the distinction between *de re* and *de dicto*:

	de re	*de dicto*
1	singular	non-singular
2	relational	notional
3	indexical	non-indexical
4	non-propositional	propositional
5	acquaintance	knowledge by description

We briefly explain what is meant by these distinctions:

(1)   A mental act is singular if it is directed to, or about, only one object (*res*); else it is non-singular.

(2)   A mental act is "relational" if it is necessarily veridical, which means that there must be a direct infallible access from the act to the object (*res*). If there is no such access, the act is rather about the concept or notion (*dictum*).

(3)   A mental act is indexical if it picks out different object in different contexts, while a non-indexical act always picks out the same object.

(4)   A mental act is propositional if it has an abstract proposition as its content; and it is non-propositional if it has a Russellian hybrid proposition as its content.

(5)   A mental act of acquaintance is directly aware of its object; no mediating concepts are needed. In knowledge by description such concepts or descriptions connect the act to its object.

So there seems to be quite a confusion about what the distinction *de re*/*de dicto* really is. There are, of course, many ways of trying to disentangle this conceptual mess. We try one of them: we trace the history of the concept *de re* to see whether there is any "original" meaning that could shed some light on the present confusion.

12.2. Aquinas and two kinds of necessity

There is a close connection between the concept of *de re* modality and the doctrine called essentialism. According to Anthony Flew's *Dictionary of Philosophy*, the most important form of essentialism is "a metaphysical view dating back to Aristotle":

It maintains that some objects – no matter how described – have essences; that is, they have, essentially or necessarily, certain properties, without which they could not exist or be the things that they are. This is often seen as equivalent to the claim that there are *de re* modalities ... (Flew 1984, 112)

According to Aristotelian essentialism, it is a *de re* necessity that man is rational, since rationality belongs by definition to the concept of man. But there is no necessity in man's being white or black, because no particular colour of skin is involved in the essence of 'man'. There is also another type of necessity. For example, if I correctly describe somebody as 'the tallest man in town', then it is necessary that he is taller than any other regular inhabitant of the town. But this necessity does not belong to his essence, to him merely "as a man" but only to him "as the tallest man", that is, only under the description ("*dictum*") 'the tallest man in town'. Therefore, it is a case of *de dicto* modality.

There is a kind of analogy between *de re* and *de dicto* modalities on the one hand and apodictic and dialectical reasoning on the other hand. Both types of reasoning are deductive in character. The only difference between them lies in the fact that the premises of apodictic reasoning are self-evident, known by intuition, whereas the premises of dialectical reasoning are "generally accepted opinions". Therefore the conclusions of apodictic reasoning are absolutely necessary since the premises are necessary truths, while the conclusions of dialectical reasoning are necessary truths only on the supposition that the premises from which they are derived are necessary truths. (See Aristotle's *Topics* I 1 and *Prior Analytics* I 1 for this distinction.)

We do not know who was the first to use the *de re/de dicto* distinction, but at least Aquinas used it to distinguish two ways in which a property can be said to belong necessarily to a thing: (1) the property belongs to the essence of the thing itself, and (2) the property necessarily belongs to the thing owing to some supposition that has been made on our part. The former is *de re* or metaphysical or absolute necessity and the latter *de dicto* or logical or conditional necessity.

The theological significance of the distinction is well brought out in the following quote from Aquinas's opusculum XXVI *de Rationibus Fidei ad cantorem Antiochenum*. By means of this distinction it is possible to combine divine foreknowledge and man's free will. In this passage he does not use the terms '*de re*' and '*de dicto*' (but he does so in an almost identical passage that we will quote later):

At the height of eternity God regards all things from above the movement of time. Events that come to be in time are already present to him. When I see Socrates sitting down, my knowledge is certain and infallible, but it imposes no necessity on Socrates to sit. And so God, in looking at things which to us are past, present, or future, infallibly and certainly knows them as present realities, yet without imposing on them the necessity of existing. (Aquinas 1951, No. 310)

Here Aquinas seems to argue that if I see that Socrates is sitting, then it is necessary that Socrates is sitting. But it is not absolutely necessary (for he might have been standing as well) but only necessary *under the supposition* that I veridically see him sitting. Similarly, God's foreseeing me committing a sin at a later moment does not impose any necessity on my doing it; therefore He is justified in inflicting a punishment on me.

In *Summa theologica* Aquinas again distinguishes these two kinds of necessity without, however, using the terms '*de re*' and '*de dicto*'. The passage is worth quoting at length because of its clarity:

There are two ways in which a thing is said to be necessary, namely, absolutely, and by supposition. We judge a thing to be absolutely necessary from the relation of the terms, as when the predicate forms part of the definition of the subject; thus it is necessary that man is an animal. It is the same when the subject forms part of the notion of the predicate; thus it is necessary that a number must be odd or even. In this way it is not necessary that Socrates sits, and so it is not necessary absolutely, though it may be so by supposition; for granted that he is sitting, he must necessarily sit, as long as he is sitting. (Aquinas 1952, I 19 3)

To alter the example, it is an absolute necessity that a ball is round, because a ball is by definition a round body. But there is no absolute necessity that, say, the thing in my bag is round: it may be or it may not be. But if we describe the thing in my bag in some way, for example by using the phrase 'that spherical thing in my bag' then there is a conditional necessity in the statement that the thing in my bag is round.

In his *Summa contra gentiles*, when dealing again with the problem of the relationship between God's foreknowledge and man's free will, Aquinas uses the terms '*de re*' and '*de dicto*' to distinguish absolute from conditional necessity:

If God knows everything as if he saw it before him, then that which God knows necessarily exists, just as Socrates is necessarily sitting if he is seen to be sitting. But this [i.e., that Socrates is sitting] is not absolutely necessary ... but only necessary under [the] condition [that he is seen to be sitting]. For this conditonal proposition is necessary: 'If somebody is seen to be sitting, he is sitting'. If this conditional proposition is turned into a categorical one, 'He who is seen to be sitting is necessarily sitting', then its *de dicto* ... reading is evidently true, its *de re* ... reading false. (Aquinas 1934, I 67; quoted in Latin in Kneale and Kneale 1966, 237; our translation)

If the expression 'It is necessary that P' is symbolised by 'N (P)', then the sentence 'He who is seen to be sitting is necessarily sitting' can be interpreted in two ways:

> *de dicto*: **N** (S is seen to be sitting —> S is sitting).
> *de re*:   S is seen to be sitting —> **N** (S is sitting).

In the *de dicto* interpretation *necessity* is a property of the whole sentence (*dictum*). This interpretation does not imply that the property "is sitting at **t**" belongs to Socrates's essence. In the *de re* interpretation necessity attaches to the thing (*res*) called Socrates. It claims that it belongs to Socrates's essence to be sitting at **t**.

12.3. Two kinds of belief

The distinction *de re/de dicto* has become a stock in trade in modern modal logic. There the distinction is signalled by the order of the quantifier and the alethic operator. (The quantifier is the logical counterpart of the everyday expression 'all' or 'some'; and the modal operator is the logical counterpart of the words 'necessarily' or 'possibly', symbolized by 'N' and 'M', respectively.) Thus, of the two expressions,

> (1)   (Ex) M[Fx]

and

> (2)   M[(Ex)Fx]

the first is *de re* and the second *de dicto*. (1) says that there is an x that is possibly F while (2) says that possibly there is an x that is F. At first blush, these two sentences seem to say the same thing, but there is after all an important difference: while (1) picks out an actually existing individual and says of it that it is possibly F, (2) says that it is possible that there is an individual which is F but it does not assert that there actually exists such an individual.

Or, to put it in the idiom of possible words, (1) says that there is in *this* world an individual such that it is F in some possible world; but (2) says that in *some* possible world there is an individual which is F in that world. The difference is, therefore, that (1) is committed to the existence in this world of the individual to which the property of being possibly F is ascribed, but (2) is not committed to the existence of anything in this world.

This commitment to the existence of an individual seems to have been the central idea that was carried over to the mental sphere when the *de re/de dicto* distinction was introduced there. And it was also believed that the whole thing can be explained by resorting to the order of the quantifier and of the epistemic operator.

As we just saw, the logical modalities *de re* and *de dicto* are distinguished from one another by means of the order of the quantifier and the alethic operator:

(1)   *de re*:   (Ex) M[Fx]
(2)   *de dicto*:   M[(Ex) Fx]

Similarly, mental acts, e.g., belief, can be divided into two kinds:

(3)   *de re*:   (Ex) B_a [Fx]
(4)   *de dicto*:   [(Ex) Fx]

Here (3) says that A believes of some really existing thing that it is F, while (4) says that A believes that there is a thing which is F. The difference lies, again, in the fact that (3) presupposes the existence of a thing of which A believes that it is F whereas (4) is not committed to the existence of any other thing than the person A. This is the received view of the mental version of the distinction. Often it is combined with the doctrine that there really are *de re* acts, that is, acts with a complete guarantee that their objects exist.

12.4. Uses of the distinction

The usefulness of the *de re/de dicto* distinction can hardly be denied. It can be used to solve many philosophical puzzles, e.g., the following ones.

> *Puzzle 1*. Electra knows her brother. Electra does not know the masked man in front of her. The masked man is Electra's brother. Now, does Electra know the masked man or not? (cf. Kneale and Kneale 1966, Ch. III, Sec. 1)

Solution: *de re*, Electra knows the masked man; but, *de dicto*, she does not. That is, Electra knows the man in front of her because he is her brother and she presumably knows her brother; but she does not know that the man in front of her is her brother. (Or, to put in in terms of the the distinction between acquaintance and knowledge, Electra is acquainted with her brother and with the masked man but does not know that in reality they are one and the same man.)

> *Puzzle 2*. Should we obey the voice erring conscience? (Aquinas 1952, I–II 19 6)

Solution: *de dicto*, we should never obey erring conscience; but we sometimes obey what is, *de re*, erring conscience and are right in doing so. In other words, we should always follow the voice of our conscience – as long as we take it to be right – although we can never know whether it errs or not, the presumption being that it is the only source of our knowledge of good and bad. We cannot say: 'My conscience commands me to do X but I believe X is wrong.' This would be as weird as G.E. Moore's paradox: 'It is raining but I do not believe that it is raining.'

> *Puzzle 3*. A case from J. O. Urmson's book *Aristotle's Ethics*: "I go out, as I honestly claim, on a tiger hunt. I come across the spoor of a leopard, ignorantly mistake it for the spoor of a tiger and follow the spoor. The question is whether I am hunting a tiger or hunting a leopard." (Urmson 1988, 58)

Solution: *de re*, Urmson is hunting a leopard but *de dicto* he is hunting a tiger. Urmson himself does not use the concepts '*de re*' and '*de dicto*' but solves the problem by using the concepts of 'intentional object' and 'extensional object'. He says that the tiger is the intentional object of his hunting, while the leopard is the extensional object (Urmson 1988, 58). In this traditional scholastic terminology that Urmson is using, the intentional object of a mental act is its "internal object" or, as we have called it, the content of the act; and the extensional object is the "external object" or the real object in the external world. (Therefore, the extensional object could also be called the external object, and the intentional object could be called the internal object. And, taking into account the possibility of being mistaken about the object of one's mental act, the extensional object could be called the real object, and the intentional object the apparent object.)

Urmson does not go beyond the mere statement of his solution; he does not, for instance, tell us anything about the ontological statuses of the two objects. Since his example raises many interesting questions, it is worth while to examine it a little closer. There are three main problems about the relationship between extensional objects (henceforward 'EOs') and intentional objects ('IOs') that remain unsolved on Urmson's account.

12.5. Three problems

In describing the mental attitudes of other people, an observer has two possibilities: either he sticks to the vocabulary that the subject himself would have used to describe his own mental state (e.g., 'J.O.U. is hunting a tiger', etc.), or, wanting to display his superior knowledge, he uses words that the subject himself could not have used owing to ignorance of some feature of the object (EO) of his mental act (e.g., 'J.O.U. is hunting a leopard', etc.).

Descriptions of mental acts in terms of their IOs are necessarily accepted by the subject of the act because such descriptions are made from the subject's point of view. Descriptions in terms of the EO may or may not be accepted by the subject because they are made from an observer's point of view which may (but need not) radically differ from that of the subject.

According to a suggestion made by Risto Hilpinen in a private discussion, the *de re*/*de dicto* distinction is not a distinction between two kinds of *beliefs* but between two kinds of *descriptions* of beliefs. As Hilpinen put it: "To say that a belief is *de dicto* is to characterize it by means of its content; to say that a belief is *de re* is to characterize it by means of its object." If we simplify matters a little and stipulate that the content of an act is its IO, and its object is the EO, we get:

> *de re* acts   = acts described by means of EO
> *de dicto* acts   = acts described by means of IO

It is clear from this formulation that it is somewhat misleading to speak of '*de re* acts'. It would be more correct to speak of '*de re* descriptions of acts' because the mental acts themselves are neither *de re* nor *de dicto*; this distinction is applicable not to the acts themselves but only to their descriptions. Let us, however, provisionally suppose for the sake of the argument that it makes sense to speak of *de re* and *de dicto* acts. Later we will consider a strategy of eliminating all such talk. Now let us have a look at the three problematic cases and see whether the epithets '*de re*' and '*de dicto*' are applicable to them.

(P1)   Sometimes one and the same object seems to be both the IO and the EO. Consequently, one and the same act is both *de dicto* and *de re*.

Are the IO and the EO two ontologically different objects? At first sight, it seems that they are not, because at least for the well-informed hunter the real and the apparent objects of hunting coincide: he thinks he is hunting a tiger and in fact he is hunting a tiger. But does this mean that the IO and the EO coincide or are identical? But how could such utterly different entities as a mental picture of a tiger and a really existing tiger ever coincide? The problem is analogous to (or even identical with) the one we encountered in connection with Locke's problems with the resemblance between an idea and its object.

There we argued that, strictly speaking, an idea cannot resemble its object; it can only represent the object. In the same spirit, we could stipulate that the IO and the EO of an act coincide if and only if all the properties *presented* by the IO are *exemplified* by the EO.

Thus it is possible that the two objects of a mental act coincide in the loose sense although they are ontologically quite different kinds of entities. (Remember, however, that to say that the IO and the EO are the same object or that they coincide is just a picturesque and ontologically loaded way of saying that the subject of an experience or action, who sees it in terms of its IO, accepts an observer's description of the experience or action, given in terms of its EO.)

(P2)   Sometimes the EO seems to be missing altogether. Consequently, some acts can be only *de dicto*.

It is obvious that, at least in the simplest cases, the IOs are in the mind whereas the EOs are out there in nature. But suppose that Mr. X has been drinking heavily for several days. One morning he wakes up and starts chasing the pink rat which is standing on his bedside table. The problem is now whether or not he is chasing a pink rat. In a sense he is not, for there certainly is no EO, i.e., pink rat, at all. Yet something is going on inside Mr. X's mind: he is having a mental picture of a pink rat, and therefore there is an IO for his act. Therefore, to give a complete account of his state, we must say that an IO appears in his mind, but there is no corresponding EO. Therefore, the act must be *de dicto*.

(Of course it could be argued that there are mental acts *de re* that are directed to non-existent objects. Whether there are such acts depends on how one can identify and name such objects: for example, if one imaginary being has two names or definite descriptions, it is possible that a person who imagines it "under one name" does not know "under another name" that he is imagining it.)

(P3)   Sometimes there seems to be, as it were, a third object which "contains" both parts of the IO and parts of the EO, although the IO and EO themselves are mutually incompatible. Consequently, the act would be partly *de dicto* and partly *de re*.

Consider Urmson's hunting example again. The IO of his hunting is a tiger whereas the EO is a leopard. Suppose now that somebody were to ask Urmson, "Are you hunting a tiger?" He would surely have replied "Yes". But he would have answered "No" if he had been asked whether he is hunting a leopard. But suppose now that someone had asked him whether he was on a big cat hunt. He would have answered "Yes". And therefore the IO of his hunting is a big cat. But it also seems that the EO of his hunting is a big cat, for he is, after all, chasing a big cat. Thus there are several descriptions of Urmson's hunting activity, e.g., the following:

(1)   J.O.U. is hunting a tiger.
(2)   J.O.U. is hunting a leopard.
(3)   J.O.U. is hunting a big cat.

Now, according to Urmson's suggestion, the tiger in (1) is an IO, while the leopard in (2) is an EO. But the problem is now: to which category does the big cat in (3) belong? It seems that it is simultaneously both an IO and an EO, for both the really existing leopard and the mentally existing tiger are big cats (although in different ways: the former by exemplifying big-cat-hood and the latter by presenting properties characteristic of big-cat-hood). So the inevitable conclusion seems to be that the big cat is both an IO and an EO, which, to be honest, is a dubious ontological view.

According to our characterization of *de re* and *de dicto* acts, we could say that 'J.O.U. is hunting a big cat' is a *de dicto* description because it is in harmony with J.O.U.'s mental state: he would have accepted it himself. It would, however, be a rather odd thing if J.O.U., when asked, would use it, instead of the sentence 'I am hunting a tiger' as the description of his activity. For it seems that the former description violates the pragmatic requirement of maximal information, according to which it is not permissible to conceal some essential information about the object. Thus, if we try to decide which of these acts are *de re* and which *de dicto*, we immediately run into big difficulties. Could we seriously offer the following conclusion that seems to follow from our definitions?

In (P1), the act is both *de re* and *de dicto* because the EO and the IO coincide; in case (P2), the act is *de dicto* because it has only an IO; and in case (P3), the act is *de re* to the extent that the EO and IO overlap and *de dicto* as far as the rest is concerned.

The only reasonable answer to such a suggestion is "No". We argue that this solution is unacceptable, for there is a simpler solution: To say that a belief is *de dicto* is to characterize it by means of the subject's concepts; to say that a belief is *de re* is to characterize it by means of the observer's concepts. Anything that can be done by using the distinction between IOs and EOs can be done more economically by contrasting the first person and third person viewpoints, or phenomenological and ontological viewpoints.

Moreover, the comparison of viewpoints does not commit us to the existence of such strange entities as IOs.

But are there *de re* acts? The common belief that there are such acts is due to language. We do say such *"de re"* things as 'Oedipus wants to marry his own mother', but this does not mean that there really is such things as Oedipus's desire to marry his own mother, because this sentence does not give a reliable picture of what is going on in the mind of the subject himself. This can be seen from the fact that if Oedipus knew about the real identity of Jocasta, there would be a dramatic change in his attitude towards the object of his desire.

12.6. Analogy: De re *acts and unintentional actions*

The line of demarcation between *de re* and *de dicto* acts seems to be quite blurred, for as we have seen one and the same act can be both *de re* and *de dicto*. To show this, we must proceed slowly and indirectly by using the analogy between *de re* acts and unintentional actions. This procedure is justified by the fact that we do not have clear intuitions about *de re* acts. But our intuitions about the intentionality and unintentionality of actions are clearer. We argue that the Davidsonian distinction between *voluntary*, *intentional* and *unintentional* actions (see Davidson 1980, Essay 3) is completely analogous to the distinction between mental acts, *de dicto* acts and *de re* acts. Schematically:

mental act	≈	(voluntary) action
de dicto act	≈	intentional action
de re act	≈	unintentional action

The terms 'voluntary', 'intentional' and 'unintentional' are taken here in their Davidsonian sense: An action is voluntary if and only if it has been willed under some description.

In fact 'voluntary action' is a pleonasm; it does not say anything more that mere 'action' says. For we call actions only those bodily motions that have been caused by an act of the will. And if a bodily motion is caused by an act of the will, then there is a description such that the agent believes that the action that he is now performing falls under that description. For instance, if I now perform the action of opening the window (and do not inadvertently cause it to be opened), then there must be a description such that I now accept it as a description of my act, e.g., 'I am opening the window of my study.' But there may be descriptions that I would not accept, e.g., 'I am causing a draught that will make me catch a cold.'

Instead of descriptions we might, perhaps more clearly and less misleadingly, speak of mental images. Thus the difference between an action and a non-action (e.g., a spasm or a reflex movement) is that, for every action, there is an accompanying mental picture of the action (e.g., of the kind, result and circumstances of the action) in the mind of the agent. In short, an action is differentiated from a non-action by the fact that, in the case of an action, the agent has a picture of what he is doing (and this picture somehow directs what he is doing).

But now a problem arises. When Oedipus said 'I will' to the priest of Thebe, he performed a voluntary (linguistic) action. At the same time, however, he intentionallly married Jocasta and unintentionally married his own mother. How is this possible? The answer is this: One and the same action, the one that Oedipus performed when saying 'I will', can be intentional under the description 'Oedipus marries Jocasta' but unintentional under the description 'Oedipus marries his own mother.' At the time of the wedding ceremony, Oedipus would not have accepted the latter as a description of his action.

Note that in general there are several true descriptions that apply to a given action. In Oedipus's cases, there are at least the following: 'Oedipus marries Jocasta', 'Oedipus marries his own mother', 'Oedipus marries the Queen of Thebe', 'Oedipus marries the widow of the man he killed', and so on. And it is only under some of these descriptions that Oedipus's action is intentional. Note that the point can also be generalized to mental acts: one and the same desire can be *de dicto* when described in one way, e.g., 'Oedipus wants to marry Jocasta' but *de re* when described in another way, e.g., 'Oedipus wants to marry his own mother.'

If we accept the Davidsonian analysis of action-concepts, we must also accept its consequence: intentional and unintentional actions do not form any well-defined classes. For simplicity, we will call such well-defined and sharply circumscribed classes *natural classes*. For example, the class of horses is a natural class because it is possible to tell of every object whether it is a horse or not. On Davidson's view, voluntary actions form a natural class, because it is possible to say definitely of every bodily motion whether it is an action or not. But intentional actions do not form a natural class, because one cannot say of a given action whether it is intentional or unintentional *unless one specifies the description from whose standpoint the action is regarded.*

In short, because an action can be intentional under one description and unintentional under another, the expressions 'intentional action' and 'unintentional action' do not divide the class of actions neatly into two well-defined sub-classes. Similarly, it is not possible to divide the class of mental phenomena into two distinct classes, *de re* and *de dicto* acts, for one and the same mental act may be both *de re* and *de dicto*, depending on the way it is described. We conclude, then, that if the analogy between mental acts and bodily actions is valid and if unintentional actions do not form a natural class, then *de re* acts do not form a natural class, either.

12.7. The existence of de re acts

We have argued that the distinction *de re/de dicto* is not a distinction of acts but of descriptions of acts. The terms '*de re*' and '*de dicto*' do not apply to acts as such (to "bare acts") but to *pairs of acts and descriptions*, or – what amounts to the same thing – to acts described in a certain way. From this one could hastily conclude that there are no such things as *de re* acts. But are there such things? So far we have not given a clear answer, but the analogy between *de re* acts and unintentional actions obliges us to say that *de re* acts exist precisely in the same way as unintentional actions. Thus, if there are unintentional actions, then there are also *de re* acts.

The distinction between intentional and unintentional actions is very important e.g., in forensic practice; it makes a big difference whether an act of causing death is judged to be a murder, a homicide or an accidental causing of death. The mode of existence of unintentional actions is peculiar. In a sense, the agent cannot know while performing an action whether the action is intentional or unintentional; he can know it only after the action has been completed and a description of it has been proposed (by an observer). Of course, in another sense, all actions, if they are actions, are intentional when considered from the viewpoint of the description (or mental picture) that the agent has in mind while performing the action. But if the real consequences of the action do not correspond to the intended consequences (i.e., are not included in the mental picture of the action), then the action is unintentional to the extent that the intended and unintended consequences do not match.

Analogically, a person cannot know whether or not the mental act he is experiencing is *de re*. The distinction between and comparison of the subject's and an observer's viewpoints is a necessary condition for the existence of *de re* acts or, rather, of *de re* talk. Therefore, from an introspective point of view, *de re* acts do not exist. (More exactly, *de re* acts do not exist for the subject himself, except after the act, and even then only provided that the subjects gets new information, in the light of which the act turns out to be somehow deficient.)

This shows again that the traditional distinction between phenomenology and ontology must be revived in modern philosophy. We believe that many difficult problems in modern philosophical logic and in the philosophies of language and mind can be solved – or at least seen in a new and clearer light – if one keeps in mind this elementary lesson: don't confuse phenomenology with ontology. The rule is simple but exceedingly difficult to follow in practice.

13. THE EXPERIENCE OF REALITY

13.1. The feeling of reality

If we give up the central doctrine of the theories of acquaintance, indexicality and *de re* acts, namely, the idea of a direct access to reality, is there any way of explaining why we unmistakeably *feel* that some experiences are about reality while others are not? Our question is, then, "What makes an experience an experience of reality?" And, to begin with, our approach is internalist or phenomenological, which means that we try to get along with intramental things as far as we can. As we go on, it turns out that it is impossible to give a proper phenomenological account of the problem of reality without considering the experience of identity as well. Therefore that topic will be taken up in the next section.

To forestall misunderstandings, we repeat that the question of the experience of reality is not a question about the truth of the experience, i.e., of its correspondence with the facts (which would be an externalist question), but about the subjective feel of the experience (which is an internalist question). So, it is a question about feeling and not about "fact". In other words, the problem is not an ontological but a phenomenological one. For instance, we cannot solve the problem by saying: "What makes an experience an experience of reality is the fact that the experience is caused by reality, that is, by an really existing object." This will not do because, on the internalist approach, we cannot be sure whether there really is something out there that causes the experience. All that we can know is that we definitely feel that there is something that causes our experiences. For instance, the perception of a dog feels different from a memory or an imagination of a dog.

13.2. Phenomenology vs. ontology

The ontological thinkers want to explain a person's experiences in the scientific fashion, by assigning them external causes about which the subject may be totally in the dark. Thus they adopt the third person point of view and regard the first person point of view as subjective, unscientific and unreliable. James is not one of them. On the contrary, he explicitly distinguishes the two points of view and recommends the use of the first person viewpoint in psychology. He calls the confusion of the two points of view "the psychologist's fallacy". He writes:

The mental state is aware of itself only from within; it grasps what we call its own content, and nothing more. The psychologist, on the contrary is aware of it from without, and knows its relations with all sorts of other things. (James 1950 Vol. 1, 197; e.r.)

That is to say, the psychologist may know more about the object than the subject, but he must not let his superior knowledge show in the explanation of the mental state if he is going to give a phenomenological (or psychological, as James would have said) explanation of it. Therefore:

We must be very careful ... , in discussing a state of mind from the the psychologist's point of view, to avoid foisting into its own ken matters that are only there for ours. (James 1950 Vol. 1, 197)

Thus James warns against the confusion of phenomenological and ontological talk. In his *Psychology*, he also makes another methodological distinction, which will turn out to be useful for our purposes. It is the distinction between two ways of studying mental phenomena:

There are ... two ways of studying every psychic state. First, the way of analysis: What does it consist in? What is its inner nature? ... Second, the way of history: What are its conditions of production, and its connection with other facts? (James 1950 Vol. 2, 283)

It is clear that James's first way is phenomenological or internalist, for to study the inner nature or internal structure of a mental state is to stay within the bounds of the mind (as internalism requires). But what about the second way? At first sight, it might seem as if the way of history is the causal way (forbidden by internalism); for how else can the "history" of a mental state be studied if not by studying the causes that brought it about?

The internalist's native tendency to reject "historicism" must, however, be resisted. It is perfectly possible to pursue James's second way by using internalist means. A phenomenological study of mental phenomena does not exclude "historical" considerations, provided that one delimits one's attention to those "historical" factors that can be found solely within the stream of consciousness. For example, it is not forbidden to explain the reality-character of an experience of remembering by referring to an earlier perception of the object remembered. But it is forbidden to explain the reality-character of an experience of perceiving by postulating an external object that causes the perception.

But to what extent can these two ways be used in the study of experiences of reality? It seems that the way of analysis does not take us very far. All that can be said about experiences of reality in general is that those experiences take their object to exist or be real. It seems that we are acquainted with the feeling of reality but we cannot explain its inner nature. Therefore, the way of history is more promising. From a historical point of view, two essential phenomenological properties of experiences of reality can be discerned:

(1)   All experiences of reality either are perceptions or are founded on perceptions.

Perceptions are what we, following Edmund Husserl and Alexius Meinong, will call original acts. Their reality-character is in themselves; it has not been borrowed from other acts. But the reality-character of all other types of acts has been borrowed from original acts of perception. This borrowing, however, presupposes that the object of the non-original non-perceptual act is recognised to be the same as the object of the original perceptual act, otherwise the transfer of the reality-character will not succeed. Consequently,

(2)   The ability to recognize the present object as the same as a previous one is a precondition of non-perceptual experiences of reality.

We will expound these two theses in turn, (1) in the remainder of this section and (2) in the next section.

13.3. The birth of reality-character

Do all experiences really get their reality-character from perception? On a superficial reading, William James seems to think that any experience whatever has reality-character unless it is contradicted by other experiences:

Any object which remains uncontradicted is *ipso facto* believed and posited as absolute reality. (James 1950 Vol. 2, 289; e.r.)

As a rule we believe as much as we can. We would believe everything if we only could. (James 1950 Vol. 2, 299)

But is this true? Do we immediately assent to any proposition that is not contradicted by propositions that we already accept as true? It seems that James is wrong, if we take these statements quite literally. For I do not automatically assent to any flight of imagination that occurs to me and is not contradicted by the propositions that I take to be true. For instance, it may occur to me that it is raining heavily in Maputo at this very moment. Nothing that I know or believe contradicts this idea, yet I do not take it to be true, because there is no reason or ground whatever why I should do so. Nor do I take it to be false; it is just a vain disconnected thought.

In fact, what James really seems to hold is not that we believe as much as we can but that we accept as many of our perceptions as we can, for he wrote:

But no mere floating conception, no mere disconnected rarity, ever displaces vivid things or permanent things from our belief. A conception, to prevail, must *terminate* in the world of orderly sensible experience. (James 1950 Vol. 2, 301)

Thus, perception seems to be, after all, for James the foundation of the feeling of reality. He concludes:

Sensible objects are thus either our realities or the tests of our realities. Conceived objects must show sensible effects or else be disbelieved. (James 1950 Vol. 2, 301; e.r.)

Thus the first essential property of experiences of reality is that they all either are perceptions or are founded on perceptions. Immanuel Kant agrees: "... perception ... is the only criterion of reality." ("... die Wahrnehmung ... ist der einzige Charakter der Wirklichkeit" (Kant 1966, 302; B 273)). That is to say, if we take the way of history and trace the feeling of reality back to its source, we find that it is always perception.

13.4. Three properties of mental acts

We can see what this means if we distinguish three closely related concepts: veridicality, assertoriness and originality. They can be defined as follows:

> An experience is *veridical* if and only if its object exists.
> An experience is *assertory* if and only if its object is taken to exist.
> An experience is *original* if and only if its object is perceived to exist.

From the historical point of view, originality is the basic category because it is through perception that experiences get their reality-character in the first place. But once they have got it, they can lend it to other (non-original) experiences which have (or, more exactly, are experienced to have) the same object. Thus, if I have once seen the Eiffel Tower, all subsequent acts having it as their object will have reality-character or assertoriness. (This is not quite exact, however, for if I think: "When Caesar conquered Gaul, he did not see the Eiffel Tower", I am not committed to the existence of the Eiffel Tower at Caesar's time. And if I get reliable evidence to the effect that the Eiffel Tower has been completely destroyed, then all my subsequent acts having the Eiffel Tower as their object will lack the reality-character – at least until the evidence has turned out to be false.)

Note that both originality and assertoriness are internalist (phenomenological) concepts, while veridicality is an externalist (ontological) concept. The relationship among the three concepts seems to be the following: Original acts constitute a proper subset of assertory acts, and both original and assertory acts may be either veridical or non-veridical.

13.5. Reality and indexicality

But what feature in perception gives it its character of reality or assertoriness? It seems that an answer is to be found in the close connection between the experience of reality and indexicality. As James puts it:

"The candle exists" is equivalent to "The candle is *over there*". And the "over there" means real space, space related to other reals. The proposition amounts to saying: "The candle is in the same space with other reals." (James 1950 Vol. 2, 290; fn 1)

And this space is not the space of physics but the subjective, phenomenological space. That is, it is the experiential space – the space as I experience it. And I am the center point of this space. Thus anything that is real for us stands in some relation to us, here and now.

John Searle has a somewhat similar idea (Searle 1983, especially Chs. 2 and 8). He explains the difference between seeing X and imagining X (or, more generally, between original and non-assertory acts) by the structure of their content: the content of an act of seeing is more complex than that of an act of imagining in that its is indexical or causally self-referring. Their difference can be expressed as follows:

I see (there is an X before me & the X causes this experience).

I imagine (there is an X before me).

This is a simplified version that does not require the use of Searle's technical terminology, but we believe that it is faithful to Searle's essential insight, namely that the feeling of reality that accompanies perception is due to the second conjunct ('the X causes this experience') in the content of this visual experience. This crucial feature is *causal self-reference*; it is causal because the X is felt to be the cause of the experience; it is self-referential because the content contains the word 'this' (or rather its mental counterpart). Consequently, an act of "seeing" that would lack this feature would have the following type of content:

I see (there is an X before me).

But this would not be a full-fledged act of seeing because it lacks the feeling of reality. Rather, it would be an act of imagining (or of pseudo-seeing).

Note that this Searlean account is totally internalist and phenomenological: the causal element (the second conjunct) belongs to the content of the experience. In other words, what we have here is experiential causality and not "real" causality. Therefore the phenomenological description of the act of seeing is not committed to the real existence of an X in the external world. All that it is committed to is the feeling that there is an X out there. And this feeling is explained by means of the causal self-reference of perception.

Searle's account of perception can easily be applied to so-called *de re* acts. The strongest argument for the existence of *de re* acts is that there are acts that are essentially contextual, that is, acts which cannot be individuated by means of general concepts. Instead, it is argued, they must be individuated in terms of their object (plus, perhaps, an incomplete proposition á la Perry).

Following Searle, it could be argued that such acts do in fact have contextual features, but these features belong to the content of the experience. It is not necessary to postulate any strange inflow of the physical context into the abstract content. These contextual features are closely related to the causal self-reference of perception (which is no wonder because the typical "*de re*" act is a perceptual act). For instance, the content of the alleged *de re* act of seeing that man over there can be described phenomenologically as follows:

I see (there is an X before me & the X causes this experience & the X is a man)

Thus there is no need to suppose that in *de re* acts (or in acts of acquaintance) we have a direct and infallible access to reality. The fact is that we have only one kind of access to the world, one mediated by contents. These contents, however, can be either indexical (self-referential) or non-indexical.

14. THE EXPERIENCE OF IDENTITY

14.1. The sense of sameness

After having examined the genesis of the feeling of reality, it is time to turn to the second problem of the historical approach, namely the transfer of the reality-character from an original experience to a non-original one. As we have seen, this presupposes the ability to re-identify the object of the non-original act as the same thing as the object of the original perceptual act. In other words, perception gives the reality-character to the objects of some experiences and then this reality-character accompanies those objects ever after, even though they are not perceived any more. For example, having seen a tree in the yard, I continue to believe in its existence even if I do not see it at the moment. It follows that a creature that lacks the ability to have the feeling that "this is the same thing as ..." cannot have non-original assertory experiences.

It might be asked whether it is necessary to speak of 're-identification', because 'identification' without a prefix would be enough. For all identification seems to be re-identification: to identify a thing as "the so-and-so" or even as "a so-and-so" is to classify it in some way, to subsume it under a concept, be it a singular or a general concept. However, to emphasize the significance of memory for the experience of sameness, we use 're-identification'.

William James emphasises that this "sense of sameness", as he calls it, is a phenomenological or subjective phenomenon: it does not guarantee that the object that is felt to be the same as an object seen (or thought) earlier really is the same. Or as James puts it:

... we do not care whether there be any *real* sameness in *things* or not, or whether the mind be true or false in its assumptions of it. Our principle only lays it down that the mind makes continual use of the *notion* of sameness, and if deprived of it, would have a different structure from what it has. (James 1950 Vol. 1, 460)

James regards the sense of sameness as the fundamental fact of the human mind; it "is the very keel and backbone of our thinking" (James 1950 Vol. 1,

459). Also non-human beings may have it but not to the same extent: "In the consciousness of worms and polyps, though the same realities may frequently impress it, the feeling of sameness may seldom emerge" (James 1950 Vol. 1, 460).

By the expression 'the sense of sameness' he means our ability to recognize or re-identify an object *as the same object* as the one we met with before. The connection with the everyday concept of acquaintance is plain: if one is acquainted with X, one is able to recognize X as the same object that one has already encountered somewhere. (This ability is part and parcel of the everyday sense of 'acquaintance' but not of Russellian acquaintance.)

14.2. Sameness, similarity and conception

James radically departs from the views of the empiricists. To put it crudely, the empiricists argued that we can never know whether we see the same things or just deceivingly similar things. The sameness of the tree is only inferred from the sameness of the idea. Thus all apparent identity of objects is based on the identity of the ideas that we have of them. James, however, pointed out that the mind is not a collection of eternally returning self-same ideas, but a dynamic process, a stream. There simply are no lasting mental atoms out of which the mind is constructed. Therefore, the experience of encountering "the same object" is not a matter of having "the same idea" again. (In fact, we will see in a moment how James proves that the occurrence of the same idea could not give rise to the sense of sameness.)

Of course, James readily admits that we often have the experience of encountering the same object again, and it is this experience that he calls the sense of sameness. However, for him, it is a phenomenological, not an ontological matter. That is to say, while the empiricists are interested in the real identity of the objects, James is interested only in the experience of identity. He writes:

Note, however, that we are in the first instance speaking of the sense of sameness from the point of view of the mind's structure alone, and not from the point of view of the universe. We are psychologizing, not philosophizing, That is, we do not care whether there be any real sameness in things or not, or whether the mind be true or false in its assumptions of it. (James 1950 Vol. 1, 459–460)

In short, for James (1) sameness is a matter of immediate experience, not of inference on the basis of identical ideas, and (2) sameness is experiential or phenomenological not ontological. (He made the latter point in the quotation above by distinguishing "psychologizing" from "philosophizing".)

James makes an extremely important observation when he says: "In short, it is logically impossible that the same thing should be known as the same by two successive copies of the same thought" (James 1950 Vol. 1, 480). In other words, he points out that, for purely conceptual reasons, one and the same object cannot both be represented in two identical copies of one idea and be recognised as the same object. To see this, suppose that two identical copies of one idea could occur in the stream of consciousness. But now we have a dilemma: (i) If the two ideas are qualitatively identical, there cannot be a sense of sameness in the second idea. (ii) If the second idea involves the sense of sameness, the two ideas cannot be qualitatively identical. Therefore, the sense of sameness can occur only if the two ideas are different. Or, to put James's argument in an explicit form:

Hypothesis: Two successive copies of one idea, I_1 and I_2, can know the same object or are experienced to be about the same object.

(1)   Ideas I_1 and I_2 are qualitatively identical. That is, there is nothing in I_2 that is not in I_1, and vice versa.

(2) I_1 and I_2 refer to the same object.

(3)   Moreover, I_2 knows that it refers to the same object as I_1.

(4) I_1 does not know that it refers to the same object as I_2 does because I_1 occurs before I_2.

(5)   Therefore, there must be something in I_2 – that is, reference to I_1 – that is not in I_1.

(6)   Therefore, either I_1 and I_2 are not qualitatively identical or I_1 and I_2 are not experienced to refer to the same object.

(7)   Therefore, the Hypothesis must be rejected.

(For the original argument, see James 1950 Vol. 1, 480–482).

There is a close connection between the sense of sameness and the function of the mind that James calls 'conception'. In fact, both have to do with with the identification of an object. James defines conception and concept as follows:

The function by which we ... identify a numerically distinct and permanent subject of discourse is called conception; and the thoughts which are its vehicles are called concepts. (James 1950 Vol. 1, 461; e.r.)

We are aware of objects, not of concepts. We use concepts to refer to things, but seldom refer to the concepts themselves, except on philosophical reflection. It is one thing to use concepts in perceiving and re-identifying an object and another thing to be able to say which concepts (or features of the object) were used in the act of re-identification. We simply cannot observe what happens in our minds when we recognize or "cognize" objects. We are aware of the objects, not of the contents of our minds. This is the point James made in connection with acquaintance: we know that this tastes of pear, but we cannot define or describe that taste. (Incidentally, this experiential fact shows that there are things in the mind that phenomenology cannot reach.)

Moreover, conception seems to be an acquired ability, since without having seen an X before, one cannot see an X (in the ordinary *de dicto* sense). Or, as James puts it:

... the only things which we commonly see are those which we preperceive, and the only things which we preperceive are those which have been labelled for us, and the labels stamped into our mind. (James 1950 Vol. 1, 444; e.r.)

That is to say, we can only see things whose concepts we possess; or more exactly, we cannot see a thing as an X unless we already have the concept of X, but we can, of course, see it as a Y or as a Z if we have those concepts. These quotations show that James's conception is a clearly conceptual activity. It has little in common with Russell's non-conceptual acquaintance. This impression is further strengthened by a passage in another book where he writes:

Educated as we already are, we never get an experience that remains for us completely nondescript; it always *reminds* of something similar in quality, or of some context that might have surrounded it before, and which it now in some way suggests. This mental escort which the mind supplies is drawn, of course, from the mind's ready-made stock. We *conceive* the impression in some definite way. (James 1983, 95–96)

And even more clearly: "Every sensation must awaken *some* object, must be classed and interpreted in *some* way" (James 1983, 209). It is clear from the context that the object awakened is an experiential object and not a real one.

14.3. The limits of phenomenology

Now we would like to speculate a little about the possible ontological foundations of the experience of identity. Therefore, from now on, we give up our attempt to do pure phenomenology. We have gone so far as it is possible to go with phenomenological means (given our abilities). This does not mean that we consider phenomenological investigations worthless. On the contrary, we still firmly believe that much valuable research can be done and remains to be done in phenomenology. But phenomenology has its limits, and we feel that we have now reached them.

To prevent misunderstandings, we repeat that we believe that much harm has been done by not distinguishing phenomenological and ontological studies. As examples of such confusions we offered three related theories: those of acquaintance, indexicality and de re acts. Next we tried to show, with James's help, how much can be said of the experience of "direct access" to reality, even if such an access does not exist. Not much, was the conclusion. The following conclusions emerged: (1) some experiences are felt to be about reality; (2) they get that feeling from perception; and (3) the transfer of that feeling presupposes what James calls the sense of sameness.

It seems that, by using merely phenomenological means, the characteristic feeling of reality cannot be further analysed, nor can it be explained why precisely perception creates that feeling or on what the sense of sameness is based. So, we undoubtedly have the experience of the sense of sameness, but we cannot explain its nature if our explanation must be couched in phenomenological terms. But we believe something interesting can be said about this experience if phenomenology is left behind. And that is what we will do in what follows. Therefore we freely indulge ourselves in metaphysical speculations about the nature of a being that could possibly have the sense of sameness.

14.4. Real and experiential objects in James's model

A Jamesian view of the human mind can be pictured in the following way:

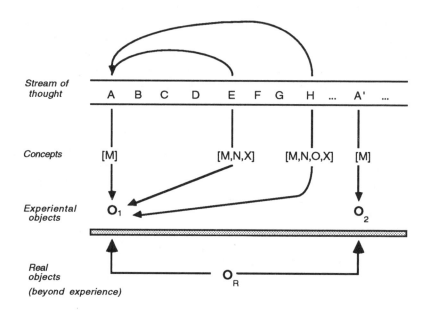

Fig.2.

This figure cannot be found in James's writings, but it is based on his ideas. It is important to keep in mind that we are not doing phenomenology here; this model is a theoretical construction that aims at clarifying the processes that there must be (or could be) in order that such things as acquaintance and the sense of sameness were possible.

The main idea in the model is simple enough. The mind is a stream consisting of overlapping and not easily distinguishable portions A, B, C, etc. And, as we have seen, it is possible that two qualitatively different portions of the stream, for instance A and E, refer to one and the same object in the external world and are experienced by the subject to do so. But it is strictly impossible that two qualitatively identical portions, A and A', are experienced to refer to the same object even though they in fact do so. The explanation is clear: A' does not involve the memory of A. Note that A' does not experience its object as different, either. It is just an object.

The model takes seriously James's thesis that the sense of sameness is not concerned with real objects but with experiential objects. (It must be admitted, however, that James himself does not clearly distinguish between real and experiential objects, but uses the term 'object' quite indiscriminately to refer now to experiential objects, now to real ones.) The relation between real and experiential objects is such that (1) one real object may be the "cause" of several experiential objects and (2) several real objects may be experienced as one and the same object. For example, (1) Jocasta occurs both in the guise of the Queen of Thebe and in that of Oedipus's mother in Oedipus's stream of thought without his being aware of their identity; and (2) identical twins may be taken to be one person.

We need the category of experiential objects because it is those "objects" that are the real bearers of information. That is, the information is connected to the objects that we experience (and not to the real objects that cause our experiences), no matter how perverse mistakes we make in identifying the experiential objects. For instance, if I mistake a statue for the Prime Minister, the real object is the statue but the experiential object is the Prime Minister, and it is to the latter that I ascribe the properties "wears a strange hat", "has a stick in his hand", "looks intently at something", and so on. Only later, when I notice my mistake, do I ascribe these properties (or their apparent counterparts) to that piece of stone in the park.

Our minds are constituted in such a way that they necessarily ascribe properties to (supposedly) permanent "objects". This means that they "objectify" experience and sometimes make mistakes in doing so. But this does not alter the fact that experiential objects are the basic units of cognition in our minds. However, instead of 'experiential objects', one could also speak, in the ontological mode, of 'memory locations'. These memory locations, no matter how realized in the brain, are the ontological counterparts of the phenomenological experiential objects. You describe one and the same fact whether you say that a piece of information is ascribed to an experiential object or that it is put into a memory location.

Using the idiom of memory locations, the fact that there is a sense of sameness can be expressed by saying that several mental acts have a memory location in common: The first act creates a memory location into which the information collected by subsequent acts referring to the same object is gathered. For instance, the fact that in our model acts E and H remember act

A (that is, E and H have the sense of sameness) can be explained ontologically by saying that A created a memory location into which the information collected by E and H about the same experiential object is gathered. (And the same fact can be explained phenomenologically by saying that both E and H contain a "memory" of A, whereas A' does not contain such a "memory".)

Now the difference between identifying and re-identifying can be expressed as follows. The identifiacation of an object (for instance, by fixing one's attention on it or by distinguishing it from the backround of other objects) just is the creation of a memory location for it, while the re-identification of an object is the act of finding an already created memory location corresponding to that experiential object.

14.5. Appropriation of content

How does one fill up a memory location with information? Consider two successive acts referring to the same experiential object, for example two acts of seeing the same thing. Sometimes the second act is richer in content than the first. This happens when we see the same object for the second time and notice more of its properties than on the first occasion. But it could be argued that even if we notice less properties on the second occasion, still the second act would be richer in content than the first act because the properties given by the first act are automatically experienced as belonging to the object of the second act (provided that the subject still remembers the information content of the first act).

Does the second act have to be richer than the first? Yes and no. (1) Yes, because the whole information content of the first act that is remembered at the time of the occurrence of the second act automatically becomes part of the information content of the second act. For the second act is just a case of storing new information into an old memory location. (2) No, because much of the information content of the first act may have been forgotten at the time of the occurrence of the second act. And if enough has been forgotten, the result will be the creation of a new memory location. Then the new information brought by the second act is assigned to a new memory location.

The second act necessarily appropriates the information content of the first act if (1) the second act is experienced as referring to the same object as the first act and if (2) the properties ascribed to the object by the first act are still remembered at the time of the occurrence of the second act. Thus it is impossible that the second act be poorer in information content than the second act, even though the information content of the first act may not be "vividly given" (or even noticed) at the time of the occurrence of the second act.

(One more point. Strictly speaking, not all the properties that are ascribed to the object on the first occasion are automatically transferred to the object on the second occasion, only somewhat permanent properties are transferred. For instance, 'wearing a red jacket' or 'being tired' are accidental properties that are not automatically expected to belong to the object on later occasions. Thus the transfer of properties presupposes an implicit theory of which properties are lasting and which are accidental in a certain kind of thing. Developing such a theory even for the most ordinary kinds of things would be an enormous task.)

14.6. The impossibility of non-conceptual access

The fact that in our model A and E refer to the same object could be explained either by saying that they have the concept or content [M] in common or by saying fact that E contains a "memory" of having seen the object before, which is symbolized by [X]. James does not use the [X] himself, but we have adopted it in order to account for the possibility that two experiences might be experienced as referring to the same real thing without there being anything in common between the contents of these experiences. Thus [X] would stand for a non-conceptual act of re-identification, if such a thing were possible.

In the figure above, three successive slices of the stream of consciousness refer to the same object and are experienced to do so. Usually the second and the third act are not – as far as their contents are concerned – mere repetitions of the first act but bring in new information about the object. Thus, the first act A acquires the information [M], the second act E acquires [N], the third act H acquires [O]. The [X] which is included in the second and in the third act guarantees that the new information is connected with the old object, and not ascribed to some other experiential object for which there is a memory location in the mind.

But what precisely is the role of the mysterious [X] in the act of re-identification? Do we really have to suppose that such a thing as [X] exists? Is it really possible that two mental acts satisfy the following conditions?

(i)   The second act refers to (is caused by) the same object as the first act.

(ii)   It is experienced to do so.
(iii)   Yet the information contents of the two acts have nothing in
         common.

The following case satisfies all three conditions:

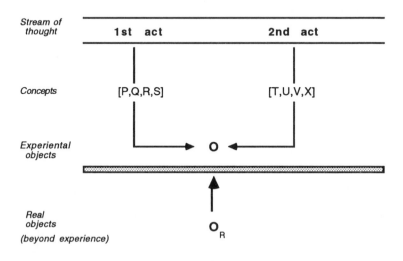

Fig.3.

Here, [X] in the content of the second act is certainly not superfluous. It is the only thing that can guarantee the sense of sameness. It cannot be taken as an abbreviation for any shared information content of the two acts, because they simply have nothing in common. However, if the *de re* theorists are right, a case like this is possible, for according to their theory, there is a direct contact between the mind and reality. And [X] is the only thing that can guarantee the experiential sameness of reference. If this case were possible, then there would have to be a non-conceptual way of referring to things – a direct access to the reality outside the stream of consciousness. Such access would be the privilege of *de re* acts or acts of acquaintance. But is it possible to find a concrete example of such a case?

Such a case could occur if there were first a veridical perception and then a total perceptual mistake (or the other way round). For example, if I first see John as John and then see him as a sparrow. (The example is fanciful, but so is the doctrine it is intended to exemplify.) Even if such a coarse perceptual mistake were possible, the normal first-person description of it would run: 'First I saw John, next he disppeared and then I saw a sparrow.' In this case, there are two distinct experiential objects. But if there were only one experiential object that appears in two incompatible guises connected by the sense of sameness, then the description of the experience would run: 'I saw John turn into a sparrow.' We find such cases bizarre, but they would have to be possible if there were such a thing as direct non-conceptual access to reality.

Note, however, that even our fanciful example of John and the sparrow is not fanciful enough, because there is one thing that remains the same: the (apparent) spatial location of the thing vis-á-vis my body. I could say both of John and of the sparrow: "It's that thing over there." But do these words express the mysterious [X] or merely an indexical content? To avoid all types of content, even an indexical one, the experience would have to be like the one that can be described with these words: "Well, first John disappeared before my very eyes and after a while he appeared as a sparrow behind my back." In this case, there would not be any continuity of ordinary properties nor of spatio-temporal location. It would be a perfect example of the sort of direct access to reality that *de re* theorists dream about. But – is it possible? It seems to us that the sense of sameness is possible, but direct access in any of its guises is not.

BIBLIOGRAPHY

Aquinas: 1934, *Summa contra gentiles*, Rome: Editio Leonina Manualis.

Aquinas: 1951, *Philosophical Texts: Selected and translated by Thomas Gilby*, Oxford: Oxford University Press.

Aquinas: 1952, *Summa theologica*, in *Great Books of the Western World*, Vols. 19–20, Chicago: Encyclopaedia Britannica Inc.

Aristotle: 1987, *Topics* and *Prior Analytics*, Selections in Ackrill, J.L. (ed.), *A New Aristotle Reader*, Princeton: Princeton University Press.

Berkeley, G.: 1972, *A Treatise Concerning the Principles of Human Knowledge and Three Dialogues in A New Theory of Vision and Other Writings*, London: Dent.

Davidson, D.: 1980, 'Agency', in *Essays on Actions and Events*, Oxford: Clarendon Press.

Flew, A. (ed.): 1984, *A Dictionary of Philosophy*, 2nd edition, London: Pan Books.

Frege, G.: 1988, 'Thoughts', in Salmon, N. and Soames, S. (eds.), *Propositions and Attitudes*, Oxford: Oxford University Press.

Frege, G. and Russell, B.: 1988, 'Selection from the Frege-Russell Correspondence', in Salmon, N. and Soames, S. (eds.), *Propositions and Attitudes*, Oxford: Oxford University Press.

Gregory, R.L.: 1981, *Mind in Science*, Harmondsworth: Penguin.

James, W.: 1950, *The Principles of Psychology*, Vols. 1 and 2 (First published in 1890), New York: Dover Publications.

James, W.: 1983, *Talks to Teachers on Psychology*, Cambridge MA: Harvard University Press.

Kant, I.: 1966, *Kritik der reinen Vernunft*, Stuttgart: Reclam.

Kneale, W. and Kneale, M.: 1966, *The Development of Logic*, Oxford: Clarendon Press.

Locke, J.: 1964, *An Essay Concerning Human Understanding: Edited by A.D. Woozley*, London: Fontana/Collins.

McDermott, J.J.: 1985, *A Cultural Introduction to Philosophy*, New York: Knopf.

Nagel, T.: 1986, *The View from Nowhere*, Oxford: Oxford University Press.

Perry, J.: 1988, 'The Problem of the Essential Indexical', in Salmon, N. and Soames, S. (eds.), *Propositions and Attitudes*, Oxford: Oxford University Press.

Perry, J.: 1990, 'Frege and Demonstratives', in Yourgrau, P. (ed.), *Demonstratives*, Oxford: Oxford University Press.

Reichenbach, H.: 1966, *Elements of Symbolic Logic*, New York: The Free Press.

Russell, B.: 1967, *The Problems of Philosophy*, Oxford: Oxford University Press.

Russell, B.: 1972, 'Philosophy of Logical Atomism', in Pears, D. (ed.), *Russell's Logical Atomism*, London: Fontana/Collins.

Russell, B.: 1980, *An Inquiry into Meaning and Truth*, London: Unwin.

Russell, B.: 1986, 'Knowledge by Acquaintance and Knowledge by Description', in *Mysticism and Logic*, London: Unwin.

Searle, J.: 1983, *Intentionality*, Cambridge: Cambridge University Press.

Smith, D.W.: 1991, 'Acquaintance', in Burkhardt, H. and Smith, B. (eds.), *Handbook of Metaphysics and Ontology*, Munich: Philosophia.

Smith, D.W.: 1989, *The Circle of Acquaintance*, Dordrecht: Kluwer.

Urmson, J.O.: 1988, *Aristotle's Ethics*, Oxford: Blackwell.

B. ULTIMATE RELATIVISM

This section investigates the versions and consequences of relativism, starting from the conclusion reached in the preceding section. First, some versions of relativism are listed, and their interrelations are studied. Then the particular problem of cultural relativism is presented as well as the various reactions it has generated. Cognitivism is one such reaction, but it is argued to be significantly different from the others. However, in providing solutions to the problem of cultural relativism, cognitivism appears to invite a more profound version of relativism: instead of cultural, and thus modifiable constraints upon cognition, our view of what there is, is restricted by our neuronal build-up.

15. CULTURAL RELATIVISM AND COGNITIVISM

The common problem that unites different versions of relativism is the following: there appear to exist mutually incompatible entities (beliefs, values, practices, moral codes, theories, etc.), for which we do not have a common measure. The versions of relativism differ from each other in telling us what the entities are and how they are incompatible. At first sight, we have the following varieties:

- descriptive cognitive relativism
- normative cognitive relativism
- descriptive ethical relativism
- normative ethical relativism
- ontological relativism
- axiological relativism

and as an eclectic mixture, we have:

- cultural relativism

Descriptive cognitive relativism relies on the factual claim that there are apparently incompatible beliefs about the world. The apparent incompatibility means that they cannot all be true, if there exists one reality. Anthropological literature is full of examples of this brand of relativism, and there are no good grounds for doubting it: it is an empirical fact. Descriptive cognitive relativism is the fundamental form of the many versions of relativism, in the sense that the others can be seen more or less as its derivatives. In anthropology the empirical fact of descriptive cognitive relativism is the starting point of research.

There are weaker and stronger versions of descriptive cognitive relativism. The weakest version claims that there are incompatible beliefs only, but that the grounds and rules of reasoning are universal. For example, the Mestizo belief concerning the relationships between envy, witchcraft and sharp pain is apparently incompatible with the explanation that we are willing to provide in the case of bodily pain, but the methods of belief-formation are similar in both cultures. Both refer to medical authorities in explaining the symptoms, and assess the credibility of the authority on the basis of its consistency, and so on. The stronger versions propose that the incompatibility goes deeper than that: the rules of reason and even the meta-standards of rationality can be different in different cultures.

Normative cognitive relativism claims that there are no reasonable or definitive grounds for deciding between different beliefs. Therefore, we should not pass judgement on apparently incompatible beliefs; the different views make equal claims about the world. This version is also included in cultural relativism, as we shall see shortly.

Descriptive ethical relativism is another empirical claim; it holds that there are apparently incompatible moral attitudes or valuations among different groups of human beings. As time and place change, so views change concerning the good and the right. The apparent incompatibility here means that the respective valuations cannot all be satisfied in the same world.

Normative ethical relativism proposes, analogously with its cognitive counterpart, the conclusion that there are no good or sufficient grounds for putting the apparently incompatible valuations in order. Since we are without sufficient premises, we cannot tell which of the multiple valuations is better than any others.

Ontological relativism is the metaphysical conclusion that can be drawn from the fact of descriptive cognitive relativism. It holds that the apparently incompatible beliefs are grounded upon a multitude of incompatible realities. In other words, the incompatible beliefs are about different worlds. Ontological relativism can be used to base the other versions of relativism on, but from the viewpoint of empirical science, it is far more far-fetched than descriptive cognitive relativism.

Axiological relativism is the metaphysical conclusion drawn from descriptive ethical relativism. It claims, to put it briefly, that there are multiple, mutually incompatible values out there, and the fact of apparently incompatible valuations can be understood against this background. The credibility of axiological relativism is on an equal footing with that of ontological relativism.

Descriptive cognitive relativism can be seen as the most fundamental version of relativism, since ethical relativism can be at least partially reduced to the cognitive one, and the ontological as well as the axiological conclusions can be treated as conclusions drawn from descriptive cognitive relativism.

Descriptive relativism (both cognitive and ethical) can be characterized as claiming that the diversity and apparent incompatibility of beliefs is a fact. Normative relativism holds that one cannot get rid of this incompatibility. Cultural relativism is a mixture of these two positions, and for that very reason there is something wrong with it. We will substantiate our claim with an argument that consists of eight premises and a conclusion:

(1)   Descriptive cognitive relativism is true.
(2)   In cultural anthropology we should beware of culture-bound judgements, or, in other words, beware of ethnocentrism.
(3)   Therefore, there are grounds for normative relativism.
(4)   Cultural anthropology should be conducted scientifically. This means, at least, that cultural traits should be contextualized, or placed in their functional roles.
(5)   Contextualization brings about compatibility.
(6)   Therefore, incompatibility is avoidable.
(7)   Therefore, there are no grounds for normative relativism.
(8)   Statements (3) and (7) jointly imply a slight contradiction.
(9)   Therefore, there is something wrong with cultural relativism.

Many authors in cultural studies agree with the conclusion, but few have spotted the root of difficulties (cf. Finnegan and Horton 1973). At first sight there is no solution readily available – in order to avoid ethnocentrism we should support normative relativism, but in order to practise science, for example, by means of contextualizing cultural traits, we must assume some degree of compatibility. There are, however, some intelligible reactions to the problem of cultural relativism (see Rescher 1988). The reactions to the problem of cultural relativism can be divided into three groups: monistic, extreme relativistic, and cognitivist. The monistic reactions reduce the apparent and irritating diversity of beliefs into a family of constitutive human properties, U, that can have diverse manifestations in different environments. Thus, whenever we encounter apparently incompatible beliefs, we can rest content with the assumption that the appearance is not reality; there is always a family of universal properties U that can be used to reduce and explain the diversity.

There are two styles of monism: emergent and reductionist. Emergent monism claims that we can illuminate or render intelligible the apparent diversity by looking at it against the background provided by U. Reductionist monism claims that for every difference at the level of beliefs, practice and culture, there is one and only one property in the family U. In both styles of monism, biological, psychological, social, and economic universals have been proposed as candidates for the family U.

Some versions of sociobiology are apt examples of biological (or rather genetical) monism. The invariants detected in belief systems and in cultural systems in general are reduced to a family of epigenetic rules (the nomic characteristics of belief systems, for example) which, in turn, are reduced to genetic laws.

Malinowskian cultural anthropology is another example. His view could be expressed by saying that the family of universals U contains the basic biological human needs as well as the principles of economic psychology. The apparent diversity of beliefs and practices is construed as rational responses to biological needs.

Modern sociology of knowledge (or sociology of science) provides the lawful mechanisms of social groups such as the family U. Whatever the apparent diversity and incompatibility encountered, they maintain, the basic dynamics of group-formation and maintenance are always present.

So-called contextualization, or contextualism, is the tough case. It has been used as the primary tool of interpretation in studying apparently incompatible beliefs and practices. Moreover, it has been advertized as the anti-reductionist tool of cultural relativism. Anyway, contextualization, seen as the placing of cultural items in their functional roles is a version of monism. This is clear in the claims to the effect that two cultural traits are in some sense similar due to their being parts of isomorphic systems (Geertz 1973 and 1983). The search for isomorphisms between systems that contain apparently incompatible beliefs and practices is a search for uniformities which, in turn, is a search for the family U. Two systems are isomorphic when they are similar in some respect, that is, when they share a common property.

The apparent anti-monism (and pro-cultural-relativism) of

contextualization is mainly due to the fact that very few contextualists bother to tell their readers what sorts of isomorphisms they are looking for. Biological, sociological, and psychological theories are more explicit in this respect since they express clearly the variety of isomorphisms they expect to find. Of course this makes them more vulnerable to criticism than the rather more obscure method of contextualization.

There is no escape from monism: the cognitive systematization of our experience, as well as scientific understanding of phenomena, requires the monistic assumption that there is a family U of lawful properties by means of which the apparent diversity is systematized.

Extreme relativism accepts the fact of descriptive cognitive relativism and draws the normative conclusion that since there are no good grounds for deciding between different views of what there is or what should be done, we may as well be totally indifferent with respect to the whole question. Indifference follows from the fundamental incompatibility, the proponents of extreme relativism maintain, because "good ground" and "reason" are putatively universal notions that range over belief systems; since there are no such universal concepts at all, there is no content to these notions either.

A powerful counterargument against extreme relativism has been presented by Nicholas Rescher (1988). He proposes what he calls "conceptual egocentrism". It may be outlined as follows. It is not indifferent, at least to us, which beliefs or practices or rules of reasoning we endorse. Quite the contrary, we prefer our own beliefs and practices, as well as our standards of reasoning, precisely because we have the best available reasons for them. We can provide reasons for our beliefs and practices, and by the same token, reasons for not using any other, apparently incompatible systems. Another counterargument against extreme relativism is that if its proponent throws away the notion of good ground or reason, we are not supposed to accept what he is saying, or, alternatively, he should tell us what he means by acceptability. Moreover, if he disregards all elementary logic, we are not supposed to even understand him, since the identification of speech acts requires the identification of mental states, which, in turn, requires some logic.

With the above counterarguments at our disposal, it is relatively easy to get rid of extreme relativism.

Cognitivism is a version of monism. It claims that the family U of universal properties contains first and foremost those properties that are relevant to human information processing.

Intellectualist anthropology, as exemplified in the writings of Robin

Horton is one cognitivist strategy applied in cultural anthropology (Horton 1970 and 1982). Horton's main thesis is that apparently incompatible beliefs and practices have a common core, their cognitive structure. Beliefs, even the exotic ones, are parts of cognitive models. These models serve the task of information processing; more largely, the goals of understanding, explanation, and control. That is their reason for existence. One of the most debatable of Horton's claims is that Western theories are more correct than other, for example, African or Asian, theories. This prima facie colonialistic claim is a version of conceptual egocentrism, and it might turn out to be correct.

Although cognitivism is committed to the monistic reaction against the problem of relativism, it differs from the other monistic reactions in significant ways. Most importantly, the monistic versions listed above can be seen as committed to a profound contrast between the realms of rationality and causality, and accordingly, between the domains of cognitive and causal explanations (cf. Skorupski 1973). This contraposition has invited a deep chasm between two families of concepts:

> rationality – causality
> cognitive explanation – causal explanation
> person – system
> mind – body
> autonomous man – mechanical man
> reasons – causes
> unpredictable behaviour – lawful behaviour
> subject – object
> active – passive
> science – religion and magic
> us – them

These contrasts are ordered so that the top ones are more closely related to the structures of reality and to our putative explanatory strategies. The further down we descend, the more moral, political, ideological, and finally almost tribal the contrasts get. The rock bottom is the distinction between us and them, the distinction that is claimed to haunt the versions of monism, and of which the versions of cultural relativism have falsely been believed to be free. Extreme relativism is, of course, easily freed from these distinctions, but, by the same token, it is freed from sensible discussion.

The most profound distinction, the one between rationality and causality, has been commented on by various authors. Martin Hollis (1977) claims that in explaining human beliefs and practices, rationality is the strategy to be used, since rational beliefs and practices include their own explanations. Causal explanations of human behaviour are only for deviant cases, when the episode deviates from the intelligible course of belief or action. The Edinburgh school of science studies proposes, on the contrary, that there is no need for two disctinct explanatory strategies, one working when the system is in order, and the other working when the system is out of order. In the case of human beliefs and practices, and cultural entities in general, we should make do with one sort of explanation only, namely, the causal (see the articles and references in Hollis and Lukes 1982).

So much for the one-sided solutions suggested to our problem. The message of cognitivism is that the cognitive processes that are responsible for the dynamics of cognitive systems, are both rational and causal. The import of this solution is that it minimizes or even eliminates the chasm between us and them. The application of causal explanations does not need to threaten human dignity, rooted in rationality, since the very focus of the explanation is a rational process. This is the difference between cognitivism and the rest of the monistic reactions. The solution may appear simplistic, since it glues together the relevant concepts. But ongoing research on cognitive processes, on the role of clustered mental representations or schemata, and other topics explored in the above chapters, is giving us a better idea of how this commonsensical synthesis is realized. Namely, the idea that we, for instance, are systems governed by processes, some of which are both rational and causal.

16. ULTIMATE RELATIVISM

The cognitive paradigm has been immensely successful in explaining some of our mental abilities. At the same time, however, a few cognitivists have claimed that what we now understand about the mind may have important implications for what we can ever understand about the world. That is, they are suggesting that our cognitive machinery constrains our access to a true and complete account of the world.

The first cognitivist to introduce this worry was the linguist Noam Chomsky (1975). He distinguishes between problems, which human minds are in principle equipped to solve, and mysteries, which systematically elude our understanding. The reason for the existence of genuine mysteries is, according to him, that the very faculties of mind that make us good at some cognitive tasks may make us poor in others.

In 1983 Jerry Fodor exposed the same problem in his book *The*

Modularity of Mind. His general aim in this book is to sketch a functional taxonomy of human cognitive architecture as follows: there are basically two different kinds of systems in the brain-mind: modular input-systems and central systems. Modular systems are special-purpose computational mechanisms that are designed to solve only computational problems of a certain kind. If our mind consists of modular pieces like this, it is conceivable that our mental capacities have internal constraints. And because of this it might be that the best possible science or the true theory of the structure of the world is not among the theories we can understand.

Fodor (1983, 120) formulates a concept of epistemological boundedness: a psychological theory represents the mind as epistemologically bounded if it is a consequence of the theory that our cognitive organization imposes epistemically significant constraints on the beliefs that we can entertain.

Fodor thinks that we can treat cognitive systems as hypothesis-confirming devices that must have access at least to (Fodor 1983, 121):

(a)   A source of hypotheses to be (dis)confirmed.
(b)   A data base.
(c)   A metric which can compute the confirmation level of a given hypothesis relative of a given data base.

Fodor then considers how such a device might be so organized that it fails, by virtue of its organization, to pick the best hypothesis for the available data. Epistemic boundedness can be a result of our quantitative or qualitative cognitive limitations. Quantitative, or parametric, limitations are more or less trivial: the computations to be performed might be too long for the system to compute, or the critical data base too complex to represent. As Fodor puts it:

Perhaps the riddle of the universe requires one more neuron than, de facto, anyone will ever have. Sad, of course, but surely not out of the question. (Fodor 1983, 122)

The qualitative limitations of hypothesis-confirming devices are connected to what Fodor calls domain specificity. He suggests that our cognitive mechanisms are biased towards solving some kinds of problems to the exclusion of others: the class of concepts accessible to us is endogenously constrained and, consequently, there are thoughts that we are unequipped to think.

Fodor tries to show that any possible cognitive theory cannot guarantee epistemological unboundedness but, even worse, must imply epistemological boundedness. Unboundedness would require that there should be no interesting endogenous constraints on the hypothesis accessible to intelligent problem solving. A psychology which guarantees our epistemic unboundedness would thus have to guarantee that, whatever subject domain the world turns out to be, somewhere in the space of hypotheses we are capable of entertaining there is the hypothesis that specifies the structure of the world. However, any psychology must attribute some endogenous structure to the mind and, according to Fodor (1983, 125) it is hard to see how, in the course of making such attributions of endogenous structure, the theory could fail to imply some constraints on the class of beliefs that the mind can entertain.

We accept epistemic boundedness unhesitatingly for every other species: we would presumably not be impressed by a priori arguments intended to prove (for example) that the true science must be accessible to spiders. This fact, in Fodor's (1983) opinion, makes it perhaps a little easier to accept boundedness also in our own case.

Recently, Colin McGinn has taken these ideas seriously and introduced the idea of cognitive closure:

A type of mind M is cognitively closed with respect to a property P (or theory T) if and only if the concept-forming procedures at M's disposal cannot extend to a grasp of P (or an understanding of T). (McGinn 1989, 350; see also McGinn 1991)

He then argues that our minds, unfortunately, are suffering from cognitive closedness, and that there is at least one problem, namely the problem of consciousness (or the mind-body problem) that we are cognitively unequipped to deal with:

Conceiving minds come in different kinds, equipped with varying powers and limitations, biases and blindspots, so that properties (or theories) may be accessible to some minds but not to others. What is closed to the mind of a rat may be open to the mind of a monkey, and what is closed to us may be open to the monkey. Representational power is not all or nothing. Minds are biological products like bodies, and like bodies they come in different shapes and sizes, more or less capacious, more or less suited to certain cognitive tasks. (McGinn 1989, 350)

Total cognitive openness in not guaranteed for human beings and it should not be expected. (McGinn 1989, 352)

Monkey minds trying to grasp the concept of an electron or a 5-year-old child trying to understand Relativity Theory are examples of cognitive closure. So there are naturalistic scientific theories that are not accessible to these types of mind and the question arises whether there are any other true explanatory theories with respect to which the adult human mind is forever closed.

McGinn thinks that there is at least one problem that is unsolvable for any human mind just because of cognitive closure. This is the mind-body problem or the problem of consciousness: the human mind is forever closed from a general mind-body theory. Now, what exactly is "the mind-body" problem and why does McGinn think that it is unsolvable? McGinn formulates the problem as follows: how is it possible for conscious states to depend upon brain states? What makes the bodily organ we call the brain so radically different from other bodily organs, say the kidneys – the body parts without a trace of consciousness? In solving the mind-body problem, we would first and foremost like to take the magic out of the link between consciousness and the brain.

McGinn thinks, firstly, that there exists some property of the brain that accounts naturalistically for consciousness. That is, there exists some property P of the brain, by virtue of which the brain is the basis of consciousness. And secondly, there exists some theory T, referring to P, which fully explains the dependence of conscious states on brain states. If we knew T, then we would have a constructive solution to the mind-body problem. McGinn's central argument is that we are cognitively closed with respect to property P, and that we can never come to know T.

According to McGinn, we have two possible avenues to reveal the property P: neuroscience and introspection. He considers both of them are leading only to a dead end. He claims that neuroscience will not be helpful, because our perception of the brain constrains the concepts we can apply to it and the property of consciousness itself is not an observable or perceptible property of the brain. Conscious states are simply not potential objects of perception: they depend upon the brain but they cannot be observed by directing the senses onto the brain. Neither can any coherent method of concept introduction lead us to P. If our data, arrived at by the perception of the brain, do not include anything that brings in conscious states, then the theoretical properties we need to explain this data will not include conscious states either.

It seems to us that McGinn is ignoring some potentially useful methods in the search for the property P. Surely there are discliplines such as cognitive psychology and neuropsychology in addition to "introspection" and "neuroscience". And precisely in these fields interesting empirical findings (Young and DeHaan 1990) and theoretical constructions concerning consciousness (Baars 1988; Schacter 1990) have been made (see Part I). So it is simply not true that we cannot make any advance in developing theories of brain-consciousness relationships. On the contrary, it seems that it is exactly what has to be done in order to explain the experimental data. Granted, then, that at least we should use a concept of consciousness, is there still something that is missing from our theories?

Here enters the worry about the irreducible subjectivity of conscious mental states (see Nagel 1974, 1979 and 1986; Searle 1989). Also McGinn pays attention to this problem by reminding us that we have a restricted access to the concepts of consciousness: one cannot form concepts of consciousness unless one oneself instantiates those properties. The man born blind cannot fully grasp the concept of red and humans cannot conceive of the echolocatory experiences of bats.

McGinn argues that this subjectivity is a possibly unsurmountable obstacle on our way to a general solution of the mind-body problem. Suppose bats have experiences of type B and the explanatory property that links these experiences to the bat brain is Pb. By grasping Pb we could understand the link between bat brains and experiences – we would have solved the mind-body problem for bats. But how could we understand that theory without understanding the concept B that is in it? We constitutionally lack the concept-forming capacity to encompass all possible types of conscious state, and this obstructs our path to a general solution to the mind-body problem. Even if we could solve it for our own case, we could not solve it for bats and Martians.

Is subjectivity in any conventional sense a proper object of knowledge at all? Some (for example, Lewis 1983, 130–132; Lewis 1988; Nemirow 1990; Carruthers 1986, 144) have argued it is not: knowing what it is like to experience a certain kind of conscious state (for example, seeing green, tasting salt, smelling a rose, hearing the sound of a harpsichord) is not factual knowledge at all, but, instead, it is a practical recognitional capacity or ability. And no amount of factual information about bat brains (for example) will give us any of the bat's capacities: we still cannot fly although we know everything about bat flight; analoguously, we still cannot have the practical skill of recognising bat experiences without having practice in having those states.

This kind of reply only seems to beg the question. Aeronautics (or whatever you call the science of flying) has no deep metaphysical problems about the relationship between aircraft and flying, and it would be strange to claim that there is something we cannot understand about bat flight because we can not fly ourselves. Nevertheless, it seems there is something we do not understand about bat experiences just because we are not bats. If experiences were only practical abilities like flying, nobody in his right mind would ever have thought about there being a "mind-body", or "brain-consciousness" problem. We have no comparable problems in the realm of other practical abilities – not many philosophical articles have been published lately around the "foot-kicking" or "scissors-cutting" problems. In experiences there is a subjective component that practical abilities, like cutting or flying, lack, and claiming that experiences are simply practical abilities amounts only to denying this.

McGinn suggests that the nature of the psychophysical connection has a full and non-mysterious explanation in a certain science, but that this science is inaccessible to us as a matter of principle. There is no intrinsic conceptual or metaphysical difficulty about how consciousness depends on the brain: the correct science does not have to postulate miracles. It is just that the correct science lies in the dark part of the world for us. There is, in reality, nothing mysterious about how the brain generates consciousness: the sense of miracle comes from us, not from the world.

We have, then, at least one candidate theory that resists a general solution because of our cognitive closure or epistemic boundedness: it is the General Theory of Experience. Types of experience different from human experience are difficult to conceptualize and impossible to understand: we are like blind men trying to build a theory of colours. Do we have any other domains closed from our cognitive capacities? Worth mentioning but beyond the scope of this discussion are, for example, quantum physics and paranormal phenomena. The quantum world seems to be utterly mysterious and a coherent and general interpretation of quantum phenomena has not emerged despite more than 50 years of intensive theorising. Paranormal phenomena, if they exist at all, seem to escape from the grip of science time after time.

McGinn is arguing, in short, that the limits of our minds are just not the limits of reality – reality is not constrained by what the human mind can conceive. To insist the contrary would be the worst kind of anthropocentrism. To the philosophy of science, then, the bad news from cognitive science is that most likely we are some kind of cognitive prisoners, enjailed in the dungeons of our own construction. Exactly how constrained we are, we do not yet know, but anyway we should leave behind our hopes of omniscience or epistemological unboundedness.

* * *

Summarizing the good news and the bad news seems to take us, we are afraid, one step forward and two steps back. So, cognitivism helps us to solve some old problems arising from cultural relativism by pointing out a universal cognitive-model structure behind all those incompatible beliefs. The functioning of these models is both rational and causal, which saves cognitivism from a dangerous dichotomy.

However, this universal cognitive structure is based on the internal structure of the human mind which restricts the class of beliefs and thoughts we are capable of entertaining: we are "epistemologically bounded" or "cognitively closed".

Thus, we end up with a new variety of relativism, which we have called Ultimate Relativism. There are minds that are equipped with apparently different kinds of cognitive abilities, and every type of mind has some biases and restrictions in its representational powers. Thus, Ultimate Relativism seems to reside not in the differences between cultures but in the relation between our own construction and that of the real world. No type of mind has absolute, complete access to the real world or to its properties or theories about it. The way the human mind grasps the world is only different from but not superior to the worlds of monkeys, dolphins, bats, or Martians. There are some things we can grasp but they can not, and vice versa. No mind's truth is The Complete Truth, and so we lack a common measure, as is typical of relativism. The reason, however, why this particular version deserves the sinister name Ultimate is, that there is no way we, the cognitive prisoners, can escape from the dungeons of our own construction.

BIBLIOGRAPHY

Baars, B.J.: 1988, *A Cognitive Theory of Consciousness*, New York: Cambridge University Press.
Carruthers, P.: 1988, *Introducing Persons: Theories and Arguments in the Philosophy of Mind*, London: Croom Helm.
Chomsky, N.: 1975, *Reflections on Language*, New York: Pantheon Books.
Finnegan, R. and Horton, R. (eds.): 1973, *Modes of Thought*, London: Routledge and Kegan Paul.
Fodor, J.A.: 1983, *The Modularity of Mind*, Cambridge MA: MIT Press.
Geertz, C.: 1973, *The Interpretation of Cultures*, New York: Basic Books.
Geertz, C.: 1983, *Local Knowledge*, New York: Basic Books.
Hollis, M.: 1977, *Models of Man*, Cambridge: Cambridge University Press.
Hollis, M. and Lukes, S. (eds.): 1982, *Rationality and Relativism*, Oxford: Basil

Blackwell.

Horton, R.: 1970, 'African Traditional Thought and Western Science', in Wilson, B. (ed.), *Rationality,* Oxford: Basil Blackwell.

Horton, R.: 1982, 'Tradition and Modernity Revisited', in Hollis, M. and Lukes, S. (eds.), *Rationality and Relativism,* Oxford: Basil Blackwell.

Lewis, D.: 1983, *Philosophical Papers,* Vol. 1, New York: Oxford University Press.

Lewis, D.: 1988, 'What Experience Teaches', in Lycan, W.G. (ed.), *Mind and Cognition,* Oxford: Basil Blackwell, 499–518.

McGinn, C.: 1989, 'Can We Solve the Mind-Body Problem?', *Mind* 9 8, 349–366.

McGinn, C.: 1991, *The Problem of Consciousness,* Oxford: Basil Blackwell.

Nagel, T.; 1974, 'What Is It Like to Be a Bat?', *The Philosophical Review* 8 3, 435–450.

Nagel, T.: 1979, *Mortal Questions,* London: Cambridge University Press.

Nagel, T.: 1986, *The View from Nowhere,* Oxford: Oxford University Press.

Nemirow, L.: 1990, 'Physicalism and the Cognitive Role of Acquaintance', in Lycan, W.G. (ed.), *Mind and Cognition,* Oxford: Basil Blackwell.

Rescher, N.: 1988, *Rationality: A Philosophical Inquiry into the Nature and the Rationale of Reason,* Oxford: Clarendon Press.

Schacter, D.L.: 1990, 'Toward a Cognitive Neuropsychology of Awareness: Implicit Knowledge and Anosagnosia', *Journal of Clinical and Experimental Neuropsychology* 1 2 (1), 155–178.

Searle, J.R.: 1989, 'Consciousness, Unconsciousness, and Intentionality', *Philosophical Topics* 1 8, 193–209.

Skorupski, J.: 1973, *Symbol and Theory: A Philosophical Study of Theories of Religion in Social Anthropology,* Cambridge: Cambridge University Press.

Young, A.W. and DeHaan E.H.F.: 1990, 'Impairments of Visual Awareness', *Mind and Language* 5 (1), 29–48.

INDEX OF NAMES

INDEX OF SUBJECTS

247

LIST OF AUTHORS

Matti Kamppinen
Senior Lecturer in Comparative Religion
Department of Cultural Studies
University of Turku

Antti Revonsuo
Research Associate (Academy of Finland)
Department of Philosophy
University of Turku

Seppo Sajama
Associate Professor in Philosophy
Department of Philosophy
University of Joensuu

Simo Vihjanen
Research Assistant
Department of Philosophy
University of Turku

Finland

STUDIES IN COGNITIVE SYSTEMS

1. J. H. Fetzer (ed.): *Aspects of Artificial Intelligence.* 1988
   ISBN 1-55608-037-9; Pb 1-55608-038-7
2. J. Kulas, J.H. Fetzer and T.L. Rankin (eds.): *Philosophy, Language, and Artificial Intelligence.* Resources for Processing Natural Language. 1988
   ISBN 1-55608-073-5
3. D.J. Cole, J.H. Fetzer and T.L. Rankin (eds.): *Philosophy, Mind and Cognitive Inquiry.* Resources for Understanding Mental Processes. 1990
   ISBN 0-7923-0427-6
4. J.H. Fetzer: *Artificial Intelligence: Its Scope and Limits.* 1990
   ISBN 0-7923-0505-1; Pb 0-7923-0548-5
5. H.E. Kyburg, Jr., R.P. Loui and G.N. Carlson (eds.): *Knowledge Representation and Defeasible Reasoning.* 1990   ISBN 0-7923-0677-5
6. J.H. Fetzer (ed.): *Epistemology and Cognition.* 1991   ISBN 0-7923-0892-1
7. E.C. Way: *Knowledge Representation and Metaphor.* 1991
   ISBN 0-7923-1005-5
8. J. Dinsmore: *Partitioned Representations.* A Study in Mental Representation, Language Understanding and Linguistic Structure. 1991   ISBN 0-7923-1348-8
9. T. Horgan and J. Tienson (eds.): *Connectionism and the Philosophy of Mind.* 1991   ISBN 0-7923-1482-4
10. J.A. Michon and A. Akyürek (eds.): *Soar: A Cognitive Architecture in Perspective.* 1992   ISBN 0-7923-1660-6
11. S.C. Coval and P.G. Campbell: *Agency in Action.* The Practical Rational Agency Machine. 1992   ISBN 0-7923-1661-4
12. S. Bringsjord: *What Robots Can and Can't Be.* 1992   ISBN 0-7923-1662-2
13. B. Indurkhya: *Metaphor and Cognition.* An Interactionist Approach. 1992
   ISBN 0-7923-1687-8
14. T.R. Colburn, J.H. Fetzer and T.L. Rankin (eds.): *Program Verification.* Fundamental Issues in Computer Science. 1993   ISBN 0-7923-1965-6
15. M. Kamppinen (ed.): *Consciousness, Cognitive Schemata, and Relativism.* Multidisciplinary Explorations in Cognitive Science. 1993
   ISBN 0-7923-2275-4

KLUWER ACADEMIC PUBLISHERS – DORDRECHT / BOSTON / LONDON